Why Reagan Won

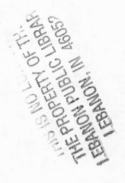

Why
Reagan
Won

A Narrative History
of the
Conservative Movement
1964-1981

F. Clifton White
William J. Gill

Foreword by William F. Buckley, Jr.
Introduction by Senator Paul Laxalt

REGNERY GATEWAY

Published by Regnery Gateway
360 West Superior Street
Chicago, Illinois 60610

Manufactured in the United States of America.

Library of Congress Catalog Card Number: 81-52142.
International Standard Book Number: 0-89526-668-7

To my grandchildren
Tabitha, Clifton III, Graham IV,
Meagan, Cameron and Garrett.
May Ronald Reagan re-establish
government as *their* servant.

—F.C.W.

Contents

Introduction by Senator Paul Laxalt   ix
Foreword by William F. Buckley, Jr.   xv
 1: Convention 1980   1
 2: A Man Who Speaks For Himself   11
 3: The Speech   20
 4: The Movement   29
 5: The Oracles   38
 6: The Think Tanks   55
 7: The Cadre   65
 8: The Governor   82
 9: The Reluctant Candidate   92
10: Countdown to Miami   105
11: The Near Miss   117
12: The Outcasts   130
13: The Changing Scene   143
14: Time of Trauma   151
15: The Split   161
16: The Long Battle   174
17: Convention '76   182
18: Between Battles   192
19: Comeback   203
20: Roundup   215
21: Election   225
22: A Look Ahead   239
Index   247

Introduction

by Senator Paul Laxalt

Ronald Reagan's political career was forged in the caldron of one of the most bitter presidential campaigns in American history. I am not speaking of the 1980 campaign which President Reagan refused to turn into a vituperative contest even after former President Jimmy Carter personally tried to label him as a dangerous warmonger. Rather, I am referring to the 1964 electoral war waged by Lyndon Baines Johnson and the Democrats against Senator Barry Goldwater.

The 1964 campaign was the first nationwide face-off between the modern conservative movement in the United States and the loose liberal coalition assembled by Franklin Delano Roosevelt in the decade of the Great Depression. Barry Goldwater lost that election by nearly 16 million votes and he won only six states with a total of 52 electoral votes. Yet his courageous campaign gave birth to a new national political force that in 1980 swept Governor Reagan to an overwhelming victory over an incumbent President, a feat unequaled since Grover Cleveland toppled Benjamin Harrison in 1892.

No man had more to do with organizing this movement than F. Clifton White. And few played a more significant role in the major steps that ultimately led to Ronald Reagan's election as President of the United States.

Clif White started the Draft Goldwater Committee in 1961–62 with no encouragement from Senator Goldwater and still less from the Republican Party's entrenched leadership. Indeed, at times it seemed as though both the conservative Goldwater and the mostly liberal, or quasi-liberal, GOP establishment were trying to outdo each other in dampening the enthusiasm of Mr. White and his young cohorts. The senator because he really did not want to run for President. The establishment because it did not want him to run, preferring Governor Nelson Rockefeller of New York or William Scranton of Pennsylvania to the man they viewed as an outspoken cowboy from Arizona.

Oddly enough, up until this time Clif White had been regarded by most Westerners, and not a few Easterners, as a certified member of the Eastern Establishment. After World War II combat service as an Air Corps navigator, White had taught political science at Cornell and at Ithaca College before entering politics in the New York state administration of Governor Thomas E. Dewey, eventually serving as state Commissioner of Motor Vehicles. He was part of the Dewey team that halted Senator Robert Taft's drive toward the Republican presidential nomination at the 1952 convention, the team that helped hand the prize to Dwight D. Eisenhower.

Clif White worked hard in both of President Eisenhower's successful campaigns and he served as director of organization for the Volunteers for Nixon-Lodge in 1960. His Eastern Establishment political credentials, on the surface at least, were impeccable. But there was something about Clif that few of his Eastern friends ever knew: his grandmother was a Westerner. In fact she had protected her cabin and her family with a six-gun on the Montana frontier in the waning days of the old West. It is my belief that she passed her strong Western independence on to Clif even though the family returned to New York state long before he was born.

Actually, Clif White is a *national* politician, in the best and truest sense of that term. Few people have greater knowledge about the widely different and intricate political machineries of each and every one of our fifty states, particularly the complicated processes for choosing presidential convention delegates. But Clif White has also shown a remarkable range of vision that embraces the whole wide spectrum of national issues and national politics. And it was this vision that led him to start the Draft Goldwater movement from an office opposite New York's Grand Central Station. He has told that story in fascinating detail in *Suite 3505: The Story of the Draft Goldwater Movement*, which he co-authored with William J. Gill, who is again co-author of this new book.

The details in *Suite 3505* were so fascinating, in fact, that the book is still recommended reading in scores of university political science courses and both the George McGovern and Jimmy Carter teams, in 1972 and 1976 respectively, bought up thousands of copies and used it as a road map in winning their party's presidential nomination.

My colleague, Senator Goldwater, summed up Clif White's role in the Republicans' 1964 nominating process in a letter he wrote Clif just after the convention.

"It was you who got this whole thing started and it was you who led the team on to victory in San Francisco," Barry Goldwater said.

In that sense, then, it was Clif White who got so many of us started in politics, because the 1964 Goldwater campaign was the incubator for the successful careers of at least a score of present United States Senators, several dozen Governors, and probably more than a hundred members of the House of Representatives, as well as untold numbers of state legislators, county and local officials.

What Clif White and the Goldwater forces wrought at San Francisco in 1964 was a revolution in American politics, first within the Republican party and more recently within the conservative-drifting Democratic party as well. He and thousands of others—27,176,799 others, if we count Candidate Goldwater's total vote—understood that the country could no longer continue its tragic tilt to the left. They were a little ahead of their time, but not as far ahead as most political observers may think. Already, in 1964, the polls showed that many more Americans regarded themselves as conservative rather than liberal, even though a clear majority had voted for a liberal President.

Ronald Reagan was one conservative who got his political start in the 1964 Goldwater campaign. Clif White tells us how this came about, with a wealth of fresh detail that only he could supply. For it was Clif who appointed President Reagan to his first job in a Republican campaign—co-chairman of the Citizens for Goldwater-Miller in California. It was Clif who served as Ronald Reagan's de facto presidential campaign manager in 1968 and very nearly stopped Richard Nixon on the first ballot in Miami. And it was Clif who as Candidate Reagan's senior campaign advisor in 1980 gave us the benefit of his unequaled national political experience in the strategy sessions that charted the final successful campaign for the Presidency.

In *Why Reagan Won*, however, Clif White tells us much more than all this, interesting as his behind-the-scenes view of President Reagan's long, hard drive for the White House will certainly prove to the average reader as well as to future historians. Mr. White and co-author Gill, a prize-winning journalist and distinguished author, tell us what no other writers could tell with such a depth of perception and first-hand knowledge—namely, that the conservative movement Ronald Reagan has led to victory is not merely political. It represents a deep and, I believe, an abiding philosophical and intellectual—and, yes, *spiritual* upheaval in America that ultimately will be felt around the world.

Ours is a true movement. It is not simply a faction or party that brought about a conventional changing of the political guard. White and Gill explore this movement in captivating detail—the people, the ideas, the beliefs, the events that formed it into an irresistible force that carried Ronald Reagan to his landslide election victory, gave the Republican Party control of the United States Senate for the first time in nearly three decades, and, I am confident, will provide us with a healthy majority in the House in 1982.

Why Reagan Won will certainly stand as one of the great political books of our time. But it is much more than a political book. It is a clear and incisive overview of America in these closing decades of the most eventful century in all history. It is the moving story of Ronald Reagan's political career and the conservative movement he so ably and so courageously represents. It is, in short, a tale well calculated to stir men's souls.

Foreword

by William F. Buckley, Jr.

I am both happy to be invited to write a foreword to the volume by Clif White on the victory of Ronald Reagan, and happily situated to do so: because I learned so very much from Mr. White, of the stuff he here purveys so lucidly and so dramatically.

I met him not so very long after I graduated from college. There the abstractness of most thought inevitably influenced me, usually in the direction of naivete. The predominant notion was that that which is true will prevail. That all ideas should be permitted to start even in the race, lest an idea that was unfashionable might suffer unnecessary encumbrances before emerging as the true idea. Light and (therefore) Truth was the motto of Yale, and not so very long after graduating I learned of that dimension in politics which strikes most people as obvious, but did not then strike me as any such thing. It is, of course, the need for organization.

But the need for organization consists in more than merely getting people to register and out to vote. The need to effect organization is, really, a need to awaken the civil community. So to speak, to arrest its attention. This I think is what Mr. White all along perceived. And it is by perceiving this that he acquired the reputation he had along the time he took up the cause of my brother's election to the Senate. This he effected, against great historical odds (only a single senator backed by a third party had been seated in this century), primarily by recognizing that the need for organization was, if properly superintended (here his skills were inestimable) largely accomplished under its own motion.

This happens to be true, I would later learn, in that extension of organization which is political fund-raising. I would learn that what was important about the lady who sent in twenty five dollars was not the twenty five dollars, most of which in any event would go to defray the costs of raising the twenty five dollars, but the mobilization of the lady herself. Not only was she likely to send money in response to the second request, but she became in a most palpable way identified with Clif's candidate—and his cause. That is the kind of organization that Clif promoted at the grass roots level.

Oh yes, he could deal at other levels. He is charmingly candid about his desertion of Reagan (though it could be phrased differently) in the great fight of 1976. There, Clif White did not have the multitudes to stir. To the extent that they were stirred for Ford, they were already risen. The sleeping multitudes, who soon awoke in formidable force, rose to the banner of Ronald Reagan, and Mr. White tells us that Mr. Ford very nearly lost the nomination to Reagan in Kansas City, and that probably the fatal mistake of Mr. Reagan had been in selecting so archly-liberal a running mate as Senator Schweicker, thus short-circuiting the great national impulse for a genuine conservative. Well . . . I knew of the choice of Mr. Schweicker before Mr. Reagan did, having been consulted in the matter by the insiders. They didn't argue the merits of Mr. Schweicker (though almost all of them now would), but insisted that the Reagan votes were insufficient to hold the line against Ford in the few weeks that lay between the Fourth of July, which Mr. Ford had all but converted into a personal birthday (no doubt aided in this by Mr. White!), and the convening of the delegates in Kansas City.

One threads one's way, then, in this engrossing book, at once attempting to discover the role of genuine enthusiasm in organization; and the extent to which genuine enthusiasm can be frustrated by manipulation. Mr. White is kind enough to his readers not to disguise the uses of enthusiasm to generate organization, or the uses of organization to frustrate enthusiasm!

Clifton White is a genuine pioneer in the technologization of the democratic art. His vision, moreover, made these skills, inevitably advancing on us, available to friends of the old ways, by which I mean the old insights of the Founding Fathers. These he understands to be served by the man he helped to make president. It is hard to imagine, in politics, a happier or more useful life than to provide critical aid to the man who will lead the country.

Stamford, Connecticut
September 4, 1981

1

Convention 1980

It was after 11:00 P.M., Wednesday night, July 16, 1980. Two hours earlier Ronald Reagan had been nominated as the Republican Party's candidate for President of the United States at the national convention in Detroit's Joe Louis Arena. This was a time for celebration, especially for those of us who had started out with Governor Reagan on his long and tortuous road to the nomination more than a dozen years before. But it had also become a time of suspense and uncertainty because of the rampant speculation as to whom Candidate Reagan would choose as his vice–presidential running mate. Everyone in that arena, and millions of citizens watching on television, felt that Reagan's own candidacy for the highest office in the land could well hang on that choice.

Much of the news media had already nominated former President Gerald Ford for second place on the Republican slate. George Bush had been swept into the dustbin of history by the commentators and Ford was being presented to the nation by the television networks as the somewhat reluctant component of the Grand Old Party's "dream ticket."

Inside the Reagan communications trailer, which I commanded

1

from the parking lot next to convention hall, I'd had the privilege of directing the roll call of the delegates as Ronald Reagan's political director for the convention. When Montana's 20 votes made Reagan's nomination official, putting him over the magic 998 he required, the convention went wild. The delegates on the floor and the spectators in the galleries cheered themselves hoarse, drowning out the brassy band and cheerfully popping the thousands of red, white and blue balloons that showered down on them from the roof of the arena.

Now, however, the cheering had become sporadic. The noise that a short time before had threatened to burst the arena's walls was replaced by long and ominous silences as the convention speakers droned on to a tired and almost lethargic audience. More than once I had to signal our people stationed throughout the arena to drum up more enthusiasm. The spontaneous celebrating had passed and the media had conditioned the people inside the convention hall, as well as the millions across the country, to accept Jerry Ford as the vice–presidential *fait accompli*. Most of the delegates were relieved by this "news," since the majority of them preferred Ford to George Bush, who had been Reagan's leading rival for the presidential nomination. Bush was anathema to the conservative majority within the Republican Party because of his primary campaign attacks on Reagan and on our candidate's conservative positions on the most emotional issues, particularly Reagan's opposition to the Equal Rights Amendment and legalized abortion.

Shortly after 11:30 the television commentators reported that Reagan was about to leave his hotel for the arena to announce his choice of Gerald Ford. In the Reagan trailer, however, we had had no official word of this and as the minutes ticked off with no signal from the Reagan suite, the tension in the trailer became almost palpable.

Senator Laxalt of Nevada, who had helped guide Ronald Reagan's nominating drive to the triumph of that night and had earlier in the evening placed our candidate's name in nomination, stood beside me in the rear room of the trailer waiting for the call from Governor Reagan. William Timmons, the quietly able Reagan convention director, stood with us, eyeing the door to the outer section of the trailer where our dozen regional political directors kept in constant touch with the delegates on the floor and the sergeants–at–arms in the galleries.

It was no secret that our staff, like so many of our delegates and the thousands of people in the galleries, were deeply troubled by the possibility that Reagan might pick a liberal running mate. They had begun to acquiesce in the selection of former President Ford, who was still regarded as a conservative even though many stalwart conservatives were suspicious of Ford's unswerving devotion to Henry Kissinger. But the chance that Ford would be passed over for Bush was something that worried all of us concerned with the management of the convention. Like Paul Laxalt and Bill Timmons, I was afraid the high expectations of a Ford candidacy raised by the television oracles might explode into an angry emotional reaction if George Bush were named instead.

Just that morning Governor Reagan had a chance to measure the depth of the anti–Bush feeling that prevailed among conservatives at the convention. Ominously, the meeting had taken place about the time a furious thunderstorm swept out the skies and literally shook the Detroit Plaza hotel. A huge black cloud descended on Detroit's Renaissance Center and enveloped the hotel tower in total darkness. Deafening thunder and fierce flashes of lightning followed and the tall hotel tower vibrated in a frightening fashion.

At Reagan's meeting with a group of conservative leaders the vice–presidential possibilities were discussed at length. The group included Phyllis Schlafly, the lady who had so courageously led the successful battle against the highly questionable Equal Rights Amendment; Nellie Gray, a leader of the anti–abortion group; the Reverend Jerry Falwell, who had enlisted more than 70,000 pastors in his Moral Majority movement and whose television programs are watched by millions; Howard Phillips, national director of the Conservative Caucus; Senator Gordon Humphrey of New Hampshire, who had strongly backed Ronald Reagan in that state's presidential primary, the first in the nation and the first to give Reagan a victory in 1980.

In his discussion with this group Reagan appeared to be leaning toward George Bush. He mentioned that three conservative Senators—Strom Thurmond of South Carolina, John Tower of Texas, and James McClure of Idaho—had all said Bush was acceptable to them. The Governor had said nothing about the negotiations with former President Ford, which he believed were confidential, although that night Ford permitted himself to be interviewed on television by CBS's Walter Cronkite and later by ABC's Barbara Walters. Broad hints of "co–presidency" were dropped and, knowing that Ronald Reagan was as surprised as I was at Ford's indiscretion, I called and asked our media people to get Jerry Ford off television before any more damage was done.

Even earlier, word of the negotiations between the Reagan and Ford camps had leaked out. Our team was represented by the Reagan campaign director, William J. Casey; Edwin Meese III, the Governor's long–time assistant; and Richard Wirthlin, his chief pollster and a key advisor.

The Ford group comprised Henry Kissinger, who was rather too obviously trying to set the stage for his own return to Washington as Secretary of State; John O. Marsh, the former Congressman from Virginia who had been Ford's chief counsel in the White House; Allan Greenspan, former Chairman of the President's Council of Economic Advisors; and Robert Barrett, another former Ford White House aide.

Of these four, it was Kissinger who roused the most opposition among conservatives. The night before I had managed to keep the gallery and delegates from booing Kissinger out of the arena when he had formally addressed the convention with a speech carefully calculated to allay conservative fears. Through our regional political directors I had given the order to the floor and galleries: *Don't boo. Let Kissinger have his say.*

Our people, realizing their every move or remark was being monitored by millions via television, let Henry speak, with only a minimum of interruption for scattered applause. Kissinger kept looking up expectantly at the end of each of his carefully tailored punch lines, waiting for the cheers that never sounded. The applause came only in widely separated ripples but our RPD's did manage to rouse the delegates and spectators for a final polite burst when Kissinger finished.

Tonight, however, the dominant conservative majority among our Republican delegates was more disturbed by the possibility of George Bush being picked as Vice President, even though (according to the TV pundits) that possibility appeared to be fading rapidly. Many of the delegates actually seemed to be relieved by Gerald Ford's seemingly certain selection.

In the trailer we had been informed that the former President had gone down one flight from his suite at the Detroit Plaza to meet with Governor Reagan. On Monday when Reagan and his family had arrived in Detroit they had attended a birthday party for Jerry Ford in the hotel. Ron Reagan, who carries his Irish wit with him wherever he goes, ceremoniously presented his 1976 rival for the nomination with an Indian peace pipe. The two old political warriors had a good laugh and I think this broke the ice for the serious negotiations that followed.

But now Ford seemed uncertain again. He told Reagan he wanted to sleep on the invitation to run for Vice President. The Governor, feeling that the suspense in the convention had been stretched out long enough, said, in effect, he wanted the decision then and there. Ford didn't see how he could give his decision that night so they shook hands and agreed to call the whole thing off. When Ford left, Reagan summoned his aides and told them: "Call George Bush." On the phone a surprised Bush promised

Reagan he would enthusiastically support him and the platform, although Bush had earlier opposed several of the more controversial planks.

A moment later the phone rang in our trailer. It was Governor Reagan's staff people informing us that he would be on his way to the arena to present George Bush's name to the convention personally. Senator Laxalt demanded to speak with Reagan himself and when he got him on the line Paul strongly urged Reagan not to come to the hall. After a moment the Senator shook his head and passed the phone to me. Reagan was still at the other end.

"Clif, I've made my choice," Reagan said to me in his forthright way. "The next Vice President will be George Bush. You can tell your gang in the trailer. But ask them not to let it out. I'm coming over to the convention right now to make the announcement."

"You can't come tonight," I replied. "I'm afraid these delegates will boo even you if you make that announcement in the convention tonight. Give us 24 hours to persuade them and you can come over tomorrow night for your acceptance address and they'll cheer you, I promise."

"No, Clif," he said, "I'm coming over."

I turned the phone back over to Senator Laxalt, who is probably Ronald Reagan's closest political friend and staunchest congressional ally. The Senator had caught the sense of the conversation and he picked up where I left off in urging Reagan not to come to the hall. Even Bill Timmons, who generally has very little to say, joined our chorus.

Nonetheless, Reagan stood his ground. He would not be deterred by the disappointment of the delegates. He would come to the hall and face whatever music he had to, no matter how discordant it might appear to be, especially to the vast television audience tuned in on the Republican convention.

When we finished talking with Ronald Reagan, I said something to Laxalt and Timmons about facing my own music and walked to the door of the outer room where the regional directors were manning their phones to the floor and galleries.

"OK," I said. "The Governor wants you to know—but he doesn't want you to let it out yet. His candidate is George Bush."

A salvo of groans greeted this announcement, followed by some unprintable expletives. One of the regional directors, who I know had worked unstintingly for Ronald Reagan for years, spit out a curse, strode to the outer door, and kicked it open. He disappeared into the night and it was 2:30 a.m. before we found him drinking off his disappointment in a bar at the hotel.

As it turned out, Reagan's appearance at Joe Louis Arena was a triumphal one. In their happiness over his victory on the roll call, none of the delegates wanted to sound a rebellious note as I'd feared they would. Indeed, their cheers seemed to lift the roof of the massive building. Even his announcement of George Bush as his candidate for Vice President was greeted with loud cheers.

Ronald Reagan's remarks that night were brief and to the point. He said it was former President Ford's decision not to run with him for Vice President but that Ford had promised to "campaign his heart out" for the Republican ticket.

He praised George Bush as a man with "great experience in government" and said that Bush had told him that "he can enthusiastically support the platform across the board." Since it was the platform that Senator Jesse Helms of North Carolina and other conservatives had labored so hard to construct, this aspect of Bush's candidacy was vital to the unity of the Republican Party.

Reagan brought the curtain down on that tense night without further ado.

"It's past the witching hour," he smiled. "It's late. God bless you. Good night. We'll see you tomorrow night."

The following night, Thursday, I was back in the communications trailer directing the roll call for George Bush, the man we had fought so hard against in the primary campaigns from January until June. I tried to make it a unanimous vote for Bush but three others received a total of 119 votes. They were Senator Helms, who received 54 delegate votes; Congressman Jack Kemp of New York, 42 votes; and Congressman Philip Crane of Illinois, 23 votes. Meager as these votes may seem next to the 1,832 cast for Bush, they are nonetheless no small measure of conservative dedication to the cause. The overwhelming majority of all the delegates at this convention were conservative but the fact that more than a hundred of them refused to go along with their presidential candidate was significant.

George Bush delivered a short acceptance address following his nomination and the stage was at last fully set for the big dramatic moment of the convention.

Ron and Nancy Reagan entered the hall with their family to the tune of "California, Here I Come" and the wildest cheering I'd ever observed at a national convention. It took more than a half–hour for the crowd to quiet down so the candidate could begin his acceptance speech. Typically, he opened with a jest. Referring to a biographical film on him that had been shown earlier, Reagan quipped:

"My first thrill tonight was to find myself in a movie on prime time."

The acceptance address had originally been drafted by Reagan's long–time public relations man, Peter Hannaford. But like all Reagan speeches, it had then been worked over thoroughly by Reagan himself. What emerged was a masterpiece of political oratory, delivered by one of the great speakers of the twentieth century.

Reagan deftly handled even the most emotional issues, like the party's anti–ERA plank, Social Security, and taxes, before moving into a broad attack on the policies of then–President Carter and the Democratic Party.

He promised that his top priority would be to continue the

quest for peace, while at the same time rebuilding America's weakened defenses.

"This evening marks the last step, save one, of a campaign that has taken Nancy and me from one end of this great land to the other," he said.

"It is impossible to capture in words the splendor of this vast continent which God has granted as our portion of His creation. There are no words to express the extraordinary strength and character of this breed of people we call Americans.

"Everywhere we have met thousands of Democrats, Independents, and Republicans from all economic conditions and walks of life. . . . They are concerned, yes. But they are not frightened. They are disturbed, but not dismayed. They are the kind of men and women Tom Paine had in mind when he wrote, during the darkest days of the American Revolution, 'We have it in our power to begin the world over again.' "

Reagan denounced those who say the American spirit no longer exists.

"I have seen it," he said. "I have felt it all across the land—in the big cities, the small towns, and in rural America. The American spirit is still there, ready to blaze into life if you and I are willing to do what has to be done—the practical, down-to-earth things that will stimulate our economy, increase productivity, and put America back to work."

Near the end, Candidate Reagan paused for a moment. Then he added:

"I have thought of something that is not a part of my speech and I'm worried over whether I should do it." He paused for one dramatic moment and went on: "Can we doubt that only a Divine Providence placed this land, this island of freedom here as a refuge for all those people in the world who yearn to breathe freely. . . .

"I'll confess that I've been a little afraid to suggest what I'm going to suggest—I'm more afraid not to—that we begin our crusade joined together in a moment of silent prayer."

He bowed his head humbly and a great silence descended upon the arena, a silence that I'm sure was emulated in millions of homes where our people were watching the convention on television. It lasted only a moment. Then Ronald Reagan raised his head and, with that winning smile that is all his own, said:

"God bless America."

2

A Man Who Speaks For Himself

It was characteristic of Ronald Reagan to insist on coming before a potentially hostile convention to personally announce a vice presidential choice he knew would be unpopular with many of the delegates. In the really tough spots, he is a man who can—and does—speak for himself. Two incidents from my personal experience with President Reagan will serve to illustrate this point. One occured the very first time I met him. The other took place on Thursday morning following his acceptance address at the Detroit convention.

At our morning strategy session, the day after Reagan presented George Bush to the convention, I revived my request for a meeting with the candidate and my regional directors. Ed Meese and Mike Deaver knew how important the regional directors would be to our coming campaign and they agreed to arrange the meeting.

The next morning, after Reagan's acceptance address, our RPD's came to the 69th floor of the Detroit Plaza and assembled in one

11

of the suites. Reagan was having breakfast in another suite with Governor William Milliken of Michigan and Mayor Coleman Young of Detroit and the breakfast lasted longer than expected. Ed Meese met me in the hall and told me that Reagan wanted to see me privately but, since his schedule was running late, he would have to cut short the meeting with our regional directors.

"No," I said. "I'll keep my meeting with Ron short. I want him to spend the time with our boys."

Meese then suggested Reagan bring George Bush with him to the session with the RPD's.

"They want a one–on–one session with the candidate," I said. "George can come in later if he wants. But we've got to give these fellows some time alone with Ron."

Reagan and I chatted for a few minutes in his suite and then I took him down the hall to meet the RPD's. He had a smile and a quip for them but some of the regional directors were still smarting over Reagan's choice of Bush and they wasted no time letting him know of their dissatisfaction.

Reagan answered their questions patiently and, where warranted, in detail. His forthright replies made sense and he won over most of the disgruntled RPD's. However, one or two die–hards kept firing tough, even hostile, questions at him. Reagan fielded them with grace and good humor but the tone of their questions kept getting more vitriolic. Finally, after one particularly rough sally, I stepped forward, intending to end the meeting.

"No, Clif," Reagan said, holding up his hand. "That's a good question and it deserves an answer." He then went on to respond in some detail and I happen to know the regional director who asked it walked out of that meeting committed to give the campaign every ounce of energy he could command, and he did.

George Bush came in toward the end of the meeting and disarmed the group with his opening remark. "Gee," he said with a mock rueful smile, "I'm sure glad to have you guys on my side for a change." The whole session ended on a friendly and cooperative note and I believe it helped bring the team more closely together for the coming campaign against Jimmy Carter and the Democrats.

There had been a lot of questions thrown at Ronald Reagan in that meeting that other presidential candidates I've known would have sluffed off or not even deigned to answer. Some might have tossed the particularly hot potatoes to their aides. But Reagan met all the questions head on, although with no show of belligerence, a trait I believe is foreign to his nature. Above all, he had insisted on answering even the toughest questions himself.

At the very outset of my relationship with Ronald Reagan I had observed this telling quality in him. My first meeting with him took place in Los Angeles in the early autumn of 1964. I have often thought that Reagan took his first step toward the White House at this meeting, though I'm sure he did not attend with any presidential vision in mind. In fact, he came to accept a leadership role in an obviously losing campaign—Senator Barry Goldwater's brave but ill-starred bid for the highest office in our land.

I had served as the original organizer of the National Draft Goldwater Committee which conceived and successfully executed history's first genuine draft of a presidential candidate.

Barry Goldwater had not sought the Republican nomination. Indeed, he did not want it. But the grassroots conservative movement, mobilized for the first time in our Draft Goldwater Committee, pushed the reluctant candidate out onto the primary campaign trail. Reorganized as the National Goldwater for President Committee in January 1964, we succeeded in winning the nomination for the Arizona Senator at the July convention in San Francisco against the formidable opposition of the entrenched Eastern Establishment, represented that year by Nelson Rockefeller and William Scranton.

After the convention we created the Citizens for Goldwater-

Miller, the organization that was to coordinate the activities of the myriad volunteer groups spawned by the Draft Goldwater movement. Jimmy Doolittle and Claire Booth Luce were named co–chairmen and I was appointed national director. It was in this capacity that I first came into contact with Ronald Reagan.

I had flown to Los Angeles from Washington with Dean Burch, the newly named Chairman of the Republican National Committee, and John Grenier, Dean's executive assistant. Two groups were struggling for control of the Citizens for Goldwater in California. One group wanted Phillip Davis, a Southern California businessman, for chairman of the Citizens committee in the state. The other wanted Ronald Reagan.

Davis came to the meeting with several of his key supporters. Reagan came alone. The Davis group felt they had earned the right to run the show in California since many of them had been among Senator Goldwater's earliest and most active supporters in that state. They had helped give Goldwater his smashing presidential primary victory over Nelson Rockefeller and had brought the largest single state delegation pledged to the Senator into the Republican national convention.

The meeting quickly warmed up and after about an hour things got rather hot and heavy. Phil Davis and the others kept talking about Ron's political inexperience. Reagan, who was sitting next to me, had not had much to say and after a particularly acerbic attack on him by the Davis group I decided to intervene. As I started to raise my voice in his defense, Reagan reached over and gently grasped my arm.

"No, Clif," he said quietly. "This is my fight. Let me handle it."

He freely admitted he did not have as much political experience as Phil Davis but he then went on to offer such persuasive arguments for his involvement in the campaign that the meeting broke up in a happy compromise: Reagan and Davis would serve as Co–Chairmen of the Citizens for Goldwater in California.

Together they helped the Senator win nearly three million votes, far more than he received in any other state. More important for the future, Reagan and Davis expanded conservative control over the Republican Party machinery in California, which just that year had become the most populous state in the Union.

I had several more meetings with Ronald Reagan during the 1964 campaign and my respect for his judgment began to grow. It became obvious to me that he was a serious, genuinely thoughtful man who bore little resemblance to the image that even then was being painted of him as a superficial actor with no real grasp of the issues confronting the country. The fact was he had a better grasp of the issues than most professional politicians, including the one who then occupied the White House, Lyndon Johnson.

It is my belief that President Reagan is an American leader in the truest and deepest sense. By that I mean he has never sought power for power's own sake, as so many of our recent Presidents have. If you study his career, and particularly if you get to know the man, you will soon realize he has always been thrust into leadership positions because of his deep and abiding sense of duty, his sincere belief that it is a citizen's obligation to serve.

Ronald Reagan has been a leader all his life, but every leadership role that he played sought him, including the presidency. Once he became committed to run for an office, however, he threw everything he had into the race. Over a period of a dozen years—from 1968 to 1980—he waged three campaigns for the Republican Presidential nomination. In every one of those campaigns he went all out, although the odds against him in 1968 and 1976 appeared to be insurmountable. Ronald Reagan is, quite obviously, not a man to back away from a fight. Nonetheless, I doubt if he ever deliberately sought one in his life. Controversy is not his style and he will go to great lengths to avoid an open confrontation. And, most important of all, he never gives up.

The high courage which the country and the world saw so dramatically during the assassination attempt on President Reagan in March 1980 is only one facet of his leadership capabilities. Another, which I think was apparent from the moment he stepped onto the national political stage in 1964, is that Ronald Regan genuinely *likes* people. In this respect he is more like Dwight D. Eisenhower than any other President of the past two decades.

I had a chance to observe Reagan's Ike–like charisma very early in our relationship. One night in October 1964 I was in Los Angeles to deliver a speech for Candidate Goldwater at a dinner rally. After the dinner, a number of people got together to give a party for me at the home of one of our Citizens for Goldwater leaders. Ron Reagan had also given a speech for Goldwater that night at another rally and he was late arriving at the party. But when he came into the room the whole party seemed to light up. I always thought this was due in part to the love for Ron reflected in Nancy Reagan's eyes. And that night I saw for the first time the warm glow that seems to radiate from both Nancy and Ron when they are together.

After most of the people had left the party about a dozen of us sat around on the living room floor telling stories about the campaign and the people involved in it. Ronald Reagan's stories were easily the best, and certainly the funniest. In no time, he had us all laughing. Yet his stories all had a point to them, and collectively they caught the brave spirit of Barry Goldwater and his adherents, the spirit of our then very young conservative movement.

None of Ronald Reagan's stories had a mean twist to them. All of them presented the cast of characters in a good light. They were not of the sophisticated stuff that party stories are usually made in Hollywood or New York or Washington. But they were good stories about real people, amusing stories pertinent to our campaign, revealing vignettes of the hard–working men and women waging a tough, so often disappointing battle against the seemingly all–powerful coalition inherited by Lyndon Johnson. Their difficulties were magnified a thousand–fold by the news media, which, in that year at least, had united into a blatant propaganda machine for the Democratic Party and its presidential candidate.

As my co-author, William J. Gill, and I observed in our book, *Suite 3505: The Story of the Draft Goldwater Movement,* Barry Goldwater had enjoyed a generally good press before he became a serious candidate for President. Working newsmen liked the Senator personally. They admired his honesty and his candor, which almost always made his statements "good copy." After the assassination of President Kennedy, however, many members of the media became almost hysterical in their opposition to Goldwater and the people who openly supported him.

John S. Knight, president of the Knight newspapers in Miami, Detroit, Akron and other cities (now the Knight–Ridder group) was *not* a Goldwater supporter. But his sense of fair play rebelled against what he called the "shabby treatment" of the Senator by "most of the news media." In the *Detroit Free Press* of June 21, 1964—months before the hysteria reached its height in the fall campaign—Knight wrote: "Of the syndicated columnists, I can think of only a few who are not savagely cutting down Senator Goldwater day after day." The same held true, he said, of cartoonists, television commentators and editorial writers. Some journalists even tried to pin the "fascist" label on Barry Goldwater. From San Francisco, columnist Drew Pearson wrote: "The smell of fascism is strong at this convention." Others picked up the fascist theme and ran with it all the way down to election day.

Under the withering barrage trained on Goldwater and his followers, the most staunchly Republican newspapers broke in a mad scramble to dissociate themselves from his candidacy. Even the Hearst chain caved in. In all America, only a handful of major newspapers stood by Goldwater editorially, among them the *Chicago Tribune, Los Angeles Times, St. Louis Globe Democrat,*

Cincinnati Enquirer and *San Diego Union.* In endorsing Goldwater on September 29, 1964 the *Cincinnati Enquirer* said:

> Barry Goldwater has become the most slandered man in American political history. . . . He is portrayed as a poisoner of chidren, as a creature of the night–riders, as a pawn of the militarists and the war–mongers. To see the viciousness of the vilification heaped upon him is to begin to understand the desperation with which his enemies are trying to cling to the perverted political order they have been foisting on America. Their purpose is to do considerably more than defeat him at the polls: they seek literally to crush him lest any other muster the courage to ask them to account for their sordid works.

Today, four presidential campaigns later, even many of the people who participated in this all-out character assassination of Senator Goldwater must realize how badly misled they were. Indeed, most of the press once again regards him kindly.

In spite of this experience, some members of the Fourth Estate tried to mount a similar campaign against Ronald Reagan in 1980. In so doing they were taking their cue from a desperate Democratic Party and from an incumbent President driven to the extreme position of attempting to label his opponent as a man not to be trusted with control over atomic weapons.

Jimmy Carter's extremism backfired badly, as the results of the 1980 election will forever testify. And I believe one of the reasons it backfired is because much of the media had the feeling they had been down that primrose path before and they did not want to repeat the excesses of 1964. Further, they saw that Ronald Reagan was not suited for the war–mongering role obviously alien to Reagan's whole personality. This, of course, was apparent to anyone who knew Ronald Reagan, as I came to know him from 1964 onward.

The drubbing Jimmy Carter absorbed in the television debate with Candidate Reagan in 1980 was due in part to the then President's amazing misreading of his opponent. It is a mistake people have often made about Reagan—underestimating his resourcefulness, his knowledge, and above all, his great ability to win people over to his views on important issues. It is probably no consolation for Mr. Carter, but this mistake was made by some of my colleagues among the Goldwater campaign's leaders. Fortunately, the mistake was corrected then. If it had not been, Ronald Reagan may never have made it all the way to the White House.

3

The Speech

Ronald Reagan's presidential star first orbited on the outer edge of the American political horizon in the autumn of 1964, when millions of television viewers almost accidentally caught a speech he gave in support of Barry Goldwater. The speech was very nearly accidental on several counts. First, it had initially been vetoed by some of Senator Goldwater's key advisors. Second, after the Senator finally gave the green light himself the election was barely a week away and the Goldwater Television Committee had to scurry frantically to get the half–hour Reagan speech on the air.

A number of versions have been given as to how the speech got on national television, and why it almost did not get on at all. The latest I have heard is Senator Goldwater's version, which he delivered, tongue in cheek, at a luncheon for my original Draft Goldwater cadre on the Saturday before Ronald Reagan's inauguration as President.

"Now you fellows can see what happens when you give a speech away," the Senator smiled. He implied the Reagan speech had originally been written for him "but some of those damn words were just too long for me so I said give it to Ron Reagan."

This is an amusing bit of apocrypha. But the version I recall from the Goldwater campaign days is that Ronald Reagan wrote the speech himself, and all the evidence indicates it was a speech he had actually been giving in somewhat different forms for a good many years. Some elements originated with the standard speech he gave touring General Electric plants when he was employed by GE as a good will ambassador. *

Campaigning for Goldwater as California Co–Chairman of our Citizens organization, Reagan polished the speech to perfection. One night he gave it at a fund-raising dinner in Los Angeles and several of our Citizens for Goldwater people who were there decided it was so inspiring it ought to be shown on television. They put up their own money, as I recall, and had Reagan repeat the Los Angeles speech as a half–hour show for TV on a local L.A. station. Then they offered it to the Goldwater headquarters in Washington.

Several of the Senator's advisors, including the late William Baroody and Denison Kitchel, the Goldwater campaign chairman, deemed the Reagan speech too "emotional and unscholarly." For some days a debate was waged at the Washington headquarters about the speech and I remember asking whether Senator Goldwater had heard the speech himself. When I was told he had not, I suggested he see it as soon as possible and make the final decision. Meanwhile, the Goldwater TV Committee was also pushing hard for the Reagan speech in order to fill a half-hour in prime time they had already purchased, and they refused to release the time for any other campaign purpose.

At last, the Senator was shown the speech and he gave his approval, as I thought he would. It was shown on national television Tuesday night, October 27th, and millions of people

*Reagan was also host of TV's highly successful General Electric Theater. This show held first place in the Sunday night prime time ratings for nearly eight years beginning in 1954 until *Bonanza* galloped over the video horizon in living color and knocked GE Theater's black-and-white offering into oblivion.

who watched the Reagan speech realized that a new political star had been born. Ronald Reagan switched thousands of voters from the Democratic fold that night. Many of them never returned.

Although it may be difficult for liberals to believe even now, what Ronald Reagan did in 1964 was to echo the innermost beliefs, thoughts and feelings of the vast majority of Americans. And he articulated them so succinctly, so compellingly that even before he finished the twenty–seven minutes on television a good many people were already thinking of Reagan as a future leader of our country.

What was it that Reagan said that struck such a responsive chord in America's half–hidden heart? A few excerpts from "A Time for Choosing," the title he gave the speech, will suffice to tell:

> For almost two centuries we have proved man's capacity for self–government, but today we are told we must choose between left and right, or, as others suggest, a third alternative, a kind of safe middle ground.
>
> I suggest to you there is no left or right, only an up or down. Up to the maximum of individual freedom consistent with law and order, or down to the ant heap of totalitarianism, and regardless of their humanitarian purpose, those who would sacrifice freedom for security have, whether they know it or not, chosen this downward path. . . .
>
> Already the hour is late. Government had laid its heavy hand on health, housing, farming, industry, commerce, education, and to an ever increasing degree interferes with the people's right to know. . . .

There were flashes of the Reagan wit in the speech, illuminating some of the darkest corners of Lyndon Johnson's Great Society, which was gearing up to spawn an additional array of federal bureaus:

> A government agency is the nearest thing to eternal life we'll ever see on this earth. . . .
>
> There are two–and–a–half million Federal employes. No one knows what they all do. One Congressman found out what one of them does. This man sits at a desk in Washington. Documents come to him each morning. He

reads them, initials them, passes them on to the proper agency. One day a document arrived that he wasn't supposed to read. But he read it, initialed it, and passed it on. Twenty–four hours later it arrived back at his desk with a memo attached that said, "You weren't supposed to read this. Erase your initials, and initial the erasure". . . .

After attacking the Democratic domestic record, Reagan turned to foreign policy. It was obvious even in 1964 that the United States was bogged down in Vietnam, and although Lyndon Johnson raised ferocious fears during the campaign about Barry Goldwater's "dangerous" stand on the war, it was President Johnson who escalated the conflict sharply the following year and pursued it in ways that guaranteed we could not win.

Characteristically, Reagan refrained from being too critical of the incumbent President's strategy in Vietnam, believing, like most of us, that you should support your country in wartime whether you agree with its policy or not. However, he spoke clearly on the larger war with Communism, of which Vietnam was only a single painful episode. And in one broad brush stroke he showed how the the conduct of that larger war depends on America's fiscal stability:

> We are faced with the most evil enemy mankind has known in its long climb from the swamp to the stars. There can be no security anywhere in the free world if there is not fiscal and economic stability within the United States. Those who ask us to trade our freedom for the soup kitchen of the welfare state are architects of a policy of accomodation. They tell us that by avoiding a direct confrontation with the enemy he will learn to love us and give up his evil ways. All who oppose this idea are blanketly indicted as warmongers.
>
> Well, let us set one thing straight: there is no argument with regard to peace and war. It is cheap demagoguery to suggest that anyone would want to send other people's sons to war. The only argument is with regard to the best way to *avoid* war. There is only one sure way—*surrender*. . . .
>
> Should Moses have told the children of Israel to live in slavery rather than dare the wilderness? Should Christ have refused the Cross? Should patriots at Concord Bridge have refused to fire the shot heard round the world? Are we to believe that all the martyrs of history died in vain?

Then Reagan finished up with a rallying call to the American people, a call they heard only faintly at first, but one they realized more and more they would one day have to answer:

> You and I have a rendezvous with destiny. We can preserve for our children this the last hope of man on earth or we can sentence them to take the first step into a thousand years of darkness. If we fail, at least let our children and our children's children say of us we justified our brief moment here. We did all that could be done.

The immediate reaction to the Reagan TV speech was overwhelming. Our Citizens for Goldwater headquarters in Washington and the state and city offices throughout the country were snowed under with telephone calls and personal visits from people who had seen Reagan on television. Checks showered in on the Goldwater campaign as a result of the brief fund–raising rider that had been given at the end of the TV program. An estimate of $600,000 has been used by several writers, but I believe the figure was far more than that if contributions that came to our local, state and national Citizen's groups as well as to the Goldwater campaign headquarters are included.

Many of these contributions were used to buy additional time for the Reagan speech on local television stations, and I did everything I could from Washington to encourage this. In some cities *The Speech*, as it was already being called, was shown as many as a half–dozen times.

Not all the reaction was favorable, of course. Some liberal editorial writers tried to pin the tired old "extremist" label on Reagan for his outspoken attack on Communism and his strong criticism of the federal bureaucracy. Reagan could laugh off most of this criticism but he was hurt when his former friends in organized labor joined the chorus. Reagan had been president of the Screen Actors Guild, an AFL–CIO affiliate union, for six terms and had served on its bargaining committees for many more.

In his 1965 autobiography, *Where's the Rest of Me*, Reagan's hurt showed through when he wrote: "My erstwhile associates in organized labor at the top level of the AFL–CIO assail me as a 'strident voice of the right wing lunatic fringe.' Sadly I have come to realize that a great many so–called liberals aren't liberal—they will defend to the death your right to agree with them."*

Reagan wrote these lines in 1965 but strangely the AFL–CIO was still clinging to its distorted picture of him and of the conservative movement in 1981, although millions of union members had voted for Reagan for President in 1980. Indeed, estimates of union rank-and-file support of Reagan in that election range from 40 to 50 percent, which suggests to me that some of the hierarchy in the AFL–CIO has not only lost touch with political reality but also with its own membership.

By the time he wrote his autobiography Reagan had reached the conclusion that the labels "liberal" and "conservative" somehow had gotten "pasted on the wrong people."

"The classic liberal used to be the man who believed the individual was, and should be forever, the master of his destiny," Reagan wrote. "That is now the conservative position. . . . The liberals believe in remote and massive strong–arming from afar, usually Washington, D.C."

This perception of the liberal and conservative positions was even then gaining currency in America. Once again Ronald Reagan was articulating what so many of his fellow citizens had come to believe, just as he had in his television speech during the Goldwater campaign.

After the 1964 election I sent a letter to all the former leaders of the Citizens for Goldwater requesting answers to seven key questions plus "an overall report of the political climate and situation" in each state. Ron Reagan replied with characteristic humility: "I'm afraid I have to yell for help." He pleaded that he

*Where's the Rest of Me by Ronald Reagan with Richard G. Hubler; Duell, Sloan and Pearce, New York, 1965. (The Reagan autobiography takes its title from a line in the scene in the movie Kings Row in which actor Ronald Reagan awakens after an operation to find both his legs had been amputated by a revengeful surgeon.)

had "not paid enough attention to the backstage operation" of politics in California to give me the full–dress report I'd requested. Nonetheless, he sent back the questionnaire "with some scratched notes that I made which only indicate to me that I wasn't the best source for this kind of information."

In spite of this self-deprecating approach, Reagan's comments on the questionnaire showed he was learning more about politics than perhaps even he realized at the time. In answer to my question about the effectiveness of the state Republican Party organization, he noted that in California it was "divided definitely along the liberal–conservative line." And on the prospects for the party in terms of the 1966 elections he wrote: "Good—depending on final decision with regard to gubernatorial candidate and if one is chosen to unite the party and avoid a bitter primary."

I knew that some of our mutual friends in California had already talked with Reagan about running for governor there but this indicated to me that he had not yet made up his mind. Actually, Reagan had been seriously approached a number of times over the years about running for public office. As early as 1948 the Democrats had tried to persuade him to run for Congress against an incumbent Republican, Donald Jackson, who had been targeted by the liberals because he was a member of the House Un–American Activities Committee. But Reagan had turned down the Democrats, although he was a respected member of that party at the time.

In 1962 some leading Republicans asked him to run for either the governorship or the U.S. Senate but he turned them down too and worked instead for Richard Nixon in his losing campaign for governor. In 1964 he was again approached to try for the Senate but he declined, probably because he felt his old friend George Murphy should have a crack at the Senate on the basis of George's long and very useful work for the Republican Party, both in California and nationally.

George Murphy's victory over Pierre Salinger, the late President Kennedy's press secretary, in the 1964 California contest for the United States Senate, may have helped nudge Ronald Reagan into seeking the Republican gubernatorial nomination in 1966. Senator Murphy, a conservative and, like Reagan, a former President of the Screen Actors Guild, had won handily against the strong Democratic tide that swept so much of the nation in '64.

In December of 1964 I had a talk with Ronald Reagan on the telephone. I mentioned the tremendous response to his television speech and asked if he would consider running for Governor.

"Clif," he asked doubtfully, "do you run for Governor on the basis of a single speech?"

"People have run on a whole lot less," I replied. "In politics, as in life, you have to take the opportunities as they come. You have a chance to catch the train now and ride it into Sacramento and the governor's mansion in 1966. If you wait, the train may pull out of the station and leave you standing on the platform. I hope you will give some serious thought to running. You've got the strong leadership qualities California and the country need very badly. I think we are going to need them even more in the years ahead."

Reagan refused to say he would run. But a few months later three of our mutual friends called on him at his home in Pacific Palisades. They were Henry Salvatori, chairman of the Western Geophysical Company of America; A.C. (Cy) Rubel, former chief executive officer of Union Oil Company of California; and Holmes Tuttle, whose Ford auto dealership in Los Angeles is one of the largest in the country.

As I had done on the phone in December, they urged Reagan to run for Governor. At the outset he turned them down but they kept working on him and before the meeting was over they had persuaded him at least to consider running.

It was nearly a month before he made up his mind. I know that he talked with his wife, Nancy, about it over and over again, and

I am certain he prayed over it every day. At last he told our friends that he would run—on the condition that the Republican Party unite behind his candidacy.

This same concern had surfaced in the notes he had scribbled on my questionnaire some weeks earlier—that Republican prospects in California for 1966 were "good" providing the GOP could find a gubernatorial candidate "to unite the party and avoid a bitter primary."

Uniting the disunited Republicans of California was easier said than done and, as it turned out, the bitter primary was unavoidable. In the end, however, Ronald Reagan did unite the party in California and it remained united on through to his Presidency.

4

The Movement

William A. Rusher, author, columnist and long-time publisher of *National Review* wrote soon after the 1980 election: "Ronald Reagan did not spring full-blown from the brow of Jove in 1980 or any recent year." Rusher, a cofounder of the Draft Goldwater Committee, also observed, quite correctly, that "the history of the modern conservative movement in this country is not widely understood, primarily because our largely liberal media and academic analysts first ignored it as long as possible, then minimized it, and continue to distort it relentlessly."

How did today's conservatism begin? Politically, it is traceable, at least in part, to Senator Robert A. Taft and his quest for the Republican Presidential nomination against Dwight D. Eisenhower in 1952. Philosophically, many historians trace the origins of modern conservative thought to a group of classical 18th Century thinkers, most prominently Edmund Burke, the 18th Century parliamentarian. More recent philosophical mentors of the movement include such diverse libertarian or individualistic thinkers as Albert Jay Nock, H.L. Mencken and T.S. Eliot, the poet of *The Waste Land*. Eliot, particularly, exerted a strong influence on modern American conservative thinkers and engaged in faithful correspondence with Russell Kirk and others on this side of the Atlantic in the immediate post–World War II period.

Those of us who returned from that war in 1945–46 found the liberal cause transcendent—in politics, in the academy, in the media. Indeed, many of us who later became leaders of the modern conservative movement considered ourselves to be liberals in those early days, Ronald Reagan and this writer among them. Yet even then we were beginning to coalesce around the three fundamental issues that have carried conservatism from a minority status to what I believe is today an overwhelmingly majority position in the United States. Those three issues are: (1) that belief in God is necessary to freedom and to a proper respect for our fellow man; (2) that totalitarianism, under whatever guise, must be resisted with all our strength; and (3) that the federal government interferes coercively in our everyday lives through oppressive taxes, restrictive regulations, and an increasing tendency of federal courts to dictate laws to states and communities.

These are the three fundamental beliefs that ultimately carried Ronald Reagan to the presidency. Yet much of the philosophic impetus behind the second, and to some extent the third, of these basic tenets of modern conservatism—that totalitarianism and the growing encroachment of government upon individual rights must be strenuously opposed—originally emanated from Europe. And a good bit of this impetus came from a group of philosopher-economists who comprised the "Austrian School"; Ludwig von Mises, Friedrich Hayek, and Wilhelm Ropke, to name a few.*

The Austrians, and a fair number of other Europeans, were provided with an intellectual base in America by Leonard Read and his Foundation for Economic Education, founded by Read in 1946 and still active today in Irvington–on–Hudson, New York. A year after Read started FEE nearly forty European and American

*Wilhelm Ropke is actually a German but he came to be identified with the "Austrian School."

scholars gathered at Mont Pelerin in Switzerland to form the society that still bears the name of that original meeting place. At the conclusion of this conference in the spring of 1947 the Mont Pelerin Society adopted a "Statement of Aims" that included the following passage, one with which today's conservatives—and, I would hope, many thoughtful liberals—will most certainly agree:

> The central values of civilization are in danger. Over large stretches of the earth's surface the essential conditions of human dignity and freedom have already disappeared. . . . The position of the individual and the voluntary group are progressively undermined by extensions of arbitrary power. Even the most precious possession of Western Man, freedom of thought and expression, is threatened by the spread of creeds which, claiming the privilege of tolerance when in the position of a minority, seek only to establish a position of power in which they can suppress and obliterate all views but their own.
>
> The group [the Mont Pelerin Society] holds that these developments have been fostered by the growth of a view of history which denies all absolute moral standards and by the growth of theories which question the desirability of the rule of law. It holds further that they have been fostered by a decline of belief in private property and the competitive market; for without the diffused power and initiative associated with these institutions it is difficult to imagine a society in which freedom may be effectively preserved.

One member of the Mont Pelerin Society attending this 1947 meeting was Milton Friedman, who in later years would win the Nobel Prize and would come to exert a strong influence on Ronald Reagan's economic policies. Looking back on Mont Pelerin some two decades later, Friedman observed: "The importance of that meeting was that it showed us that we were not alone."

Every conservative has at one time or another in the past felt this same, deep sense of aloneness, of isolation. President Reagan has shared it too, as he revealed in the speech he gave to the Conservative Political Action Conference at the Mayflower Hotel in Washington on March 20, 1980, when he asked:

"How many of us were there who used to go home from meetings like this with no thought of giving up, but still find ourselves wondering in the dark of night whether this much–loved land might go the way of other great nations that lost a sense of mission and a passion for freedom?

"There are so many people and institutions who come to mind for their role in the success we celebrate tonight. Intellectual leaders like Russell Kirk, Friedrich Hayek, Henry Hazlitt, Milton Friedman, James Burnham, Ludwig von Mises—they shaped so much of our thoughts." He paid a special tribute to the late Frank Meyer, whom he credited with helping to fashion "a vigorous new synthesis of traditional and libertarian thought—a synthesis that is today recognized by many as modern conservatism."

Friedman, Hayek, von Mises and others came to be known as "conservative economists," though in 1947 probably few of them would have owned up to being "conservative" and at least one, Hayek, disavowed the label and wrote an essay in 1960 entitled "Why I Am Not a Conservative" in which he claimed instead to be an "Old Whig."

Yet Hayek's landmark 1944 book *The Road to Serfdom* had helped greatly in stimulating interest in the conservative philosophy, whether he would accept the name or not. And with von Mises, Ropke and the others who gravitated to Mont Pelerin and the Foundation for Economic Education, they presented a very clear alternative to the prevailing academy of economists whose output was then almost completely dominated by the liberal theories of John Maynard Keynes.

President Franklin Delano Roosevelt had constructed his radical New Deal on the Keynesian model and conservatives increasingly viewed Keynes' planned economy with deep distrust. As the Keynesian epoch clanked onward, and particularly as it gained new momentum with the accession of John F. Kennedy's New Frontier and Lyndon Johnson's Great Society, the conservatives gained in credibility almost everywhere and were joined by millions of Americans in their revulsion for the planned society.

Slogans play too important a role in politics and much too

often they are misleading. I doubt if any of the Democratic Presidents who presided over the New Deal, New Frontier or Great Society concocted the slogans themselves. Indeed, in the case of Lyndon Johnson, his Great Society slogan originated with the Fabian Socialists in England a half-century before LBJ ran with it against Senator Goldwater.

In 1914 Graham Wallas, a leading Fabian theorist, published his book, *The Great Society*. The preface is a letter to Walter Lippmann, who, Wallas implies, inspired the book. Significantly, the last three chapters of *The Great Society* are revealingly titled "The Organization of Thought," "The Organization of Will," and finally, "The Organization of Happiness." In his 1964 campaign, Lyndon Johnson seemed to be emphasizing "The Organization of Happiness" but he also added another which played an even more important role in his landslide—"The Organization of Fear," a theme which Jimmy Carter tried unsuccessfully to inject into the 1980 campaign against Ronald Reagan.

It must not be imagined that all substantive political thought in America in the twentieth century came from abroad, whether it be Keynes, Wallas, Beatrice and Sidney Webb and the other Fabians exporting their brand of socialism to our shores or Hayek, von Mises, Ropke, et al shipping us their conservative–libertarian philosophy. On the contrary, America was developing its own political philosophers and a significant number of them were conservative or, at the least, libertarian.

Among the foremost younger conservative thinkers and writers of the movement's embryo period—the 1950's—were William F. Buckley, Jr., Russell Kirk and Richard Weaver.

Buckley's *God and Man at Yale*, published in 1951 soon after he was graduated from Yale, burst upon the post–World War II scene like a revelation, challenging as it did the most cherished tenets of liberal thought, not only at Yale and in American higher education generally, but in the larger body politic as well.

Two years later Russell Kirk's *The Conservative Mind* drove another wedge into the hidebound liberal academy. A study of conservative thought since the late 18th Century, Kirk's book was also a sweeping indictment of liberalism in all its forms. Looking back to Edmund Burke as the founder and fountainhead of "the true school of conservative principle," Kirk argued persuasively that any just government had to be grounded on the "belief that a divine intent rules society as well as conscience," that "property and freedom are inseparably connected, that economic levelling is not economic progress," and, finally, that there must be a "recognition that change and reform are not identical."

Richard Weaver had in a sense anticipated both Buckley and Kirk and the whole new school of conservative thought with the publication of his book, *Ideas Have Consequences*, in 1948. Many scholars believe this was the genesis of serious conservative philosophy in the post World War II period. Like Kirk, Weaver was profoundly pessimistic in his outlook and his book took as its theme "the dissolution of the West."

Everywhere he looked, Weaver saw evidence of this dissolution—in art, music, politics, education, the business world. Yet he set for modern conservatives a lofty goal: nothing less than the "driving afresh of the wedge between the material and the transcendental." Moreover, he made specific recommendations for the achievement of that goal, such as greater discipline in the teaching of languages, both English and foreign tongues, and in a revival of poety, which Weaver believed "offers the fairest hope of restoring our lost unity of mind." Willmoore Kendall, the political scientist who was Bill Buckley's mentor at Yale, wrote that *"Ideas Have Consequences* had elevated Richard Weaver to 'the captaincy of the anti-Liberal team.' " Actually, in 1948 I doubt if conservatives could have fielded a full philosophical team as large as a football eleven against the rampant liberalism of the time.

We were beginning, however, to recruit knowledgeable new activists for the squad, and many of them were coming from a rather surprising source—the far Left.

In the wake of the Hitler-Stalin Pact of 1939, which sliced Poland in half and started World War II, many American and European communists had taken a second look at their Marxist faith. Now, in the immediate post-war period, many more were shaken by the revelations of espionage in high places within the U.S. Government. Although historians today call this the "McCarthy Era," actually the most serious disclosures of Soviet spying were made well *before* Senator Joseph McCarthy first leveled his charges against the State Department.

Whittaker Chambers, the man who identified Alger Hiss as a Soviet agent in 1948, was among the first of the former Communists to come in from the cold. He was joined by Frank Meyer, Nathaniel Weyl, Will Herberg and Willi Schlamm, all of whom, with Chambers, wound up writing for William Buckley's *National Review*. Several other former men of the Left, though not ex–Communists, joined this company, most prominently James Burnham and Ralph de Toledano.

It is my belief that the people who abandoned the Left to join the conservative movement did so almost invariably as an act of conscience. The credibility of Communism or the other Leftist creeds had been stretched to a breaking point and they could not continue serving an ideology in which they no longer believed.

In *The God That Failed*, a book which appeared in 1950, six well-known intellectuals told the story of their disenchantment with Communism. They were Arthur Koestler, Ignazio Silone, Richard Wright, Andre Gide, Louis Fischer and Stephen Spender. Koestler, the author of *Darkness at Noon* and other novels about the crisis of civilization, stated the reason for his defection in vivid terms:

> At no time and in no country have more revolutionaries been killed and reduced to slavery than in Soviet Russia. To one who himself for seven years found excuses for every stupidity and crime committed under the Marxist banner, the spectacle of these dialectical tight-rope acts of self-deception, performed by men of good will and intelligence, is more dis-

heartening than the barbarities committed by the simple in spirit. Having experienced the almost unlimited possibilities of mental acrobatism on that tight–rope stretched across one's conscience, I know how much stretching it takes to make that elastic rope snap.

Many former communists, Koestler included, never moved all the way over into the conservative fold, of course. But those who did, like Whittaker Chambers and Frank Meyer, brought with them more than an intimate knowledge of the inner workings of the Communist apparatus. They came armed with an invaluable perspective of how the Communists manipulate liberals and liberalism.

Defectors from the Left added strength to the new conservatism budding in the 1950s. But the mainstream of conservative thought came from people who never flirted with the Left, or, if they had, the flirtation had been brief and transitory. A fair number of them were Roman Catholic, including Buckley, Kirk, F. Brent Bozell, Thomas Molnar, Francis Wilson and Frederick Wilhemsen. A good many others were Episcopalian, among them Anthony Harrigan, John Hallowell and Bernard Iddings Bell, the latter an Episcopal priest.

Harrigan, who now heads the United States Industrial Council, came out of Bard College, where the Reverend Bell had once been warden, joined the *Charleston News and Courier* in South Carolina where he worked with two outstanding conservative newsmen, William Watts Ball and Thomas R. Waring. Disturbed by the weakening of the moral ethical fiber of Americans, Harrigan traced it to a "fierce and subtle" modernism which was promoting amorality at the expense of traditional values. "Though the life of the country is basically decent," Harrigan wrote, "Americans are in the hands of a cultural ruling class which, having led to destruction the humane elements in our civilization, is conducting us to ruin."

In the early writings of Anthony Harrigan and others we can see the beginnings of the awakening which has now spread across much of the land.

At the time Harrigan, Buckley, Kirk, Bozell and the others first appeared on the scene, however, all the normal channels of national mass communication were virtually closed to conservatives. As publisher Henry Regnery recalls: "Liberalism reigned supreme and without question; the Liberal could believe, in fact, that no other position was conceivable." It is a measure of the early conservative movement's courage and determination that it was able to open up its own communication network, for the most part bypassing the mass media, to reach out directly to the people who were soon to become the activists in the campaign to win the mind of America.

5

The Oracles

For fifteen years before he became President of the United States Ronald Reagan was the articulate leader and spokesman of the conservative political cause in America. He was able to delineate the conservative position on both foreign and domestic policy issues in a way that won acceptability with broad blocs of voters and with influential national leaders. Quite often he was saying essentially the same things on these issues that other conservatives were saying. But instead of being obliterated by the press and other opinion moulders as Barry Goldwater was in 1964, Reagan, although frequently criticized, somehow escaped major damage. And, more than that, he actually converted many doubting Thomases to conservative positions, at least on certain key issues such as national defense and federal spending.

Nonetheless, I do not believe that even Ronald Reagan, as deftly articulate as he is, could possibly have paved the way for the 1980 landslide singlehandedly. He is, in fact, the first to say that "our victory, when it was achieved, was not so much a victory of ideas, not so much a victory for any one man or party as it was a victory for a set of principles—principles that were protected and

38

nourished by a few unselfish Americans through many grim and heart-breaking defeats."

The broad acceptance of these conservative principles by the American people was evident in virtually every national election after 1964. Only two years after Senator Goldwater's defeat, Ronald Reagan and 25 other Republicans, most of them conservatives, were elected governors of their states. In 1968 Richard M. Nixon, who claimed to be a conservative, though most people now recognize he was not, was elected to his first term as President and in 1972 he won the second biggest electoral landslide in history with only one state, Massachusetts, voting against him. Even the presidential election of 1976 cannot be viewed as a repudiation of conservative principles. Jimmy Carter won his narrow victory because he was perceived to be a conservative and if he had revealed his liberalism, as he did during the next four years, he would have been soundly trounced by Gerald Ford.

In short, the whole broad sweep of public opinion in America for the last two decades has been increasingly conservative, and the setbacks suffered by the Republican Party, rightly regarded by our citizens as the more conservative of our two major parties, have been temporary ones that have ultimately had little effect upon the forward march of our ideas and ideals.

Dissemination of these ideas and principles was not an easy task. It was, indeed, the most difficult job conservatives had, particularly in the earlier stages of the movement's development.

In the 1940s and 1950s virtually all the major national news and opinion outlets were closed to conservatives. Many of them still are closed, most notably the television news networks. But there has been a steady growth in the popularity of conservative columnists, writers, editors, and even a few cartoonists, since the mid–1960s. A large part of this mounting popularity has been due to a small group of publications which conservatives started because they found their views practically outlawed by the major media.

Ronald Reagan, shortly after he became President, paid tribute to two of these publications in his speech to the Conservative Political Action Conference in Washington in the spring of 1981. "I like to think back," he said, "about a small, artfully written magazine named *National Review*, founded in 1955 and ridiculed by the intellectual establishment because it published an editorial that said it would stand athwart the course of history yelling 'Stop!' And then," President Reagan continued, "there was a spritely written newsweekly coming out of Washington named *Human Events* that many said would never be taken seriously, but it would become later 'must reading' not only for Capitol Hill insiders but for all those in public life."

The influence of *National Review* and *Human Events* could never have been measured by their relatively small circulations. These and a handful of other conservative publications were read carefully by many opinion leaders, including an ever-growing number of journalists and other writers.

Human Events was started as a newsletter in 1944 by Frank Hanighen, Felix Morley and Henry Regnery, with William Henry Chamberlin as a regular contributor. It went through several changes, finally emerging as a tabloid-size weekly under the editorship of James Wick, and in more recent years has been operated by Thomas Winter, Allan H. Ryskind and Robert F. Latham. Ronald Reagan has been a regular subscriber and careful reader of *Human Events*, as well as one of its leading volunteer promoters, for many years.

National Review began publication in November 1955 a few days before the 30th birthday of its founder, William F. Buckley, Jr. Its original, or very early, contributors included writers representing the whole spectrum of libertarian and conservative thought—James Burnham, John Chamberlain, Whittaker Chambers, Frank Chodorov, Max Eastman, Willmoore Kendall, Russell Kirk, Frank Meyer, Wilhelm Ropke, Willi Schlamm, Freda Utley, Erik von Kuehnelt-Leddihn, and Richard Weaver.

It is a testimony to Bill Buckley's persuasiveness that he was able to bring under one journalistic tent writers who held such diverse views, stretching from what Russell Kirk called the "philosophical anarchism" of Frank Chodorov to the deep traditionalism of Richard Weaver and Kirk himself, to say nothing of the monarchism of Otto von Hapsburg, who was to become a fairly regular contributor to *National Review*.

This diverse group was, however, united on one critical point: the necessity of halting the spread of Soviet Communism. Most of these writers were also opposed to collectivism in any guise. Inevitably, there were open divisions over the years, as when Frank Meyer engaged in a running and sometimes acrimonious debate with his fellow *National Review* columnist, Russell Kirk. But by and large Buckley's coalition hung together amazingly well.

There were other journals of opinion that helped weld the new conservatism into a cohesive movement. Earlier *The Freeman* had played an important role. Originally founded in the 1920's by the aristocratic libertarian Albert Jay Nock, author of the book *Memoirs of a Superfluous Man*, the *Freeman* went through several metamorphoses, and even ceased publication for a time, before resurfacing in 1950 under the editorship of John Chamberlain and Henry Hazlitt following a merger with Isaac Don Levine's anti-Communist publication *Plain Talk*. Among the better known writers who found an outlet for their conservative views in *The Freeman* were former liberal journalists John T. Flynn, Raymond Moley and George Sokolsky.

The Freeman lasted only four years in this state of its long recurring lifespan and in mid–1954 it was taken over by Leonard Read's Foundation for Economic Education, which has published it ever since as a scholarly, practically non–political monthly magazine. Frank Chodorov was its first editor in this new garb. In recent years it has been published under the overall aegis of Leonard Read with Paul L. Poirot serving as manager editor.

Frank Chodorov is one of the more colorful characters in the early development of the modern conservative movement, and one who demonstrates how broad and tolerant the movement really is. An old-style libertarian, Chodorov's ideas at least skirted dangerously close to anarchism yet he found an intellectual home with the younger conservatives who believe in government but whose efforts have all been directed at making government work within the confines set for it by the Constitution.

In 1953 Chodorov founded the Intercollegiate Society of Individualists with Bill Buckley as its first president. ISI later changed its name but kept its initials by becoming the Intercollegiate Studies Institute. Since Chodorov's departure it has been ably headed by Victor Milione and has long had its headquarters in Bryn Mawr, Pennsylvania. ISI has reached out to many thousands of college students and provided them with thoughtful reading matter they would never have found through their courses or even in their school libraries.

One ISI publication is *Intercollegiate Review* and another important outlet which ISI has given conservative writers is *Modern Age*, a quarterly designed for the academy. Originated in 1957 by Russell Kirk through the good offices of the indefatigable Henry Regnery, *Modern Age* was boldly subtitled *A Conservative Review*. The editorial board of *Modern Age* read like a *Who's Who* of the more traditionalist wing of conservatism: Kirk, of course, Richard Weaver, Bernard Iddings Bell, David McCord Wright, Eliseo Vivas, Francis Wilson, Frederick Wilhelmsen, Donald Davidson, Leo R. Ward, Anthony Harrigan, and James Jackson Kilpatrick.

Orbis, a quarterly journal devoted primarily to foreign policy, was published by the University of Pennsylvania's Foreign Policy Research Center, headed by Robert Strausz–Hupe and, later, by William Kintner, both of whom went on to become distinguished diplomats. Although not, strictly speaking, a conservative publication, *Orbis* nonetheless published articles by conservative writers and scholars and was thus one more important outlet for members of the growing movement.

Another publication which served as a transmission belt for conservative ideas in the 1950's was the *American Mercury*. Founded by the crusty iconoclast H. L. Mencken in the 1920's, it survived under a succession of editors, including George Jean Nathan and Lawrence Spivak, who, with Martha Rountree, founded the long-running television interview show, "Meet the Press." After Spivak left in 1950 the magazine was edited by William Bradford Huie and it shifted sharply to the right.

More recently a publication which in some respects fills the role once played by *American Mercury*, particularly in its H.L. Mencken heyday, is *The American Spectator*, edited by R. Emmett Tyrrell, Jr., and published out of Bloomington, Indiana.

In addition to these publications there has been a proliferation of newsletters with a decidedly conservative coloration. One of the most influential, particularly in the 1960's, was the *Washington Report* of the American Security Council. Devoted to national security affairs, *Washington Report* also developed a "Washington Report of the Air," a radio program that had a long run on the Mutual Broadcasting Network with former Congressman Walter Judd as the regular commentator, and later, the distinguished journalist Phillip C. Clarke, winner of several top Overseas Press Club awards.

Of much more recent origin is *Conservative Digest*, published by the direct mail czar Richard Viguerie and originally edited by Lee Edwards, who was our public relations director in the Draft Goldwater Committee. Edwards was succeeded by Neil Freeman, formerly an editor with King Features, and after Freeman's departure John Lofton assumed the editorship.

Young Americans for Freedom also sponsored an important publication, *New Guard*, which has had a succession of capable editors. This lively magazine gives fledgling writers on the nation's campuses a chance to air their views nationwide and, equally important, it has given conservative political leaders a vehicle through which they could communicate with the campuses. For example, the April 1975 issue of *New Guard*, with a photograph of a smiling Ronald Reagan on the cover, contains the text of Reagan's speech to the YAF spring conference in Washington. This was the speech in which former Governor Reagan threw down the gauntlet for President Gerald Ford by concluding that "A political party cannot be all things to all people. It must represent certain fundamental beliefs which must not be compromised to political expediency, or simply to swell its members."

Although Reagan was criticized for being "unrealistic" in this speech, it is my opinion that he won a good many younger people to the Republican Party with this kind of approach. And the *New Guard* was certainly an important element in getting Reagan's position across to students on campuses up and down the country.

On the whole, Reagan has enjoyed a good relationship with the working press, if not with some editorial writers and editors. On occasion, however, he has had to correct the record and sometimes this has resulted in amusing exchanges with the media. Helene von Damm, who has been Reagan's personal secretary since 1966, tells of several of these in her book, *Sincerely, Ronald Reagan*, which is based on his correspondence, both private and official. In one exchange, Reagan corrected a story by Kim Marcus, a reporter for a California college newspaper, who wrote that in a San Francisco appearance in 1978 Reagan's face "was applied with heavy amounts of 'pancake' makeup."

"Please tell Miss Marcus," Reagan wrote her editor, "that I wore no makeup at the Commonwealth Club (I'm allergic to it). In the interest of press integrity also please tell her she has a standing invitation to do a 'white glove' test on my face the next time she is assigned to cover an appearance of mine." (Reagan has never worn makeup, even when he was in the movies and on television.)

For the most part Reagan has handled the press gently, turning the other cheek when newsmen lash out at him. Miss von Damm cites a typical Reagan letter to a reporter who strayed a bit too far from the facts:

"I couldn't help but drop you a note regarding your recent story in the Sunday *Sacramento Union*. You know I'm not given to railing at the press but in this instance I feel justified in pointing out that the overall effect your story gives of putting my foot in my mouth is based less on what I've said than on what someone else has accused me of saying. I'm sure you are not guilty of deliberate distortion but have only accepted the oft–repeated version of the incidents you used as gospel." He then went on to set the record straight in some detail on the comments in question and ended by writing, "I hope you accept this in the way it is intended. It was written only because we have had a relationship I value."

There is another aspect of Ronald Reagan's relationship with the press that must have puzzled many people. Before being elected President he was a national political figure for more than fifteen years. Yet the major newspapers and magazines seldom carried articles by him, even on their op–ed pages, although candidates like John Anderson and Morris Udall, who were never really seriously considered by their respective parties, frequently appeared in print in these publications.

One major magazine with a mass circulation that did frequently carry articles by conservatives was *Reader's Digest*. DeWitt Wallace, its founder and publisher, remained a conservative until his death in 1981 and was a generous financial contributor to conservative organizations. Dr. Walter Judd, next to Ronald Reagan probably the most articulate spokesman for conservative causes, was a roving editor for the *Digest* for many years after he left the Congress in 1963. Moreover, the staff of *Reader's Digest* tackled stories that none of the other big magazines covered adequately. Eugene Methvin wrote a number of penetrating articles on the

Far Left's disruption of our college campuses, and John Barron's monumental book *The KGB* was condensed in the *Digest*.

Until the mid–1970s, however, most other organs of national communication remained the private preserve of liberal journalists. The one notable exception was the nationally syndicated column. Even in the very early stages of the development of modern conservatism there were libertarian or conservative writers contributing columns to the newspapers via the syndicates. Holmes Alexander, John Chamberlain, Henry J. Taylor, Ralph deToledano, Alice Widener, Paul Scott, Robert Allen and Morrie Ryskind were all syndicated in the post-World War II period, and several of them still are.

Other columnists who did not consider themselves conservatives at that time, but who found common cause with our movement in their strong opposition to Soviet agression, also made a significant contribution to the awakening of the American people to the steadily growing threat of the USSR's military buildup— an issue which stirred Ronald Reagan's deep and abiding concern long before he became President. Notable among this group was the late Edgar Ansel Mowrer, dean of the *Chicago Daily News* foreign correspondents. Expelled from Germany by Hitler in the 1930s for writing articles critical of the Nazis, Mowrer covered World War II and knew intimately every major leader of the Allies, including Churchill, Roosevelt and Charles DeGaulle. Returning to America after the war he was a founder of the left–leaning Americans for Democratic Action, but soon became disillusioned by his fellow liberals' blindness toward the Soviet threat. Unfortunately, as Mowrer's columns became more and more critical of this obvious blindness, the number of newspapers carrying his column steadily dwindled. But Edgar Mowrer never wavered in his determination to expose what he called "the most important story of this century"—the USSR's quiet stockpiling of nuclear weapons aimed at America and its allies.

There were other journalists who sounded similar warnings from Washington on this and other issues that deeply concerned conservatives. Willard Edwards and Walter Trohan of the *Chicago Tribune*'s Washington Bureau were notable among them, as were David Sentner of the Hearst Newspapers; Smith Hempstone and Earl Voss of the *Washington Star*; Frank van der Linden, the *Nashville Banner*'s Washington correspondent; John Steen of the *Tampa Tribune*; Clark Mollenhoff of the *Cowles Newspapers*; Carl deBloom of the *Columbus Dispatch*; Raymond J. McHugh and Lyn Nofziger of the *Copley Newspapers*; Edgar Allen Poe of the *New Orleans Times-Picyaune*; Edward O'Brien of the *St. Louis Globe Democrat*; Hanson Baldwin and Richard Burt of the *New York Times*.

Not all of these newsmen were conservatives. But they were not afraid to cover the really tough stories their peers either ignored or, in some cases, consistently reported with a strong liberal bias.

In the late 1960s there was a marked change in the attitude of newspaper editors throughout the country. Many of them realized there was something sadly lacking in the wire and syndicated stories they were getting out of Washington and they moved to correct the sins of omission by publishing the younger conservative columnists who were beginning to gain national prominence.

Bill Buckley's "Firing Line" column, augmented by his weekly television program of the same name, blazed the trail and remains one of the most widely syndicated of the conservative columns. Patrick Buchanan, M. Stanton Evans, Anthony Harrigan, Jeffrey Hart, James Jackson Kilpatrick, John Lofton, Kevin Phillips, William A. Rusher, Jeffrey St. John and George Will all found growing markets for their columns through the decade of the 1970's. Today, I believe conservative columnists are more widely read than their liberal counterparts. In fact, the number of liberal columnists is receding as the conservative tide sweeps on.

The new breed of syndicated columnists is, however, only the tip of the iceberg. There are literally scores of young journalists entering the profession with, at the very least, a willingness to cover the stories and issues that conservatives are concerned with, whereas a decade ago there were only a handful in the country.

M. Stanton Evans, former editor of the *Indianapolis News*, is now director of the National Journalism Center in Washington. The Center provides an intensive 12-week work-study program for journalism school students in cooperation with more than a score of newspapers and other publications. The Center can accomodate thirty students in each program but, Evans says, "We are swamped with applications. In 1981 we had three times as many applicants as we could handle."

I had a personal experience with a young journalist which illustrates the way more and more media people regard the conservative position. I first got to know this young man when he worked in James Buckley's campaign for the Senate in New York, which I had managed in 1970. Later he won a Pulitzer Prize for his investigative reporting on crime for a newspaper in Stamford, Connecticut. Early in 1980 he came to see me at my home in nearby Greenwich. Expressing his admiration for Ronald Reagan, he told me, "Clif, I've just got to get involved in Governor Reagan's campaign for President." I referred him to my friend William J. Casey, who was about to take over as the Reagan campaign manager, and he was signed on the campaign team.

The young journalist is Anthony Dolan. He is today President Reagan's chief speech writer and a respected member of the White House staff. His brother John (Terry) Dolan heads up the Conservative Political Action Committee which helps finance conservative candidates for the Congress and has had some notable successes in both House and Senate races.

William J. Gavin, another writer, worked on James Buckley's

Senate staff in the 1970's. Bill Gavin, author of *The Street Corner Conservative*, also became a speechwriter for Ronald Reagan in the 1980 campaign.

Richard J. Whalen, a former editorial writer with the *Richmond News Leader* and later an associate editor of *Fortune*, is yet another who had input into the Reagan speech–writing process in 1980. Author of *The Founding Father*, a best-selling biography of Joseph P. Kennedy, and *To Catch a Falling Flag*, Whalen operates a private information service out of Washington and has served as writer–in–residence at the Georgetown University Center for Strategic and International Studies.

All this is not to say that the news media has gone conservative. It hasn't. Indeed, *The New York Times* and the *Washington Post* will, I expect, remain liberal until hell freezes over. But the *Times* and the *Post* and the newspapers, magazines, and broadcasting networks that automatically follow these twin Pied Pipers of journalism, have largely discredited themselves with the majority of Americans.

Indeed, the *Washington Post* itself reported, on August 16, 1981, the results of a survey it commissioned on public attitudes toward the major news media:

"Among the most stinging citizen complaints is a widely held belief that the news media hold back important news from the public, a sentiment that is apparently shared by more than half the people.

"Another is an even more pervasive perception that reporters and editors for TV network news operations and large newspapers such as *The Washington Post, The New York Times* and others have little or no concern for the average person. By more than 2 to 1, people believe that the news media 'frequently violate the privacy of individual citizens.' " The survey also found that no less than 59 per cent of those polled felt "reporters in the major news media often give too much of their own opinions and not enough facts."

Although the influence of *The Post* and *The Times* and their followers has dwindled substantially, they remain a powerful force, as Richard Nixon discovered when the *Post-Times* network deposed him via Watergate after he swept the country in the presidential election of 1972.

Moreover, national television news remains as biased for liberalism as it ever was, even though there is evidence local stations have become wary of the network news product. The National Television News Survey, completed in 1971, found that there were managers or news directors of 212 TV stations in 153 cities who recognized that there was what Howard K. Smith had called "the strong leftward bias of the networks." Most of these stations were, of course, network affiliates.

Radio news, although not as openly biased as its network television counterpart, unfortunately remains an essentially superficial medium of communication. However, over the years there have been many radio news commentators who refused to be stampeded in the liberal direction. Fulton Lewis, Jr., Ray Henle and Henry J. Taylor were notable in this regard in the post-World War II period. Martha Rountree, also a television commentator who won virtually every major news award for her "Meet the Press" and other shows, has had several radio news programs that always strived to "tell it like it is." And Mutual Broadcasting encouraged the invariably straight reporting of commentators like the late Robert Hurleigh, president of Mutual; award-winning newsman Phillip C. Clarke; White House correspondent Forrest Boyd, and veteran radio announcer–turned–commentator, Del Sharbutt.

Radio also developed in the 1960s and 1970s yet another group of commentators who were preponderantly conservative. They were not newsmen but clergymen and they attracted huge listening audiences who harkened to the preachers' pleas for a return to traditional Christian and American values. Many of these have also gone into television where they have reached out to millions. The late Bishop Fulton J. Sheen was among the earlier pioneers in TV and later the Reverends Oral Roberts, Jerry Falwell, Pat Robertson and others won massive viewing congregations. Although not all of these radio and television clergy were necessarily politically conservative, their clarion call for a reawakening of the fundamental values which originally forged our Western civilization certainly played a major role in the conservative revival.

In addition to network television news, there is still another liberal bastion that conservatives have cracked only occasionally— the book publishing fraternity centered in New York. This modern Mount Parnassus still functions as though nothing has changed on the American political scene since the advent of Franklin Roosevelt and his New Deal a half–century ago. Yet here again resourceful conservatives have established their own lines of communication to the book–buying public and some of the biggest bestsellers of the past two decades have been frankly conservative books. In fact, in the wake of the Goldwater campaign the Conservative Book Club was founded by Neil McCaffrey, with financial support from Randolph Richardson and from Gerald Gidwitz, chairman of the Helene Curtis Company. It is still going strong after seventeen years.

In a somewhat earlier period the publishing of conservative books was a much more difficult venture, however. Henry Regnery, whose Chicago house is publishing this book, went into the business in 1947 to bring out books which, Regnery later wrote, did not necessarily "fit the liberal ideology which so dominated publishing as to constitute a particularly effective form of censorship."

There were only two other publishers who would regularly take a chance on conservative books from 1945 to 1965. One was the late Devin Garrity, president of the Devin–Adair Company in New York. The other was James Herrick Gipson, brother of historian Lawrence Henry Gipson, who ran Caxton Printers in Caldwell, Idaho.

Yet almost from the beginning Henry Regnery found there was a market for conservative books. He had a number of bestsellers soon after he went into publishing, including Freda Utley's *China Story* and William Buckley's *God and Man at Yale*. His house continues to hit the top of the book sales lists, most recently with *Fat City*, Donald Lambro's telling exposé of the Washington bureaucracy. More important than his long string of bestsellers, however, have been the books Regnery brought out that no one else would publish. The number of writers whose first books were published by Regnery are legion: Bill Buckley, Russell Kirk, Richard Weaver, M. Stanton Evans, Duane Thorin, Earl Voss, Frank Meyer, to name but a few.

Unfortunately, many books brought out by conservative publishers were not reviewed by *The New York Times* and the other established organs of the literary world. The result was that there began to circulate in the country, beginning in the late 1940s, a veritable underground literature which contributed profoundly to the changing of American political attitudes.

In some cases, the authors financed publication of their own books. Perhaps the most notable was Phyllis Schlafly, who wrote and published *A Choice Not An Echo* during the Goldwater presidential campaign. Taking her title from the theme of Senator Goldwater's opening campaign speech in January 1964, Mrs. Schlafly's book was an instant success and by the time of the November election she had sold more than six million copies. Her attorney husband, Fred Schlafly, acted as business advisor to the Pere Marquette Press they founded to publish this book and her children helped in the sales and distribution by packing and shipping the books in the basement of the Schlaflys' home in Alton, Illinois. Subsequently, Mrs. Schlafly brought out a half–dozen more books, some in co–authorship with Admiral Chester

Ward, former Judge Advocate of the United States Navy. All sold exceedingly well, although they were virtually ignored by the *Times* and the rest of the liberal establishment press.

In a very real sense, *The Times* and its faithful followers missed the boat.* By refusing to let their readers know that most conservative books had even been published they not only failed their own obvious duty to the reading public and to book store proprietors, they ultimately discredited themselves and helped to undermine the trust Americans had traditionally placed in the news media.

At the same time, by blocking off access to the normal channels of mass communication, *The Times* and its media disciples forced conservatives to create and improvise channels of their own. The most spectacularly successful of these was direct mail, and the great entrepeneur in this field is Richard Viguerie. A Texan who went to New York to work for Young Americans for Freedom in the very early 1960's, Viguerie learned the direct mail business under an innovative pioneer, Marvin Leibman. He helped with press relations in the early stages of our Draft Goldwater effort and after the 1964 campaign he went to the office of the Clerk of the House of Representatives which had on file the names and addresses of all those who had contributed $50 or more to Goldwater. He copied the lists by hand with the help of several others and this was the beginning of his direct mail empire.

In every election from 1966 onward, the Viguerie Company and its score of imitators and spin-off firms have played a significant role in raising money to elect conservative candidates. In so doing, they also developed into an important new component of the mass media. For their fund-raising letters also brought infor-

---

* For an incisive analysis of how the *New York Times* literally shapes the news see Herman Dinsmore's *All The News That Fits*. Dinsmore adapted his telling title from the *Times'* long standing masthead slogan, "All the News That's Fit to Print." That the *Times* did not deem news of concern to conservatives "fit to print" disturbed Dinsmore, who worked for the paper nearly thirty years. Arthur Krock, Frank Kluckholm, John V. Hinkel and other former *Timesmen* were also disturbed, indeed, deeply troubled by the *Times'* de facto censorship of the news.

mation to millions of Americans, information that quite often the people could not obtain from newspapers or television or mass circulation magazines.

The liberal Democrats have tried, with only very limited success thus far, to emulate Richard Viguerie and his fellow conservative direct mail communicators. But there is yet another area of communications in which conservatives initially took their cue from the liberals and subsequently, I believe, went the liberals one better. This is the realm of the "think tanks"—the primarily academic centers that once lent an aura of scholarly credibility to liberal theories but which in the last twenty years have become increasingly conservative.

6

The Think Tanks

When Ronald Reagan first ran for public office in 1966, the academic community in the United States was almost totally dominated by liberals and all but a few of the study centers that served as research arms for the academy—and for politicians—were under the control of liberals. Ironically, this dominance of liberals in the academy had been financed by some of America's greatest fortunes, most notoriously by the golden hordes of the Fords and the Rockefellers.

Moreover, the administrators of these great fortunes helped man key posts in the liberal governments of John Kennedy and Lyndon Johnson and provided a good deal of guidance, particularly in foreign policy, for President Carter. For example, Dean Rusk, the quiet gray eminence of U.S. foreign policy for thirty years, stepped from the presidency of the Rockefeller Foundation into the office of Secretary of State in 1961 and helped Presidents Kennedy and Johnson formulate policy through the fatal "graduated escalation" period of the Vietnam War.* And McGeorge

* As Assistant Secretary of State for the Far East in the Truman Administration Rusk had played a critical role in the Korean War and is credited with keeping President Truman from ordering General MacArthur to bomb across the Yalu River into China after the Communist Chinese launched their attack on American forces in November 1951.

Bundy, who had served as John Kennedy's chief national security advisor, left early in the Johnson administration to become president of the Ford Foundation.

In addition, the revolving door fueled and financed by the great fortunes, and by the more awe–struck leaders of American industry, alternately populated the academic "think tanks" and the liberal Democrat national administrations as well as important staff posts on Congressional committees.

On entering politics, conservative Republican Ronald Reagan had few academic centers he could turn to for the kind of documented information that has become the principal ammunition of America's political wars in recent decades. Fortunately, however, two of the handful of such centers willing to develop information for conservatives, as well as for liberals, were in California—the Hoover Institution at Stanford University and a center at Claremont College. One of the people at the Stanford center was Martin Anderson, who had written the book *The Federal Bulldozer*. Today Anderson is an important member of the Reagan White House team and is in charge of policy development for the President.

But in 1966 the think tanks which would dare produce information from a conservative perspective were only beginning to emerge. In Washington, one of the earliest was the American Enterprise Institute, founded by William Baroody, Sr., an Arab-American who had worked in the New Deal's Social Security Administration some years before. Baroody had begun by rounding up scholars to supply a few conservative senators with "informational ammo." One of the senators was Barry Goldwater and Baroody became his research amanuensis in the presidential campaign of 1964. Unfortunately, Baroody knew very little about practical politics, as the results of that campaign demonstrated. However, the campaign gave his American Enterprise Institute some publicity and it was able to capitalize on that to obtain larger grants from foundations and corporations.

Although in my judgment the conservative academic centers have not made as big a contribution as most observers think they have to the changed political climate in the United States, they nonetheless have in some instances added needed credibility to the conservative point of view, particularly on defense and foreign policy issues. And they have served as a necessary "offset" to the still preponderantly liberal think tanks at Harvard, Massachusetts Institute of Technology, the Brookings Institution and others.

The development of these conservative centers is relatively recent. In the early 1960's you could count the sources of really substantial money for conservative research projects on one hand: the Lilly Foundation in Indianapolis; the Pugh Family in Philadelphia; the Realm Foundation in Ann Arbor, Michigan; the Richardson Foundation in New York; and most notably, Richard Mellon Scaife and his foundations and family trusts in Pittsburgh. Earlier, the Volker Fund in California had given grants for conservatively oriented study programs. But compared to the largesse spilled forth for liberal projects by the Ford and Rockefeller foundations, and by a host of other wealthy perrennial supporters of leftist causes, only a fractional trickle of money went to programs with a conservative "taint."

Before the Goldwater campaign roused both large and small donors to action, conservatives had for the most part been forced to develop do-it-yourself study and action projects. And seldom were they able to acquire the mantle of academic respectability.

General Bonner Fellers, chief of planning for General Douglas MacArthur in the Pacific during World War II, started the Committee Against Foreign Aid almost entirely on his own and kept it going for nearly twenty years until his death in 1974. Although he was often forced to operate on a shoestring, in the latter stages out of the basement of his Washington home, General Fellers saved the American taxpayers billions of dollars in wasteful aid through his work on Capitol Hill.

Similarly, Admiral Ben Morrell, the doughty commander of
the Seabees of World War II fame, launched the Americans for
Conservative Action as an antidote to the very liberal Americans
for Democratic Action. The ACA, like the ADA, rated Congressmen and Senators on their voting records, albeit from a
perspective 180 degrees opposite. Ben Morrell, after he retired as
chairman of the Jones and Laughlin Steel Corporation in Pittsburgh, devoted virtually full time to ACA, with relatively little
financial support from other sources. Two executive directors of
ACA, General Thomas Lane and Charles McManus, worked
virtually as volunteers in this cause, as many of us did for various
organizations in the earlier stages of the conservative movement.

Martha Rountree and her Leadership Foundation, a non–partisan
research group that was not afraid to examine the conservative
side of controversial questions like school prayer and busing, also
struggled along for years on a modest budget. However, Miss
Rountree's impact on these and other issues was substantial and in
1979–1980 her Leadership Action organization helped Senator
Jesse Helms pass his Senate amendment to restore school prayer
to the nation's schools. Miss Rountree's effort came within a few
votes in the House of helping Congressman Philip Crane force
the House version of the amendment out of Chairman Peter
Rodino's Judiciary Committee in 1980. If the measure had reached
the House floor, as it is almost certain to do next time around,
Martha Rountree had more than enough votes to get it passed.

Phyllis Schlafly has had a notable success with her own private
"think tank," which she operated out of her home in Alton,
Illinois. Mrs. Schlafly's wide–ranging Eagle Forum stopped the
Equal Rights Amendment dead in its tracks by enlightening state
legislators on precisely what ERA would do if it was ratified and
made part of the Constitution. She has also played a significant
role in awakening citizens across the country to the critical need
for a stronger national defense.

Although some of these projects like Miss Rountree's and Mrs. Schlafly's have in the last few years developed a broad base of public support through direct mail, they have seldom benefited from the large grants still enjoyed by liberal projects. However, other conservative study programs have received substantial private funds.

The Edison Institutue, headed by David Jones, has had an important influence on students participating in its education programs, particularly the program in comparative economic systems run by Dr. Lev Dobriansky of Georgetown University, which has attracted national attention.

The Georgetown Center for Strategic and International Studies first gained prominence under Admiral Arleigh Burke, the former chief of Naval Operations, in the early 1960s. Headed in recent years by David Abshire, Assistant Secretary of State for Congressional Liaison in the Nixon-Ford administrations, the Georgetown Center has provided a harbor for scholars and others representing a wide variety of political persuasions, and has become one of Washington's leading "celebrity hideouts." Alexander Haig, Richard Allen, Henry Kissinger, Admiral Thomas Moorer (the former Chairman of the Joint Chiefs of Staff), and a squadron of others have hung their hats at the Georgetown Center when they were "between engagements." Although only a few of these may be classified as conservative, the important point is that the Center does not deliberately *exclude* conservatives, as the Brookings Institution and other liberal think tanks have done for decades.

The Institute for American Strategy, an educational foundation operating out of Boston, Virginia, has similarly provided conservative scholars with a base for serious study of national security issues. The Institute and the American Security Council are both headed by John M. Fisher, a former FBI agent–turned–direct–mail entrepreneur. Probably the American Security Council's most notable contribution was the production of the highly publicized study, "The Changing Strategic Military Balance: U.S.A. vs U.S.S.R." Originated by my co–author, William J. Gill, and produced in 1967 for the House Armed Services Committee, then under the chairmanship of the late Congressman Mendel Rivers, this study was certified by a blue ribbon panel of defense experts. They included ex–Air Force General Bernard A. Schriever, Chairman; Dr. Edward Teller; General Thomas S. Power, former chief of the Strategic Air Command; Major General Dale O. Smith, advisor to the Joint Chiefs on nuclear warfare; and General Albert C. Wedemeyer, the man who planned our global war for World War II.

This landmark study was the first real balance sheet assaying the relative strategic strength of the United States and the Soviet Union. The Defense Department, under Robert Strange McNamara, had worked on a similar assessment for years without coming up with an authentic balance sheet. The result was that McNamara was retired from Defense by President Johnson after the publication of this study and for the only time in thirty years the Congress increased its relative appropriations for strategic defense during the next three fiscal years.

In more recent times the American Security Council sponsored the Congressional Coalition for Peace through Strength, one of the biggest caucuses on Capitol Hill. This coalition played a major role in halting Senate ratification of the Salt II Treaty in 1979–1980, thanks to the efforts of John Fisher and the people who work with him in the American Security Council and the Institute for American Strategy, among them Ambassador Elbridge Durbrow; General Daniel Graham, former commander of the Defense Intelligence Agency; Colonel Raymond Sleeper, who commanded the Air Force Systems Command super-secret Foreign Technology Division; and journalist Philip C. Clarke.

Another organization devoted to national security issues is

Frank Barnett's National Strategy Information Center, which in the 1970s spun off the Committee on the Present Danger, a group which included Richard V. Allen, President Reagan's national security advisor. The Committee also helped in the campaign to stop Salt II.

There have always been a number of organizations devoted to business interests. In the days of Franklin Roosevelt they were identified as "conservative" but in latter years as often as not they identified themselves with liberal issues and causes. The Chamber of Commerce of the United States is notable among them, although I believe local Chambers have by and large remained essentially conservative. The National Association of Manufacturers has also listed to starboard on a number of issues, as has the prestigious Business Round Table.

However, one business group that has remained steadfastly conservative is the United States Industrial Council, headed by Anthony Harrigan, the philosopher–journalist. The Council is headquartered in Nashville, Tennessee, and it has been gaining spectacularly in membership in the last few years with most of its growth in the Northeastern, Midwestern and Far Western states.

I believe the growth of Tony Harrigan's USIC may be attributed to the perceived leftward drift of the older business groups. As they moved away from issues conservative businessmen are interested in, or even moved *contra* conservative principles in some cases, more and more members of the business community sought out the United States Industrial Council as a conservative alternative.

A similar phenomena has been noticeable in the broader issue think tanks. As the American Enterprise Institute, the George-town Center and the Hoover Institution at Stanford shifted away from issues that concerned conservatives, or at the least demonstrated a greater ambivalence toward them, more conservative Senators and Congressmen looked for other research sources that represented their interests more closely. Beginning in 1974 they were able to find such a source in the Heritage Foundation. Started with a grant from Colorado brewer Joseph Coors, Heritage got a lot of press attention during the Reagan Administration's transition period when it came up with a lengthy "agenda" for the incoming President. Although Reagan has not acted on all Heritage recommendations by any means, he has incorporated a number of them into his various programs.

Chairman of the Heritage Foundation is Ben Blackburn, a former Georgia Republican Congressman, and the large staff located in several renovated buildings on Capitol Hill is headed by Edwin Feulner, a former aide to Congressman Philip Crane. The Foundation has had a formidable output of policy studies on a wide range of subjects and its quarterly publication, *Policy Review*, edited by John O'Sullivan, is becoming widely respected in Washington.

The Heritage Foundation, along with a surprising number of other think tanks that are either conservative-oriented or do not bar the door to conservatives, have received substantial funding from the Scaife–Mellon family and foundations in Pittsburgh through the good offices of Richard Mellon Scaife. In the spring of 1981 the *Pittsburgh Post–Gazette* ran a series of front page articles on Dick Scaife, who has been far-and-away the most generous of all supporters of conservative causes and study groups. The newspaper listed the leading recipients of funds from the Scaife trusts as follows, with the amounts they have received from the trusts since 1970 only:

American Enterprise Institute, $5,312,500; Georgetown University Center for Strategic and International Studies, $3,891,200; Hoover Institution at Stanford, $3,430,000; National Strategy Information Center, New York, $5,165,822; Foreign Policy Research Institute at the University of Pennsylvania, $1,451,000; Institute for Foreign Policy Analysis, Cambridge, Massachusetts,

$1,775,000; New York University (mostly national security study programs), $2,298,750; the Center for Advanced International Studies, University of Miami, $1,958,514; the Heritage Foundation of Washington, D.C., $2,664,600.

There were others, a total of 110 organizations by the newspaper's count, and most of those listed above as the *Post-Gazette* noted, had received substantial support from Scaife before 1970, so the aggregate amounts they received were actually quite a bit higher. The Georgetown Center, for instance, has received closer to $5,000,000 from the Scaife trusts and foundations, and the Hoover Institution at Stanford almost $6,000,000 over the last fifteen years. The *Washington Post*, several months later, estimated Scaife had given upwards of $100,000,000 to conservative think-tanks and causes.

The *Pittsburgh Post-Gazette* counted "no less than 11 Reagan advisors, from Cabinet officers to White House aides to transition team members, [who] have worked in programs and institutions funded in part by the Western Pennsylvania millionaire." These included Secretary of State Alexander M. Haig; Richard V. Allen, the President's National Security Advisor; Ambassador to the U.N. Jeane Jordan Kirkpatrick; Edwin Meese, the White House Counselor; Martin Anderson, the Special Assistant to the President for policy development; and James Watt, Secretary of the Interior.

Knowing Richard Scaife, it is conceivable to me that some of these people may never have met him or may not even have known the institutions they worked for were funded by Scaife money. Dick Scaife is one of the most modest men I have ever met and I would doubt seriously he would ever call on President Reagan or any of the above advisors or cabinet officials for any political favors.

Nonetheless, in June 1966 right after Ronald Reagan won the Republican gubernatorial primary in California, he stopped off in

Pittsburgh to have dinner with Dick and Frannie Scaife and a few friends en route to Washington where he was to address the National Press Club. "Ron Reagan knew where the priorities lay," one of the friends later quipped. That probably was so because Richard Mellon Scaife was certainly an important member of the nationwide conservative cadre which ultimately produced Governor Reagan's landslide victory in the 1980 presidential election.

7

The Cadre

In the election of 1980 the polls and the pundits were amazed by the magnitude of Ronald Reagan's victory. Only a very few, including both authors of this book, predicted that Reagan landslide *and* the Republican ascendency in the United States Senate.

In 1966 a somewhat similar situation developed in Ronald Reagan's first bid for political office. Early in the Republican gubernatorial primary campaign that pitted Reagan against San Francisco Mayor George Christopher, the Field Poll showed Reagan slightly ahead among Republicans but trailing Christopher by five full percentage points (40-45%) among Republicans and Democrats combined. In a state where Democrats then outnumbered Republicans 3–2, this boded badly for Ronald Reagan. Yet, in the June 7 primary he beat the liberal Christopher better than two-to-one—1,417,623 votes to 675,683.

Reagan's general election campaign against Governor Pat Brown, who had defeated Richard Nixon in 1962 and Senator William Knowland four years before that, was almost a statistical rerun of the primary. In October the final polls showed Reagan ahead, but only by a relatively small margin with a fairly sizeable undecided vote that could swing the election to Governor Brown. But Reagan swamped

Brown by nearly one million votes, receiving 3,742,913 to 2,749,174 for Brown. This represented a formidable margin of 15 percent, or 57 percent for Reagan as against 42 percent for Brown.

I was not involved in Ronald Reagan's campaigns for governor. However, two close friends, Thomas Reed and Lyn Nofziger, were key members of the Reagan team in 1966 and again in his successful reelection race in 1970. I was "available for consultation," of course, and I received frequent calls from Reed and Nofziger during those campaigns.

Moreover, I was involved in setting the stage for Ronald Reagan's campaigns for the Presidency, although in 1965 and 1966 my stage–setting had not yet totally focused on him as a candidate. I was chiefly concerned in those years with consolidating and expanding the conservative cadre which we had developed within the Republican Party through the Goldwater draft and campaign.

Although virtually every columnist and commentator had counted us out after President Johnson's stunning defeat of Senator Goldwater, the fact was that our cadre gained steadily in strength and influence from 1964 onward. Indeed, immediately after the 1964 election I had telephone calls and letters from people in every state asking that we continue our efforts in behalf of the conservative cause.

In January 1965 two news articles appeared, one in the *Wall Street Journal* and the other in *National Review*, revealing that I was back in New York working out of Suite 3505 of the Chanin Building in my continuing effort to coordinate conservative political activities nationally. These articles brought another flood of calls and mail urging me to reactivate the cadre.

On Sunday, January 31, 1965 our original Draft Goldwater group met at the O'Hare Inn near the Chicago airport. This was essentially the same group which had assembled in Chicago on October 8, 1961 to plan for conservative control of the Republican National Convention and presidential nominating process. To this 1961 group were now added others who had joined our effort in its very early stages.

The charter members of this group, which we appropriately called *The Hard Core*, included three ladies—Mrs. Ione Harrington, a Republican National Committeewoman from Indiana; Mrs. Patricia Hutar of Chicago, and Miss Rita Bree, my loyal executive assistant for many years before she joined the Yale University development office and then went on to a successful career in business. Other members of the group were: William Middendorf, the treasurer of our Draft Goldwater Committee, former Secretary of the Navy, and now Ambassador to the Organization of American States; Roger Milliken of South Carolina, chairman of Deering, Milliken, Inc.; the late J.D. Stetson Coleman of Virginia, who served on the boards of a number of corporations, including Pennzoil and the Los Angeles Rams football team; and the late Charles Barr of Illinois, an executive with the Standard Oil Company of Indiana (Amoco) in Chicago.

Other charter members were: William A. Rusher, syndicated columnist and publisher of *National Review*; Anderson Carter, later a candidate for the U.S. Senate from New Mexico and still later Ronald Reagan's political director (with Charles Black) in the 1980 primary campaigns; Eugene Perrin of Michigan, an executive of the Dow Chemical Company; William McFadzean of Minnesota, a former official of the 3-M Company; and John Tope, for many years the Washington representative for Republic Steel Corporation.

Charles Thone, Republican state chairman, member of the National Republican Committee, and currently governor of Nebraska, remained a member of *The Hard Core*, as did Sam Hay of Wisconsin, an executive with the Allen Bradley Company in Milwaukee; Ned Cushing, a young bank president from Downs, Kansas; and Greg Shorey, Republican state chairman in South Carolina in the early 1960's.

Roger Allen Moore, a prominent Boston lawyer, president of the Beacon Hill Civic Association, and now chief counsel of the Republican National Committee, faithfully attended our group's meetings as did two other distinguished members of the legal fraternity, David Nichols, later a Justice of the Supreme Court of Maine, and Judge Edward Failer of Iowa.

Two Texans we could always count on were Tad Smith of El Paso, a former Republican state chairman, and Albert E. Fay of Houston, a champion sailboat racer and member of the Republican National Committee.

John Keith Rehmann, an Iowa businessman who was, like most other members of our group, repeatedly a delegate to Republican national conventions; Ty Gillespie, an old Michigan friend of mine who had helped keep the Draft Goldwater effort alive in its early stages by raising vitally needed funds; and Tom Van Sickle, then a young state senator in Kansas, who had married one of our prettiest Goldwater Committee volunteers, Suzie Galvin of Ohio, all were involved.

Tom Reed, the brilliant young physicist who was Ronald Reagan's strong right arm in both Reagan campaigns for governor, remained a member of our *Hard Core* through much of the 1960's and 1970's, as did Robert Matthews of Indianapolis, a former state Republican chairman in Indiana, and one of the ablest politicans I have ever worked with, and Jerry Harkins of Kansas City, who had served as our Goldwater co–chairman in Missouri with Mrs. Nell Reed, widow of U.S. Senator James A. Reed.

Frank Whetstone, the Cut Bank, Montana, newspaper publisher who became Candidate Reagan's Western states director in the primary and presidential campaigns of 1980, never missed a *Hard Core* meeting for fifteen years, and others we could always count on were Jim Campbell of Texas, Charlie Klumb and Wirt Yerger of Mississippi, Don Pearlman of Washington state, Denzil Garrison and John Thomas of Oklahoma, Jim Mack of Illinois, and Sullivan Barnes, a South Dakota lawyer and former national chairman of the Young Republicans.

It is true that our group was strongly represented by Westerners, Midwesterners and Southerners. But there were several New Englanders, as you have seen, and our New York contingent took a back seat to none. Besides Bill Rusher and Bill Middendorf and myself, other New Yorkers, or suburbanites from the New York area, who remained a part of our cadre were Jeremiah Milbank, Jr., member of a prominent New York legal–financial family, and Gerrish Milliken, brother of Roger Milliken of Deering, Milliken, Inc., and a resident of Greenwich, Connecticut, where I have lived since moving from Rye, N.Y., in 1972.

Congressman John Ashbrook of Ohio, later chairman of the American Conservative Union, was always considered part of our original group, although the demands of Congress prevented John from attending many of our meetings through the years.

When our cadre started the Draft Goldwater operation in 1961–62, we were for the most part still relatively young. (The average age was 37.) We were to grow considerably older before Ronald Reagan finally was elected President in 1980, but we brought in a lot of younger people as we went along, many of whom you will meet later in this book.

At our *Hard Core* meeting in Chicago at the end of January 1965 I was pleased to report that an Opinion Research poll taken after the 1964 election showed that no less than 65 percent of all Republicans still considered themselves to be conservatives. Only 14 percent said they were liberals and 21 percent thought they were "in between." What this proved was that the Eastern Establishment and major media people who persisted in claiming the GOP for the liberals—or, as they euphemistically called them in those days, "moderates"—were way off the true beam of the party.

Even more significant in terms of our future chances of electing a conservative President and Congress, the same poll found a healthy 41 percent of *all* Americans regarded themselves as con-servative, a comfortable ten percent more than those who clung to the "liberal" label. The remainder, or 28 percent, decided they were somewhere "in between."

This pattern also held up among the numerous independent voters. Fully 41 percent of the independents, who are not regis-tered in either major party, felt they were conservatives and only 29 percent admitted to being liberal.

Even 30 percent of the Democrats polled classified themselves conservative, while another 28 percent refused to be tagged as liberal, revealing the liberals as a minority within the party they claimed as their traditional preserve.

This poll proved what most of our group had sensed years before, i.e., that the conservative cause was on its way toward becoming the majority political force in America. The reasons for this varied somewhat from state to state and from region to region. But all across the country there was a growing perception that the liberals had simply not delivered on their clearly implied promise that the government would take care of virtually all our problems—provided we coughed up sufficient tax money to sup-port government's free-spending schemes.

Although this mounting frustration was daily bringing more converts to the conservative cause, it also had the rather perverse effect of broadening the base of support for some liberal organiza-tions as well. Eventually, Ralph Nader and his galaxy of "public interest" groups and John Gardner and his Common Cause both were launched to provide answers for the ever growing mass of disenchanted citizens who wanted desperately to make their gov-ernment work.

As early as the January 1965 meeting of our group, we could sense that America's institutions were about to be subjected to the most severe tests they had suffered since the Great Depres-sion, and probably since the Civil War. The ominous rumbles of the "Filthy Speech Movement" at the University of California in

Berkeley were echoing on other campuses and were soon to give way to the violent wave of anti-war protests as President Johnson escalated America's involvement in Vietnam.

Many of our cities and communities were even then feeling the financial strain they had imposed upon themselves by accepting federal funds which they had to match in whole or part from local taxes. Crime rates were climbing at an alarming rate in spite of record expenditures for police protection. People were beginning to see that the courts were more concerned with protecting the criminal than his innocent victims. The illegal drug traffic was gaining momentum and pushers were starting to invade the schools. Alcoholism was on the rise everywhere, including among teenagers, and the great foundation stone of our civilization, the family, was showing serious cracks.

The educational system, in which we had placed so much hope only a few years before, was being seriously questioned as permissiveness weakened the authority of teachers and other experimental programs failed to improve academic standards. Indeed, standards everywhere—in the home, in school, in factories and other workplaces—all standards appeared to be on the decline.

In short, the *institutions* which shored up our society and which had made it function so well in the past now looked as though they were in danger of crumbling, just as they had in other great civilizations which had fallen in centuries past. Analogies between the American and Western declines and the ancient declines of Greece and Rome were being drawn with increasing frequency. And although many liberals tried to say conservatives were taking too pessimistic a view of things, many other liberals joined conservative thinkers and communicators in raising the alarm.

It was almost pitiful to see the bewilderment of liberals at the obvious failure of the "social programs" they had foisted upon us at such a tremendous cost, not only in money but in the disillusionment and loss of faith in government. Yet many of them clung tenaciously, *fanatically*, to their disproven theories and it was during this same period of the mid-1960s that Lyndon Johnson, the man who wanted to be loved by everyone, pushed through the Congress the most sweeping social revolution since the founding of the republic.

There was something for everybody in LBJ's Great Society: more free food for the poor—and the not-so-poor; more loans for students, which had the effect of raising educational costs astronomically so young people and their families went deeper into debt every year; more and more programs for minorities, which never seemed to solve the primary problem of providing decent jobs for most of the people they were supposed to help; more money for public housing, which too often destroyed old neighborhoods and replaced them with huge inhuman modern slums. In brief, *more of everything for everybody.*

Everybody, that is, except the average hard-working citizens whose taxes kept going up to pay the bills. And even these citizens appeared to benefit in the early stages of this reckless game of social roulette. The government-induced inflation raised their wages and other income so they were able to buy larger homes, more cars, expensive appliances and take "dream vacations" to luxurious resorts.

Not since the Roaring Twenties had America been on such an extended binge. And in this one we were also engaged in an expensive and painful war that was placing additional stresses on the society as the casualty lists grew tragically day by day.

Lyndon Johnson had decreed a "guns *and* butter" policy. Somehow the costs of the war would not effect fulfillment of the rising expectations engendered by his Great Society. The era of the Fabian Socialists' "Organization of Happiness" was upon us and the war in far-off Vietnam was treated as a shameful sideshow that eventually would go away if we just kept increasing the pressure on the Communists there. Johnson and his advisors actually tried to apply the same prescription to the war problem as they were trying on our domestic social problems. On April 17,

1965, in a speech at Johns Hopkins University in Baltimore, the President offered the Viet Cong and North Vietnamese billions of dollars in aid if they would just behave themselves and stop the war. He was to repeat this offer several times, both in public and through emissaries. And each time the aid ante went up.

The veteran Texas politician simply could not understand why the Communists had to be so ornery. His vision, obscured by the poor intelligence and bad advice he was receiving from his ideological subordinates, was incapable of seeing that the Communists were interested in humbling the United States and not in money, though they would be glad to take the money, too, *after* they had scored their victory.

While President Johnson diligently pressed the war policies that were to bring about the end of his Presidency, Ronald Reagan was dealing with some of the war's side effects from the governor's office in Sacramento. The University of California campus at Berkeley had been the incubator of the war protest riots that had spread to scores of campuses. Governor Reagan and the state board of regents acted to fire the university president, Clark Kerr, for failing to maintain order on the Berkeley campus. The Governor also cut the university's budget request by more than $40 million to help his all-out effort to reduce state spending and balance the California budget.

The protests that followed these actions failed to ruffle Reagan. He stuck to his guns. The result was that more and more people looked upon the California governor as a leading possibility for the Republican presidential nomination in 1968.

In the vanguard of this movement to make Reagan President was a group I had worked closely with during the Goldwater campaign—Young Americans for Freedom—and one new group which had come into being as a direct follow-on to the Goldwater effort, the American Conservative Union.

Young Americans for Freedom (YAE) had been founded in September 1960 at a meeting at Bill Buckley's family home in

Sharon, Connecticut. Bill Rusher was there, as were M. Stanton Evans, Frank Meyer and several others associated with *National Review*. Among those in on the early launching of YAF were David Franke, Howard Phillips, and the late Robert Schuchman. Others who came in at the beginning or at a very early stage included Carol Bauman, Douglas Caddy, Jamieson G. Campaigne, Jr., Terry Catchpole, Bruce Eberle, Lee Edwards, James McFadden, Mike Thompson and Richard Viguerie.

The purpose of YAF was to give young conservatives a central organization they could work through to increase their effective participation in the political process, to serve as a clearing house for new concepts and ideas, and to provide a network of chapters on college and university campuses to at least begin to loosen the iron-fisted liberal control over our academic institutions.

Young Americans for Freedom caught on immediately, showing the deep-seated need that was felt for such an organization, particularly in the academy. Chapters sprouted on campuses, large and small, in every section of the country and even high school students flocked to YAF.

Richard A. Viguerie, who had served as Harris County campaign chairman for John Tower in John's first race for the Senate in 1960, came to New York from Texas and succeeded Doug Caddy as executive director of YAF. "Actually," Viguerie says in his political autobiography, "the job was to be Marvin Liebman's account executive for the YAF account." It was under the tutelage of Liebman, a Manhattan public relations man, that Richard Viguerie first broke into the direct mail business.

Letters signed by several senior conservatives, including one by journalist George Sokolsky, were sent to the *National Review* and several other mailing lists. The response was one of the early success stories of the conservatives' use of direct mail as a major medium of communication.

Among the young people who received the Sokolsky letter was David Jones, then teaching at a high school in Clearwater,

Florida. Dave started one of the first YAF chapters on the West Coast of Florida. Soon he became state chairman of YAF and, since he was the mentor of his school's debating team, he was able to sow the seeds for other chapters when the team was on the road. Within a year Jones' efforts were recognized by the YAF national organization and after the headquarters were moved from New York to Washington Richard Viguerie brought Dave Jones in as YAF executive director so Viguerie could become business manager and concentrate on direct mail. Jones remained executive director for the next eight years as YAF grew from an essentially campus protest movement into a major political organization.

Lee Edwards, the first editor of YAF's magazine *New Guard*, became our public relations director in the Draft Goldwater committee. And a host of other YAF members and alumni were active in both the Goldwater draft and presidential campaigns.

The spectacular success of our giant Draft Goldwater rally at the Washington Armory on July 4, 1963 was largely due to the Young Americans for Freedom. Peter O'Donnell, the state Republican chairman in Texas who became co-chairman with me of the Draft Committee, brought his entire GOP staff up from Texas to help put the rally over. But I'm sure Peter will concede it was the YAF effort that made the July 4th rally the huge success it turned out to be.

Donald Shafto, whom we came to call "Rally Don," had previously filled Madison Square Garden in New York for two YAF rallies. But he and his YAF friends outdid themselves in Washington. The Armory was not only packed, it was bursting at the seams that Fourth of July. Normally it seated 6,500 but that night more than 9,000 people jammed the Armory before the fire marshalls closed the doors and several thousand more people stood outside in the streets and parking lot.

Barry Goldwater, who even at this juncture really did not want to run for President, was not there, but this crowd had turned out to urge him to become a candidate. The speakers included Senator Tower of Texas, Senator Carl Curtis of Nebraska, Governor Paul Fannin of Arizona and Congressman John Ashbrook of Ohio. A group of Hollywood personalities also appeared—Walter Brennan, William Lundigan, Chill Wills and Efrem Zimbalist, Jr.

Senator Tower gave the principal address at the end of the rally and the demonstration that followed went beyond anything I have ever seen at a national convention, before or since. Moreover, the rally produced the most extensive publicity our Draft Goldwater effort had received to that point. It got big headlines everywhere, even in New York, and the *Washington Star* actually ran two stories on its front page, one by Mary McGrory and the other by David Broder, who is now with the *Washington Post*. Arthur Krock, the veteran *New York Times* columnist, wrote that the Goldwater "boom attained high visibility with a wildly enthusiastic Fourth of July rally in Washington by citizens, predominantly youthful, from all parts of the country."

This rally proved to be a big breakthrough for our Draft movement, not only in terms of news coverage but also in persuading Senator Goldwater and other Republican leaders that ours was a serious effort. Young Americans for Freedom could take a large share of the credit for this breakthrough and literally hundreds of young people, who in later times became important supporters of Ronald Reagan, cut their eye teeth in politics through this YAF rally and other projects for Goldwater in 1963–64. A few among so many who come to mind are:

Philip Crane, a teacher in Illinois and now in his seventh term as a Congressman from that state's 12th district; William Lowery, now a Congressman from California's 41st district; Alfred Regnery, an aide to Senator Laxalt during the 1980 Reagan campaign and presently an official in the Justice Department, who started working with YAF as a student at the University of Wisconsin; and Dana Rohrbacher, now a Reagan speechwriter on the White

House Staff, who came into the conservative cadre via YAF in California.

Among the journalists and writers who belonged to YAF are Pat Buchanan, nationally syndicated columnist and a former White House aide; Donald Lambro, author of the best-selling *Fat City*, formerly an editor of *New Guard*, and presently a nationally syndicated columnist with United Features; William Schulz, Washington bureau chief of *Reader's Digest*; Richard J. Bisirjian, author of *A Public Philosophy Reader*, and now an official in the U. S. International Communication Agency; and Jamieson Campaigne, Jr., editor of a group of suburban Chicago newspapers and now a book publisher.

Young Americans for Freedom gradually blended with the Young Republican National Federation and although the two organizations maintain their distinct identities the YR leadership now comes almost exclusively from YAF. This "blending" is due in large measure to the tireless efforts of Dave Jones during his tenure as YAF executive director.

Actually, Bill Rusher and I had worked with the Young Republicans for years and in 1963 conservative Donald E. (Buz) Lukens defeated the candidate backed by Nelson Rockefeller's team for the YR chairmanship in a significant victory for the Goldwater forces. Buz Lukens, later elected a Congressman from Ohio, was succeeded in 1965 by Tom van Sickle, a state senator from Kansas and a charter member of our original Draft Goldwater group.

After Tom van Sickle's chairmanship, there was a temporary lapse of conservative leadership in YR, a lapse that was to prove harmful to Ronald Reagan's initial bid for the Republican presidential nomination in 1968. However, from 1971 onward every chairman of the Young Republican National Federation has been a member, or former member, of Young Americans for Freedom— Donald Sundquist of Tennessee in 1971, Richard Smith of Florida in 1973, Jack Mueller of Wyoming in 1975, Roger Stone of

New York in 1977, and Rick Abel of Pennsylvania in 1979. Abel, who was also on the national board of YAF, threw the YR effort solidly behind Reagan's candidacy in 1980.

Republican politics were not YAF's exclusive concern in the 1960s and 1970s by any means. In fact, in the mid-1960s YAF was primarily focused on providing a non-violent answer to the increasingly violent anti-war protests. YAF set up a program to fund Vietnam veterans to speak on campuses and to send other young people to Vietnam so they could see for themselves what was going on in that country and report back to their peers in America.

What many of these veterans and other young people saw in Vietnam was that there were actually *two* wars being fought there. The first, the one most Americans were familiar with, was the media war, or at least the version of the Vietnam War brought into our homes every night courtesy of the television networks. The other was the real war, the one which our armed forces actually won more than once, only to be deprived of their victory by the no-win policies followed by the administrations in Washington.

Indeed, the Tet Offensive of 1968, which was presented by the media as a disastrous defeat for the American and South Vietnamese forces, was in reality a major victory for them. Whole divisions of the North Vietnamese Army were routed and fled back across the DMZ in disarray. If President Johnson had not declared a halt to the bombing of North Vietnam just before the 1968 presidential election there is a good chance South Vietnam and Cambodia might not be living through the terroristic nightmare those countries have suffered through for the past half-dozen years.

Young Americans for Freedom did their best to support our troops in Vietnam and they also mounted boycotts of the growing transfer of American technology to the Soviet Union. It is one of the supreme ironies of our age that America began to significantly increase its shipments of technology and engineering know-how to the USSR while we were deeply engaged in a shooting war with the Soviet's surrogates in Vietnam.

YAF effectively challenged the growing technology transfer to the USSR and it did so by organizing boycotts against the International Business Machines Corporation, Firestone Rubber Company, and others engaged in selling high technology plants and equipment to Russia and its satellites.

Working closely with YAF on many of its projects was the American Conservative Union. The ACU was formed immediately after the 1964 election by virtually the same group which had initiated YAF: Bill Buckley, Bill Rusher, Brent Bozell, Frank Meyer, and Marvin Liebman. They were joined at the founding meeting in Washington by Congressman John Ashbrook, former Congressman Donald Bruce, James Burnham of *National Review* and others.

Bill Rusher had sounded me out on the possibility of my becoming the first chairman of the American Conservative Union but I felt I could be more effective working from within the Republican Party. Don Bruce, who had been a two-term Congressman from Indiana, was named chairman, a post he held until 1967 when my old friend John Ashbrook took over.

Although the ACU had some uncertain moments in its early years, it became an effective force in American politics. Its peak membership was about 300,000, or more than the total number of Republican National Committee contributors up until the Goldwater campaign.

Moreover, ACU has spun off a galaxy of other organizations, including the Conservative Victory Fund, the first successful conservative political action committee; the American Legislative Exchange Council, run by Kathleen Teague, a group that gives conservative state legislators an important communication vehicle; and the Educational Research Institute, which in turn spawned the National Journalism Center headed so effectively by Stan Evans.

ACU has also born the brunt of a number of important legal battles conservatives have been engaged in, including the successful fight to have the courts strike down restraints on independent campaign expenditures, a measure that would have put the political action committees out of business. In this battle, ACU lined up with several liberals who also saw the danger of these restraints, including former Senator Eugene McCarthy of Minnesota and the New York Civil Liberties Union.

With the advent of the American Conservative Union and its affiliate organizations, the emergence of Young Americans for Freedom as a potent political force both in and out of Young Republicans, and the continuance of our original Draft Goldwater Committee as an ad hoc political group, the conservative cadre was now complete for its first big test—the effort to win the Republican presidential nomination for Ronald Reagan in 1968.

Many individuals and organizations have joined the conservative movement since then, of course. But this was the structure of our cadre as we went into the 1968 campaign to do battle for Ronald Reagan with Richard Milhous Nixon. Before that battle was joined, however, Governor Reagan had a number of tough tests to pass in Sacramento as well as on the national political stage.

Ronald Reagan was sworn in as Governor of California in a televised midnight ceremony at the state capitol on January 3, 1967. Right after he took the oath Reagan turned to his old friend and fellow actor, United States Senator George Murphy, and smiled broadly: "George, here we are on the late show again." Then, becoming serious, he gave a short speech in which he quoted Benjamin Franklin as saying: "If someone could take public office and bring to the public office the teachings and precepts of the Prince of Peace, he would revolutionize the world . . ."

"I don't think anyone could ever take office and be so presumptuous to think he could ever do that or that he could follow those precepts completely," Reagan said. "But I can tell you this: I'll try very hard. I think it is needed in today's world."

From many personal experiences with Ronald Reagan over the past seventeen years I can tell you that he meant every word he said.

8

The Governor

The conservative political revolution in America was conceived in the Goldwater movement prior to 1964 and was consummated by Ronald Reagan's victory in 1980. In between, conservative candidates for public office—from local, county and state levels to the Congress of the United States—advanced steadily, winning more and more elections in every section of the country.

To a very large extent conservative fortunes have been tied to the Republican Party, although in the first year of the Reagan Presidency we have witnessed a wholesale shift of Congressional Democrats to the conservative side. Actually, however, the shift toward conservatism nationally was already discernible in the 1966 elections. Ronald Reagan was not the only prominent Republican winner that year. The GOP swept 25 of the 34 gubernatorial contests and, equally significant, captured governorships in eight of the ten most populous states in the Union.

Reagan's nearly one–million vote plurality in California was easily the most impressive Republican gubernatorial victory. But Nelson Rockefeller won handily in New York, George Romney in Michigan, Raymond P. Shafer in Pennsylvania, John Volpe in

Massachusetts, Claude Kirk in Florida, James A. Rhodes in Ohio and Richard B. Ogilvie in Illinois.

Paul Laxalt beat a Democrat incumbent to take the governorship of Nevada and Dewey Bartlett coralled 56 per cent of the gubernatorial vote in Oklahoma to succeed Henry Bellmon, the first Republican governor in Oklahoma history.

Not all of these Republican governors were conservatives, of course. But they were almost all *more* conservative than their Democrat opponents. The same was generally true of the successful GOP candidates for the Congress. In the House, the Republicans scored a net gain of 47 seats and in the Senate the party added three more members.

Conservative leaders fared well in these 1966 Congressional races. John Ashbrook of Ohio, one of the very earliest of our Draft Goldwater adherents in the Congress, won easily despite the gerrymandering of his district designed to help the Democrats. John Rhodes of Arizona, a staunch ally of our Draft organization and now minority leader of the House, was returned to Congress with a comfortable plurality. Edward Derwinski, our Illinois Goldwater chairman, won handily, as did other Congressmen prominently identified with the Goldwater movement, including William Brock of Tennessee, later Republican National Chairman and now President Reagan's U.S. Trade Representative; Durwood G. Hall of Missouri; James F. Battin of Montana; and Albert Watson of South Carolina, who switched from Democrat to Republican that year.

Similarly, the Goldwater brand proved no handicap to Republicans running for the United States Senate in 1966. John Tower of Texas scored a smashing victory, capturing nearly 57 per cent of the vote in his race for reelection to Lyndon Johnson's old seat. Carl Curtis of Nebraska, our Goldwater floor manager at the 1964 national convention, galloped in with a 61 per cent plurality, and Strom Thurmond of South Carolina, running for the first time as a Republican, proved conclusively that the GOP could win in the South. In Wyoming, Governor Clifford Hansen, another Goldwater advocate, moved into the Senate without much difficulty, and Senator Karl Mundt of South Dakota chalked up 66 per cent of the vote, outdone only by Margaret Chase Smith of Maine with 69 per cent.

Of the 32 Senate contests that year, Republicans captured 18. Several of these were won by liberal Republicans, most prominently Charles H. Percy in Illinois, Edward Brooke in Massachusetts and Mark Hatfield in Oregon.

However, virtually all of the so–called "peace" candidates who advocated wholesale withdrawal of U.S. forces from Vietnam were soundly trounced in House and Senate races and this certainly represented a repudiation of the liberal position. In addition, there was growing discontent with President Johnson's Great Society programs, mounting inflation, and spreading disgust for the ever more violent civil rights and anti–war demonstrations. In fact, these demonstrations had an effect diametrically opposite to the one the demonstrators sought to achieve. Instead of winning people to their side, they turned off most people and many who joined the conservative movement in the ensuing years did so in repudiation of the demonstrators.

Immediately following the 1966, election speculation rose concerning the possible Republican Presidential candidate for 1968. Ronald Reagan, although a newcomer to politics, earned prominent mention because of the stunning victory he had won in the nation's most populous state. But George Romney and Nelson Rockefeller were both given an even better chance to take the GOP nomination, showing that much of the news media and many political experts had not yet grasped that conservatives had taken firm control of the Republican nominating process with Barry Goldwater's win at the San Francisco convention in 1964. Richard Nixon had supposedly withdrawn from politics after his 1962 defeat for the California governorship and his failure to stir any interest at all for the Presidential nomination in 1964. But we all expected a strong comback attempt by Nixon and I knew he was busy organizing his campaign.

I was in the curious position of being approached by all four major Republican candidates to help them with their 1968 campaigns for the party's presidential nomination. George Romney invited me to Michigan several times after he became governor of that state. Romney and I became good friends but I did not feel we were philosophically close enough to join in a presidential campaign, though two former associates of mine did end up guiding the Romney effort. They were Leonard Hall, the wise old former Republican national chairman, and Travis Cross, who had worked with us in the Goldwater campaign.

Nelson Rockefeller tried to bring me into his campaign at a somewhat later date. I did not seriously consider joining him, although I never felt Governor Rockefeller was quite as liberal as many of my conservative friends believed. On national defense issues he was, in many ways, as staunchly conservative as Barry Goldwater and in his very first term as Governor of New York he had tried hard, albeit unsuccessfully, to persuade the state legislature to adopt a law requiring the construction of bomb shelters in all public buildings in New York.

Richard Nixon made a fairly determined effort to get me to come aboard his 1968 bandwagon. I had known Nixon during his years as Vice President and had been director of organization in the Volunteers for Nixon–Lodge during the 1960 Presidential campaign. After John F. Kennedy's razor–thin victory in that election I thought that I had persuaded the Nixon campaign team, which was headed by Len Hall, to contest the blatant vote frauds in Illinois, Missouri, South Carolina and Texas—frauds that I am convinced brought Nixon down to defeat. * However,

* In a story on Chicago's Mayor Richard J. Daley entitled "The Last Dinosaur Wins Again," the *Saturday Evening Post* of April 11, 1964 reported: "The 1960 election, in which the [Daley] machine carried Illinois for President Kennedy by 8,858 votes, featured widespread accusations of crookedness. More than 600 election workers were charged with fraud. Only one was convicted." *The New York Times Magazine* of September 11, 1966, in another story on Mayor Daley ("A Minority Objects; But Daley Is Chicago") said: "John F. Kennedy frankly called Dick Daley 'the man who got me elected'."

in the end Nixon decided not to contest the election and Kennedy got his highly questionable "mandate" for the revolution he and Lyndon Johnson were to bring about in America's foreign and defense policies as well as the costly spending programs for domestic "reform."

Early in 1967 Nixon sent Peter Flanigan, whom I had worked with in the 1960 Nixon–Lodge Volunteers, to see me at my office in Suite 3505. I told Peter quite frankly that whatever message he was bringing from Nixon would have to be given to me by Nixon himself before I could consider it. Peter was puzzled by this but he left and arranged for me to meet with Nixon personally.

The meeting took place at Nixon's law office in Manhattan. His secretary brought us two cups of coffee and then Nixon popped the question about my involvement in his campaign for the nomination. I told him that I was not prepared to make a commitment to work for any candidate in 1968. I also said that I would not make a unilateral decision on a candidate without consulting with my 1964 Goldwater group. This apparently was not the answer Nixon expected, because as I finished he spilled his coffee.

The second meeting took place some time later at Nixon's Fifth Avenue apartment. This time he offered me scotch whisky and poured a glass for each of us. We sat side by side but in separate chairs in his living room.

"I want you to be the Republican National Chairman after I'm nominated," Nixon said.

"No thank you," I replied, "I don't want to be National Chairman."

This time Nixon spilled his scotch all over the rug. When he recovered himself he asked, with obvious surprise, "Why don't you want to be Chairman?"

"Because," I said, "the power is in the White House and if you are elected President what you should do is run the National Committee from the White House."

He thought this over for a minute and said: "Of course, you're right. That's what we'll do."

We chatted a bit more and when I finished my drink I left. After the 1968 election Nixon did follow through on my advice. He created a new post of political counselor to the President and gave it to John Sears, one of his young law firm associates. Sears held the job only a short time and was succeeded by Harry Dent, Senator Thurmond's former aide. Dent, a capable political operator, did help the Republican Party increase its inroads into the South but I don't believe he actually fulfilled my vision of controlling the Republican National Committee from the White House.

Ronald Reagan, of all the potential Republican candidates for 1968, was the only one I really wanted to see nominated. In his book *The Making of the President—1968*, Theodore White tells the following story:

> Within ten days of his election [as governor], Reagan had gathered his inner circle together, on Thursday, November 17th, 1966, at his home in Pacific Palisades for a first discussion of the Presidency. There, too, was named a captain for the adventure—young Tom Reed, a distinguished physicist turned successful industrialist. . . . Reed, in the next two weeks, was to engage as counsel for the campaign the master architect of the Goldwater nomination of 1964, F. Clifton White of New York. Together the two were to draw up a meticulous master plan for seizure of the nomination, timed in five phases and date–deadlined from December, 1966, to nomination in August, 1968. That all their work was to come to naught . . . was less their failure than accident and tragedy.

White goes on to explain that a homosexual scandal in the Sacramento state house in the summer of 1967 stayed the Governor's hand at a critical time: "Shocked, Reagan purged his immediate staff, then withdrew to the circle of his oldest friends. . . . The plans of Reed and White were put on ice. From this blow, the Reagan campaign never recovered."

It is not difficult to understand the Governor's shock. But it is my belief that he recovered much quicker than White indicates.

Essentially, however, any delay in implementing plans in the months preceding the start of the Presidential primary season can prove fatal.

I remember shortly after the 1966 election Governor Reagan came east with Tom Reed and we had dinner with Tom's father, Gordon Reed, at the Blind Brook Country Club in Greenwich. I got the distinct impression Reagan was much more interested in doing the job he was elected to do in California than in making a serious run for the Presidency. And I recall telling him that evening: "Ron, as governor of the largest state in the Union, you will automatically be one of the leaders of the Republican Party nationally." I added that whether he ran himself or not, he was bound to be considered for the Presidential nomination.

I certainly was not alone in this. Earlier, at the beginning of his general election campaign, Reagan had made a pilgrimage to Gettysburg to have lunch with former President Eisenhower. Asked afterward if the visit meant he was endorsing Reagan, Ike replied: "Any candidate elected governor of any big state would have to be considered by the party [as a possibility for President]."

"Mr. Reagan is a man of great integrity and common sense and I know he's a Republican and I'm for Republicans," Dwight Eisenhower said in his inimitable manner.

Toward the end of the year I met Reagan at the Republican Governors Conference in Colorado Springs. Chatting one night in the bar with Sander Vanocur, the television correspondent, he told me he had been in the lobby of the Broadmoor when Reagan arrived.

"All eyes were on him," Sandy said. "I've only seen this kind of magnetism in one other public figure—Jack Kennedy."

I smiled and said: "What about Ike?"

Sandy didn't disagree, but he kept his focus on Reagan. "This guy has *got* it," he repeated several times.

There was no doubt that Vanocur was right. Reagan *was* the center of attention at the Conference, overshadowing other Republican governors like Rockefeller and Romney who were getting much more attention in the press as Presidential possibilities.

In California, the new governor was also very much in the public spotlight. He had inherited a long trainload of problems from his free–spending predecessors and he was forced to tackle them hard. Reagan had been in office only a few weeks when the *The Wall Street Journal* ran a lengthy article which led off:

> A change last year in the method of accounting state revenues, which delayed the state's day of reckoning, has helped put California Governor Reagan into a fiscal hole at the start of his administration.

The *Journal* went on to report that Reagan had already ordered state agencies to cut back expenditures 10 per cent. He had also halted the purchase of new cars except in emergencies, banned out–of–state travel by state employes and prohibiting the hiring of new employes. In March he initiated the phase–out of 3,000 state jobs, out of a total of some 110,000. The loudest protests of these budgetary cuts came from the state university system, which had considered itself sacrosanct until Reagan came to office.

The Governor also moved quickly to dampen the demonstrations that had disrupted many campuses in California. In addition to working with the state regents to ease out Clark Kerr as president of the riot–torn Berkeley campus of the University of California, Reagan insisted that order be restored at San Francisco State College, also the site of wild disturbances. Ultimately, the president of the college resigned and was replaced by semantics professor S.I. Hayakawa, whose firm administration at San Francisco State catapulted him into the United States Senate.

Eventually, most other governors followed Ronald Reagan's lead and in February 1969 the National Governors Conference adopted a policy statement condemning campus disorders. But in 1967 Reagan was one of the very few governors who was prepared to take strong action to control campus rioting.

Reagan didn't win every battle in California, of course. In the summer of 1967 the Board of Regents, by a lopsided 14 to 7, voted against the Governor's proposal to charge tuition at state colleges and universities. Asked at a press conference if he regarded the regents' vote as a defeat for him, Reagan replied: "No, but it is a rebuff to the people of California, who have so well supported the university, and I feel they deserve better."

"Do you believe your national prestige will be hurt by the regents' action?" a reporter persisted.

"I am not concerned about national prestige," Reagan responded. "Any man would like to be loved by all, but my job is in California."

Nonetheless, Governor Reagan was beginning to win recognition nationally. Columnist Nick Thimmesch was later to write that Reagan scored important political points in 1967:

> To the dismay and surprise of many liberals, Reagan far outshone Senator Robert F. Kennedy on a nationally televised question–and–answer 'Town Meeting of the World' program on America's image. And when Reagan appeared at a $500–a–plate Republican dinner in Washington alongside Richard Nixon, Governor Romney, and Senator Percy, he got the most applause and the best press notices.

By the fall of 1967 Ronald Reagan was receiving, as the *Wall Street Journal* put it, "generally high marks" for his performance as governor of California. As early as July of that year a statewide poll showed that he had won the approval of no less than 74 per cent of the voters in the state. And on his first visit to Washington as Governor, Reagan passed muster with the press.

Willard Edwards, the highly respected veteran Capitol Hill correspondent for the *Chicago Tribune*, reported after a Reagan meeting with the press that the Governor "emerged smiling and unscathed from a cross–examination on his political ambitions and beliefs" by more than 150 representatives of the media. Edwards quoted "a columnist of liberal views" as saying: "He handled every curve ball thrown at him; he didn't fall into a single trap."

There were, however, more traps on the 1968 nominating trail than either Ronald Reagan or I could have anticipated when we started out together. And the traps were not set by the press but by Richard Nixon, who cajoled many people who should have been our strongest supporters into backing Nixon himself.

9

The Reluctant
Candidate

I have been asked, usually by political professionals, why I worked for Ronald Reagan in 1968 when I had been invited by all three of the Republican front-runners—Richard Nixon, Nelson Rockefeller and George Romney—to help them win the Republican nomination for President. There were two reasons.

First, and most important, I was then and am now philosophically on the same frequency with Ronald Reagan.

Second, many people believed Robert F. Kennedy would be the Democratic candidate in 1968; I was convinced the Republican Party would never nominate Richard Nixon to run against another Kennedy, and I was even more convinced Ronald Reagan was the only Republican who had a chance of beating Bobby Kennedy.

Our primary problem in 1968 was persuading Ronald Reagan to run. A secondary problem, and the one that ultimately proved insurmountable, was convincing the conservative Republican leaders that Governor Reagan would run and that it would be prudent for them to withhold endorsement of Richard Nixon or any other candidate until the convention at Miami in August.

Very early in 1967 we had talked Reagan into accepting a "favorite son" role from the California delegation. Traditionally, this role does not commit the "favorite son" to a serious candidacy but it permits him to keep all his options open and still control his own state's delegation at the convention. In 1968 this placed Reagan in a particularly strong position since California would be sending 86 delegates to Miami, the second largest state bloc. Only New York, with 92 delegates, would have more than California.

However, even in this "favorite son" role, the Governor was assumed to be running for the nomination and the Presidency and the press naturally was on the lookout for any evidence that indicated Reagan was something more. In June 1967, for example, David Broder spotted the Governor conferring with me and some of my old Draft Goldwater cadre during the Western Governors Conference in a hotel in Montana's Yellowstone National Park.

The next day Broder's story in the *Washington Post* led off: "A number of key Republicans are now willing to bet that it is only a matter of time before Ronald Reagan has the third fully-fledged organization in the battle for the Republican presidential nomination . . . and its operating head will be none other than F. Clifton White."

Dave Broder was a little premature in this surmise, but through the years I've noticed his crystal ball is usually accurate and this story was no exception.

Other articles of this nature kept popping up after that. Several weeks later the UPI wire carried a story out of Sacramento by Norman Kempster that started off:

> If California Governor Ronald Reagan wanted to capture next year's Republican presidential nomination he would make a few out-of-state speeches, deny he is a candidate, sit back and wait.

That is just what he is doing.

He also would accept a limited number of invitations to appear on nation-wide television and would discuss such major issues of the day as Vietnam and the Middle East.

He is doing that, too . . .

It is doubtful that at this stage the freshman California governor could defeat either Mr. Nixon or Michigan Governor George Romney in head-to-head primary contests.

But if Governor Reagan sticks to the role of non-candidate while keeping his name alive with potential national convention delegates, he could be in a position to pick up the pieces if the GOP front-runners falter.

This, in a nutshell, was the strategy Tom Reed and I had concocted. Our problem was that our candidate didn't take it very seriously at first, though, like the good trouper he is, Ronald Reagan went through the motions. He allowed us to step up his appearances at Republican fund–raising dinners, events for which he was always much in demand, and this gave us a chance to introduce him to party leaders in the states he visited. By the end of 1967 Reagan had raised more than $1,500,000 for the party at these fund raisers, far more than any of the active candidates for the nomination.

I attended a number of these events with the Governor and was impressed by his speeches and by the enthusiastic reaction of his audiences. His one–liners always got a good laugh. A few of them, I think, are worth recording:

• "I've never been able to understand how the Democrats can run those $1,000–a–plate dinners at such a profit, and run the Government at such a loss."

• "You have to admire the administration's anti–crime program. They're making the money so cheap it's not worth stealing."

• "According to [some history teachers], it is the United States that has aggressive ambitions which cause the Soviets to arm defensively for protection. Logic obviously is not part of the approved course for at least some history professors."

• "Man in his entire history has adopted about four billion

laws—and we haven't improved on the Ten Commandments one iota."

• "We are told God is dead. Well, he isn't. We just can't talk to Him in the classroom anymore."

In December of 1967 he spoke at Yale University where *Time* magazine reported "Reagan fielded questions with aplomb and wit." He apparently surprised some of the more *outre* elements in New Haven because, as *Time* also noted, he proved "unbaitable and well read in his homework."

This is a facet of Ronald Reagan's character that I don't believe most people even now are fully aware of; he is a man who *reads* and who thinks things out for himself. He also writes his own speeches, something no other President has done almost since the last century. Reagan will take a draft of a speech prepared by his staff and read it over. But then, as I first noticed traveling with him in 1967–68, out comes a pocketful of three–by–five file cards and by the time he is finished making notes on them the original speech may bear little resemblance to the one he actually delivers.

As 1967 ended, Reagan began to increase his appearances around the country substantially and in January 1968, while the official candidates were knocking each others' brains out in New Hampshire, Reagan was addressing fund–raisers and other friendly audiences in Pittsburgh, Philadelphia, ˙St. Louis, Tulsa, New York and other cities.

In Pittsburgh he drew loud cheers from a largely student audience in a hall on the edge of the University of Pittsburgh campus.

"There is a youth rebellion because not enough of us have been living by those rules of conduct which we preached," Reagan told the crowd. James Helbert, the political editor of the *Pittsburgh Press*, reported that "young and old applauded" when Reagan charged there was a morality gap in government. He said the Great Society "is a complete failure" and urged that "we stop being our brother's keeper and become our brother's brother so that he can take care of himself." Reagan further charged that some politicians want to "institutionalize" the poor by "keeping them in poverty and degredation. They buy the people's votes with the people's money."

Whenever he was asked about his being a candidate for President, as he was everywhere he went, Reagan had a stock answer, as he did in Pittsburgh on January 18: "No. I am not a candidate," he said. "I find it strange that there are so many references to two unannounced candidates. I think [the nomination] is still open and will be decided at the convention. I will work for [whoever is] the nominee."

Alvin Rosensweet of the *Pittsburgh Post-Gazette* caught the essential reaction of people everywhere to Ronald Reagan:

> Even determined Democrats would admit that Reagan, at 56, generates excitement. A handsome man with a ruddy complexion, trim physique, and thick head of dark brown hair—"it's hereditary," he explained— he charmed 1,000 persons who crowded the (Syria) Mosque basement. They had paid $100 for three luncheons—$33.33 per event—and had chicken yesterday. Reagan had this to say:
> "I know the price of this luncheon and unless we win, this will be the regular price for lunch."

About this time rumors began to circulate that Reagan would make an ideal Vice–Presidential candidate—on a ticket with, of all people, Nelson Rockefeller. It wasn't difficult for Reagan and me to figure out who started that one. And we took appropriate action to scuttle Governor Rockefeller's idea of a "dream ticket."

Reagan not only rejected the whole idea of running for Vice President, he came as close as he ever did in his whole political career to repudiating a fellow Republican. In an interview with James Reston of the *New York Times*, Governor Reagan spelled out his political differences with Rockefeller in some detail.

"I would say that Governor Rockefeller, maybe because he has been in office a much longer time, would come closer to the other party's approach in method, in the belief that government can do all these things," Reagan told Reston. Specifically, he disagreed with Rockefeller's plan for clearing city slums by financing such projects with huge state bond issues. "This is contrary to my approach," he said.

Rockefeller was not our real problem, however. Nor, in a sense, was Richard Nixon. It was the conservative Republican leaders who were so determined to get a "winner" in 1968 that they could not hold back on committing themselves to the man all the "pragmatists" thought would be the best candidate, Dick Nixon.

Very early in the game I was aware of the curious game being played by three Southern gentlemen who should have been staunch Reagan supporters, if for no other reason than the vast majority of Republicans in their states wanted Reagan, not Nixon, as their candidate. The three were all state Republican chairmen: Harry Dent of South Carolina, Bill Murfin of Florida, and Clarke Reed of Mississippi.

For the consumption of their constituencies, all three appeared to be backing Reagan. But the fact was they were quietly working for Nixon, and ultimately their efforts prevented me from stopping Nixon on the first ballot in Miami.

Harry Dent played the most important role in this game for the simple reason that Harry had Strom Thurmond's ear. He had worked in the Senator's Washington office for some years and had his boss's complete confidence. Harry Dent was one member of a triumvirate who helped bring Strom Thurmond into national prominence as an expert on national defense issues during the 1960's. The other two were Colonel Philip J. Corso, who had first blown the whistle on the Kennedy–Johnson administration's plans for nuclear "parity" with the Russians, a policy that amounted to unilateral disarmament for U.S. strategic forces, and J. Fred Buzhardt, later to become chief counsel of the Department of

Defense and subsequently White House general counsel during Watergate. (He was not personally implicated in that scandal.)

I'd had several heart–to–heart talks with Senator Thurmond about the possibility of Governor Reagan emerging from his favorite son cocoon to spread his wings as a full-fledged candidate in Miami. The Senator seemed most enthusiastic and he always assured me how highly he regarded Reagan. He was quoted as telling people who asked him about the Governor: "I love that man. He's the best hope we've got."

With Thurmond behind Reagan I thought we could count on most, if not all, of the 334 delegates the Southern states would send to the convention. As things turned out, I was much too sanguine about the prospects of my candidate sweeping the South. One complication was the candidacy of George Wallace for the Democratic presidential nomination. Wallace siphoned off a good bit of the Southern support that would have gone to a conservative Republican. Another was that the Southerners felt that Barry Goldwater had not paid enough attention to them in 1964 and this time they were playing much more hard to get. Peter O'Donnell, the state Republican chairman in Texas, appeared to be taking this attitude. In the end, however, I think he and many of the other Southerners would agree that they outsmarted themselves.

O'Donnell, who had served with me as Co–Chairman of the Draft Goldwater Committee, had decided to keep his big Texas delegation tied to Senator John Tower as a favorite son in the obvious—and perfectly legitimate—hope he could trade off delegates *en bloc* for power and patronage. There was an additional motive for the Texas strategy, and one that should not be minimized: John Tower was strong for Nixon.

But O'Donnell and Tower had a subsidiary problem in the spontaneous Reagan committees that were springing up all over Texas. Eventually they appointed J.R. (Butch) Butler, a wealthy oil geologist, to keep these groups under control. And then they promptly lost control of Butler, who was really a Reagan backer. He was also one of the most independent men I've ever encountered in politics.

At one point Butch Butler flew to Massachusetts, totally on his own, and offered Governor Volpe the Vice-Presidential nomimation on a ticket with Reagan. Only Butch had neglected to check with Reagan on this "offer" and the next time they met, in California, Reagan felt compelled to tell Mr. Butler he might have to repudiate him. Butch just smiled and drawled, "Well, it's a free country, even for governors."

There was still another complication to the Texas problem, one that Rowland Evans and Robert Novak zeroed in on in their joint newspaper column early in January 1968. "If liberal Senator Ralph Yarborough is the Democratic nominee for Governor," they wrote, "Republicans will need support from the conservative Democratic establishment to beat him. If that means conceding the state to Lyndon Johnson for President, many Republican politicians would consider that a fair trade in return for the Governor's mansion. That is not the least of the reasons for the absence of presidential fever among Texas Republicans going into 1968."

Few people expected President Johnson to get knocked off in the New Hampshire primary by the ascetic junior Senator from Minnesota, Eugene McCarthy. The handsome McCarthy was more poet than politician, but his dedicated anti–war followers pulled out all the stops in New Hampshire and McCarthy wound up in a dead heat with the President. *

Bobby Kennedy was the real winner, however. On March 13, the day after the New Hampshire primary, he let it be known he was "reassessing" his plans and immediately Kennedy stole ·Senator McCarthy's thunder—and his candidacy. A few days later, on

*President Johnson received 27,243 Democrat votes in New Hampshire against 23,280 for Senator McCarthy. However, McCarthy garnered enough write-in votes from Republicans to give him a combined total of 28,791, only 230 less than Johnson's combined total of 29,021.

March 16th, Kennedy officially announced he would run for the Democratic nomination and the Presidency.

Then, on March 31st, Lyndon Baines Johnson went on national television and announced: "I shall not seek and I will not accept the nomination of my party for another term as your President." Robert Kennedy had, in effect, won the Democratic nomination without a struggle. The Vietnam War had beaten Lyndon Johnson; or, more accurately, he had beaten himself by failing to win the Vietnam War.

The President's abject surrender to Bobby Kennedy galvanized our Reagan camp, and particularly Governor Reagan. Up to this point, I felt he was merely going along for the ride, acquiescing in the plans Tom Reed and I had drawn up for him, but regarding himself as a real "favorite son" and nothing more. But now, with Kennedy's comet in orbit, he was forced to make a decision as to whether he wanted to launch a real campaign for the nomination and for the Presidency.

I don't think Ronald Reagan ever hesitated after that. He knew that a Kennedy victory would be a victory for all the forces he had fought against for so long. If anything, Senator Kennedy would, as President, far surpass Lyndon Johnson's free–spending social programs. And, more important, the forces of appeasement, which Lyndon Johnson had tried at least to keep at bay, would come howling into power with Bobby Kennedy.

It had been Bobby Kennedy who had stayed his brother's hand during the Bay of Pigs crisis and persuaded Jack Kennedy to refrain from giving the Cuban freedom fighters the air support they needed to survive that abortive invasion.

It had been Bobby Kennedy who had blackjacked (some say "wiretapped") the Nuclear Test Ban Treaty through the Senate in 1963 even though leading scientists like Dr. Edward Teller had warned the treaty would lock the U.S. into a position of strategic inferiority vis a vis the Soviet Union, a warning that tragically came to pass.

It had been Bobby Kennedy who supervised the destruction of our internal security laws and regulations by sending one of his Justice Department henchmen to the State Department with orders to get rid of Otto Otepka, the working chief of security at State, because Otepka had insisted on upholding the law and refused to give clearance to known security risks whom Kennedy wanted to install in the State Department. *

In short, it was Bobby Kennedy who had permitted himself to be manipulated by the Left as both Attorney General and as the junior United States Senator from New York. Ironically, Bobby originally came to Washington in 1953 to work for Senator Joseph McCarthy's Government Operations Subcommittee, which was conducting its controversial investigation of communists in government. McCarthy had been a good friend of the Kennedys, staying with them on summer weekends at their home on Cape Cod and dating Patricia Kennedy before she married Peter Lawford. But Bobby got into a running argument with McCarthy aide Roy Cohn and once he and Cohn even came to blows. As public opinion shifted against McCarthy, Bobby resigned from the committee and he wound up helping pave the way for the Senate censure of the Wisconsin Republican.

Now, in 1968, Bobby had preempted the candidacy of another McCarthy. Although many people disagreed, I felt Bobby would get the Democratic nomination. Ronald Reagan must have been of like mind because, from the moment Bobby Kennedy announced, Reagan became a thoroughly motivated candidate, though for strategic purposes he still had to cling to the cloak of favorite son.

In his fine book, *The Real Reagan*, veteran Washington correspondent Frank van der Linden says that I, as "Reagan's companion on his travels, gave him his first lessons in delegate-hunting on the national scene and found him an eager student, quickly

*Otepka's telephones were tapped, his files rifled, and his home placed under surveillance by John Francis Reilly, whom Kennedy sent to State from the Justice Department in 1961. Reilly and another State Department official were fired when a Senate committee proved they had ordered the wire taps.

absorbing the lore of Republican politics in various states." This is true: Ronald Reagan proved to be a very quick study.

We traveled thousands of miles together up and down the country that spring and early summer. During that period I feel that I got to know him as well as anyone with the exception of his wife, Nancy, who also became a close friend of mine. Observing Ronald Reagan in such close proximity day after day, I found there were several key aspects to his character that are not universally recognized even now that he is President. I have touched on a few of these earlier, most prominently his willingness to speak for himself when the going gets rough in politics, as it inevitably does, and his insistence on doing his own homework and writing the finished drafts of his speeches. There are some others that should be noted.

First and foremost, Ronald Reagan is a man at peace with himself. I believe this peace derives from his deep and abiding faith in God.

There is no sham about the President's religious beliefs. He doesn't go to church for political purposes. He goes, like most Americans, to offer his respect and gratitude to his Maker, and he does his best to live by the precepts of Christianity.

Secondly, and I think rooted in his belief in God, Ronald Reagan genuinely likes people, as I mentioned before. There is no hypocrisy or sham about this element of his character either. He draws strength from people. He *enjoys* being with people, even people who consistently disagree with him on political issues. He was not trying to con the Speaker of the House at the outset of his Presidency: he *likes* Tip O'Neill, and I think the Speaker has felt that, too.

Third, President Reagan is a good listener, a rare trait in politicians. Devoid of ego, he never feels the need to assert himself to get the attention of others. Moreover, he is sincerely interested in what other people have to say. This is more than courtesy, though it springs from that, too. The President, probably since boyhood, has had a great hunger to learn, and he feels he can do that better by listening to people than by talking himself, though he is a good talker and certainly anything but taciturn.

Others have remarked on his courage, which became so obvious to the nation and to the world during the assassination attempt on March 31, 1981. They have also duly noted his great sense of humor, which flashed brightly even on that day. Moreover, I suspect millions of words have now been written about his patriotism, and I don't think that anyone except the most hopelessly cynical person would question the sincerity of his lifelong love affair with America.

Like his love of God and his family, the President's love for his country is always with him. It is the great motivating force in his life, the propellant that has kept him going forward when most men would have simply rested on their oars and coasted with the tide. From this springs his sense of duty and his attitude toward public service: it is a responsibility first, an honor second, and never something to be sought for power's sake alone. Ronald Reagan did not seek the Presidency to wield power for power's sake, as I have already observed. He sought the office because he felt the country needed leadership and, although he is a genuinely humble man, he realized, because so many people he respects persuaded him to realize, that he had those qualities of leadership America required at this particular time in our history.

These are the qualities that stand out in Ronald Reagan's character and career. His faults? Every man has them, of course, but I doubt if any man in public life has had his faults culled so meticulously as Reagan's. For seventeen years, since he delivered the television speech in support of Barry Goldwater in 1964, every real or imagined fault of Ronald Reagan has been held up to public scrutiny, not just flashed on a television screen and then turned off, but held up permanently so that his faults acquired the status of myths. Yet I have noticed that most of these myths have evaporated in his tenure as President. On the closer scrutiny that is perhaps the most demanding price one must pay for occupying the White House, the myths about Ronald Reagan's faults have been found to have little substance.

History will be the final judge of his faults, though President Reagan would undoubtedly protest that. I can see him now, shaking his head with that mock rueful smile, and saying, "No, Clif. *God* will be my final judge."

It is not that he doesn't care what history will make of him. It is just that Ronald Reagan knows that history is written by men, and all men have their faults, historians included.

Reagan's concern transcends ego and hunger for power, and his decisions as President are made on the basis of something far more important to him—his *conscience.* And it was his conscience that made Reagan run in earnest for President after Robert Kennedy tossed his hat in the ring in March 1968.

10

Countdown to Miami

No other spring in our nation's history has been more eventful, more packed with tragedy than the spring of 1968.

The war in Vietnam escalated dramatically with the Tet offensive early in the year and Tet II raged on into May and June. Anti–war riots erupted anew on campuses from coast to coast, were augmented by clashes over racial issues, and disrupted or virtually shut down classes at Columbia University, Stanford, Northwestern and a score of other schools.* The Pueblo crisis, involving the seizure of a Navy electronic intelligence ship and its 83–man crew by the North Koreans, dragged on interminably. President Johnson's March 31 announcement that he would not seek reelection left the ship of state temporarily rudderless and increased the people's disenchantment with their government.

Martin Luther King's murder in Memphis on April 4 touched off bloody rioting in 125 cities, leaving 46 dead, some 2,600 injured, and the jails jammed with more than 20,000 arrested rioters. Washington, Baltimore, Chicago, Kansas City and Pitts-

---

*Columbia University reported that of the 700 persons arrested in the rioting there, 181 were not even students or members of the faculty. The 239 Columbia College students arrested represented less than 9% of the college's enrollment and the 111 arrested from affiliated Barnard College were only 6% of the Barnard student body.

burgh were among the hardest hit and thousands of fires started by arson left large areas of many cities charred ruins.

Then, on June 5, as he left the party celebrating his California primary victory, Robert Kennedy was gunned down by Sirhan Sirhan, a Marxist Jordanian Arab who had lived in the Los Angeles area for eleven years.

For the second time in five years a Marxist assassin's bullets had killed a Kennedy. And both times they killed my chances of managing a successful presidential campaign for a Republican opponent of a Kennedy.

Now, I have already made the point that Barry Goldwater was beginning to surge ahead of Jack Kennedy in the polls just before President Kennedy's assassination in November 1963. It is my belief that Ronald Reagan would similarly have surged ahead of Robert Kennedy in the 1968 election. Most assuredly, he would have taken the Republican nomination after Bobby's win in the California primary, which had virtually sewed up the Democratic candidacy for Kennedy.

But with Bobby Kennedy's assassination, the whole political scene had shifted once again. Vice President Hubert Humphrey, the choice of President Johnson and the Democratic party professionals, was certain to be nominated in Chicago. Eugene McCarthy had never had a real chance for the nomination, although he had played an important role in persuading Lyndon Johnson that the time had come for Johnson to step down.

The Republican landscape was not quite so clearly etched, but I knew that Richard Nixon was going to be much more difficult for us to beat with Bobby Kennedy gone. Indeed, one of the arguments for a Reagan candidacy that I'd earlier found most telling after Bobby's decision to run was that Dick Nixon, who had blown a huge lead to lose to Jack Kennedy in 1960 by a doubtful wafer–thin margin, could not beat another Kennedy in 1968.

The other Republican candidates were no longer a factor, although, strangely, influential elements of the press persisted in giving Nelson Rockefeller the best chance to beat Nixon at Miami. George Romney had removed himself from consideration even before the New Hampshire primary had played out its quadrennial giant–killer role. Mayor John Lindsay of New York had never been in the running and, indeed, there was a question as to whether Lindsay was even a Republican, a question he later answered by seeking the Democratic nomination in the next Presidential election.

There was only Reagan and Nixon in 1968. Nelson Rockefeller may have had more committed delegates than Ronald Reagan going into the Miami convention. But those were *all* the delegates he could ever hope to get. Our delegate buildup had just begun. And we were gathering steam in spite of the odds, in spite of all the polls, in spite of the hard fact that most of the conservative leadership, which should have gone for Reagan, had long since declared for Nixon.

Nixon's campaign had been a clever one. He had clothed himself as a pragmatist running against ideological candidates: Rockefeller, Romney and Lindsay, the liberal ideologues, and Ronald Reagan, the heir to Barry Goldwater's conservative ideological mantle. At the same time, however, Nixon was careful to cast himself as a *conservative* pragmatist, since he knew conservatives controlled the Republican nominating process.

The great irony was that Barry Goldwater himself had been among the first of the conservative leaders to announce for Nixon. I had tried to persuade him to hold off any endorsement until the convention. But Nixon's courtship of Barry, which had begun when Nixon went all out in support of Goldwater's presidential candidacy in 1964, bore fruit early in the 1968 quest for the nomination. One March day in Phoenix, Senator Goldwater called in the reporters and told them he was backing Richard Nixon.

More serious, however, was Strom Thurmond's support of Nixon. Senator Thurmond was the key to the South and Nixon simply stole our key. The kidnapping of Strom Thurmond took place in Atlanta on June 1, 1968. Nixon had flown in the day before to meet with the Southern Republican chairmen. He had succeeded in smoothing over all their fears but the Southerners raised a new one that Nixon probably hadn't considered too seriously before— the strong possibility of George Wallace taking enough of the Southern states in November to deny Nixon the election. The chairmen advised Nixon that only Strom Thurmond could hold the South and they urged him to stay over and meet with the Senator the next day.

In the end, Thurmond was won over not on the race issue, as some claimed, but on what was and is for him the overriding issue of our time—national defense. During their meeting in Atlanta, Nixon promised Thurmond he would go all–out to restore America's defenses, which were already falling seriously behind the advancing Russian nuclear buildup. It was a promise that was to go up in the heady smoke of *detente*, though like most of Nixon's promises it probably had no substance to begin with.

However, Thurmond had given his word that he would support Nixon. And once the Senator had given his word, nothing could have made him go back on it. I knew that, but I flew to Washington next day to meet him at his office there to make sure the reports were right, that it was a real commitment, and to get his thoughts on the convention, still two months away.

Senator Thurmond lectured me for an hour on how much he thought of Governor Reagan. But he made it plain that his was a firm commitment to Nixon. As I got up to leave, the Senator walked me to the door. On the way he paused at a photograph of Ronald Reagan hanging on the wall of his office. "This one's getting a little old," he said. "Do you think the Governor would send me a new one? With an appropriate inscription, of course."

I told him that I would see that he got an autographed picture from the Governor in the near future. We shook hands at the door and said goodbye.

The Senator's declaration for Nixon was a severe blow, but it failed to slow us down. In fact, Reagan and I stepped up our travelling substantially in June and July of 1968. By this time I had been officially retained as a counsel to the California delegation and I was able to operate more openly than I had in the recent past.

The Governor still maintained he was only a favorite-son candidate and this did cause some serious problems along the way. Actually, it may have set the stage for Senator Thurmond's support of Nixon because on May 19, when we were in New Orleans to meet the Southern state chairmen at the Roosevelt Hotel, Reagan had protested his candidacy a bit too much and I'm afraid most of the chairmen present felt after that the Governor would never seriously seek the nomination. However, he had not shut the door; he had said he would accept a draft, provided it was a broad–based draft that had its origins in the grass roots.

The trouble was it was too late for that kind of draft. Spontaneous, and perhaps some not–so–spontaneous, Reagan–for–President organizations had sprung up all over the country. Henry Bubb, a savings and loan company executive in Topeka, Kansas, had set up an unofficial National Draft Reagan headquarters in Topeka to coordinate the activities of the various groups on a national scale. Henry did a good job, with Tom Reed's guidance, but he simply was not equipped to organize a major draft operation of the sort we had organized in 1964.

Nonetheless, some political pundits insisted on detecting a full–blown Draft Reagan organization operating underground. Tom Wicker of *The New York Times* turned up in Boise, Idaho, for a Reagan speech toward the end of April and he must have been looking for Clif White Goldwaterites under his bed at the hotel. At any rate, this is what Wicker wrote:

> Reagan's links to the Clif White "syndicate" that won the nomination for Goldwater can be detected in Idaho. Secretary of State Pete Cennarusa, chairman of the Reagan for President committee, is married to the closest friend of Mrs. Gwen Barnett, the Republican National Committeewoman, and one of White's lieutenants. Wayne Crow, co-chairman of the group, is another White associate.

Wicker wasn't too far off. In many instances, however, I'd never heard of the people who were starting the state organizations for Reagan. In Pennsylvania, for example, a group of people got together in Pike County and declared themselves the "Pennsylvanians for Governor Reagan for President." L.W. McCormick was the Chairman; Richard T. Hoober was Secretary–Treasurer, and Victor A. Bihl was General Counsel. How did I know? I read it on their letterhead.

Like others of these groups, the letters they sent out took the occasion not just to back Reagan but to fight some state battles as well. Hugh Scott, later the minority leader of the United States Senate, was the particular target of Mr. McCormick *et al.* "Whoever accused Scott of being Republican?" they quoted a Pennsylvania newspaper as asking. They also went after my friend Governor Shafer for increasing the state sales tax and a few other things.

On the whole, however, these spontaneous groups probably helped our cause. In this case, Hugh Scott was, as usual, backing Nelson Rockefeller and, I'm sorry to say, so was Ray Shafer. Rockefeller had rounded up a rather impressive list indeed of fellow governors in support of his candidacy. Besides Ray Shafer, they included his brother Winthrop Rockefeller of Arkansas, Spiro Agnew of Maryland, Harold LeVander of Minnesota, John Chaffee of Rhode Island, John Love of Colorado, Tom McCall of Oregon, and Nils Boe of South Dakota. Some of them later got on the Nixon bandwagon, as did a number of Senators and Congressmen and other national political figures who backed Rockefeller earlier in 1968. But they were for Nelson when he came out for this, the final round of his marathon twenty–year quest of the Presidency.

It was probably this formidable array of party leadership backing Rockefeller that threw the press and other observers off the main threat to Nixon's candidacy—Ronald Reagan. It is also a testimony to the devotion of our cadre and their adherents that so many delegates were willing to oppose their state's governors and other leaders to support Reagan in 1968.

What so many people didn't seem to grasp was that the delegates to the 1968 convention would be essentially the same delegates who had voted overwhelmingly for Goldwater's nomination four years earlier. And, as a matter of fact, basically the same delegates controlled the decision in 1980, as they will again in 1984. Some of the faces have changed, of course. A number of 1964 delegates have dropped out of politics and a few have died. But we were a very young group twenty years ago when we started the conservative revolution within the Republican party and few of us are very old even today.

The great trouble in 1968 was that the conservative delegates had been preempted for Nixon; preempted, moreover, by the conservative leadership. Besides Barry Goldwater, Strom Thurmond, and John Tower, I could look down lists of names of the delegates from virtually every state in the union and find our 1964 leaders, including members of my original cadre. In Ohio, John Ashbrook, who had been, with Bill Rusher and me, one of the three founders of the Draft Goldwater movement, was now for Richard Nixon. In Alabama, Jim Martin, among the very earliest members of our cadre in the South, was fighting tooth and nail to hold the majority of his delegation for Nixon. In Georgia, it was Bo Callaway; in Louisiana, my old friend Charlton Lyons; in Nebraska, Senator Carl Curtis, to name but a few.

Even the ranks of Young Americans for Freedom had been

broken by Nixon. Tom Huston, a former YAF chairman, was for Nixon, as were several others. However, most of the 1968 YAF leadership held fast for Reagan, thanks largely to the efforts of its executive director, David Jones.

The Young Republican Federation was something else again. Jack McDonald, the YR president that year, was a conservative, but Nixon's people had brought him over to their side and Bill Timmons, another former YR leader, was Nixon's convention manager at Miami.

In short, everywhere I looked I saw my old conservative cohorts carrying the Nixon standard. Yet I knew their hearts were not with Nixon. And it was on this knowledge that I built my own hopes for Reagan's ultimate victory at Miami.

To stop Nixon on the first ballot, however, we needed help. The only other candidate who had a sizeable bloc of delegates committed to him was Nelson Rockefeller. It was in our mutual interest to halt a first ballot blitz by Nixon; neither Reagan nor Rockefeller had a prayer unless they were able to survive into a second ballot. Nelson knew this as well as I and so did my old mentor, Leonard Hall, who was managing Rockefeller's team, having lost his original candidate, Romney, in the snows of New Hampshire. Len or George Hinman or Bruce Bradley frequently contacted me with information on the Nixon camp. But there was no collusion between our camps; it was simply a matter of exchanging mutually beneficial intelligence.

I had difficulty reconciling Governor Reagan to any contact with the Rockefeller group, however. In fact, he suffered through a meeting with Rockefeller himself in New Orleans only because I urged him to do so when the New York Governor crashed Reagan's room at the Roosevelt hotel in May. Rockefeller and Reagan merely exchanged pleasantries and sat together, but when Nelson left he went into the corridor and held an impromptu press conference, hinting broadly that he had made a deal with Reagan.

Reagan went out into the corridor a few minutes later and he politely denied any "deal."

It was after this meeting that Dan Thomasson, now the able Washington bureau chief for the Scripps–Howard Newspapers, reported that Governor Reagan was "apparently moving toward a coalition" with Governor Rockefeller to block Nixon. Rockefeller also told the press in New Orleans that Reagan appeared to be "pretty well set for the top spot" when reporters asked him if he would name Reagan as his running-mate should he, Nelson, be nominated.

What Rockefeller hoped to do was split the conservatives down the middle, help us stop Nixon on the first ballot, and then make a deal with Nixon to deliver Nixon delegates to him. Nelson should have known that the majority of those delegates didn't really belong to Nixon, except on that critical first ballot. After that, given their own choice, they would have come over to Reagan *en masse*.

It must have become apparent to Rockefeller that there was something wrong with his strategy. Everywhere he went he could see that Reagan was getting all the crowds, all the enthusiasm, and he was getting hardly any. In Tulsa, for example, 2,500 people showed up at the airport to welcome Reagan in mid–June while Rockefeller was lucky to draw a few hundred when he arrived.

Once Rockefeller did outdraw Reagan, however. In New Orleans Nelson was given an uproarious, if somewhat tipsy, welcome by a huge throng, most of them young people, while Ron had to be content with several thousand, and, by comparison, much more sedate greeters. Later I found out that the Rockefeller team had taken an advertisement in a student newspaper offering free beer to anyone who rode the Rockefeller buses from the campus to the airport.

In California, meanwhile, some rabidly anti–conservative groups had started a petition to recall Governor Reagan. They got a lot of publicity, of course, all of it detrimental to Reagan, though in the end the recall boomeranged. In mid–July Mervin D. Field's California poll showed that "if the entire California public were voting today on the issue of recalling Reagan he would retain his office by a two-to-one majority vote—a larger plurality than he achieved in first winning the office almost two years ago."

More serious, two youths tried to set fire to the Reagan home in Sacramento with Molotov cocktails. As they stalked up the driveway the night of July 9, they were driven off by a warning shot fired by one of the Secret Service agents guarding the home. At the time Ron and Nancy were in the house with their two youngest children.

This was one of the few nights the Governor was home during July. He and I were traveling almost constantly that month and although the odds against us were overwhelming I don't remember Ron ever complaining. He just did what he felt he had to do and he always seemed to be in good humor. Once we ran into Bob Hope in a hotel corridor and the two of them stood there for a half–hour exchanging one-liners, thoroughly enjoying themselves.

Our campaign was beginning to have its effect as we neared the opening of the convention. Rowland Evans and Robert Novak accurately reported on our success in Birmingham, Alabama, in winning delegates away from Nixon. "Some 90 delegates and alternates from Alabama, Mississippi, South Carolina, Louisiana, and Georgia who met with Reagan at Birmingham's Tutwiler Hotel reflected a pattern of small Nixon losses and small Reagan gains throughout the South," Evans and Novak wrote.

They noted that "although one careful delegate count in June gave all 26 of Louisiana's votes to Nixon, Reagan now has nearly half the delegation and may move to a majority." They also reported our people from Mississippi estimated that state's 20 delegates were "split evenly with either side a possibility to win the entire delegation under Mississippi's unit rule."

Many of the delegates who came to Birmingham to meet the Governor were ostensibly for Nixon. But Evans and Novak wrote that the Nixon delegates "say privately they will switch quickly to [Reagan] if and when they feel Nixon slipping. That explains why a first-ballot win for Nixon . . . is becoming an absolute necessity for him."

My many friends in the South were going all-out to help. For example, Roscoe Pickett, the Republican National Committeeman from Georgia, flew more than a dozen delegates in his own plane from South Carolina to meet Governor Reagan in Birmingham.

Nixon, meanwhile, was exuding confidence, though I doubt if he felt really confident the closer we got to the convention. While Reagan and I were working the National Governors Conference in Cincinnati July 21, Nixon met with the California delegation in Los Angeles. He piously promised he would not "raid the delegation." It was an easy promise to make because he knew a raid would not have been very successful anyway.

When we landed in Cincinnati there was a tumultous reception for Reagan. There were at least a thousand people and there must have been over a hundred signs, reading "Welcome President Reagan," "Reagan, the Next President," and other such slogans. The Governor smiled as he got off the plane and he couldn't resist a quip. "I keep trying not to look at those signs," he said.

Our last foray at the very end of July took us to several more cities. Then I went on to Miami while Reagan stopped off in Winstom–Salem, North Carolina, to meet with the 26 delegates from that state. Congressman James C. Gardner, the chairman of the delegation, was one of the few Southern leaders who resisted Strom Thurmond's strong pitch for Nixon. "I'm for Ronnie," he told the Senator straight out in Miami. And he was able to announce sixteen votes for Reagan when the balloting finally came.

The day I arrived in Miami there was a veritable shower of

polls hailing down on us, showing how Nixon could beat Vice President Humphrey in November by a larger margin than Reagan; how Rockefeller could take more states in the Northeast than either Reagan or Nixon; how George Wallace would hurt Nixon and Reagan more than he would Rockefeller because the New Yorker would hold the North while the other two lost the South *and* the North, and so on, ad infinitum.

I must have been a little weary that day because Charles Whiteford of the *Baltimore Sun* quoted me as saying, "The people are tired of polls. I don't believe the delegates will be paying as much attention to them as people think."

Actually, that may have been true. But the delegates, at least from the South, *were* paying attention to Senator Thurmond, as Ronald Reagan and I could testify.

11

The Near Miss

"The lightning struck. I have been in politics for I don't know how many years, and I have never seen anything like it."

Thus spoke Harry Dent, the architect of Richard Nixon's 1968 Southern strategy, when he recalled the electrifying sensation that shot through the Republican National Convention in Miami when the announcement was made that Ronald Reagan would shed his favorite–son mantle and openly seek the Presidential nomination.

Reagan had held off making it official until the last possible moment: at 4 p.m. on Monday, August 5, a few hours before the convention was called to order. The setting was the California delegation's caucus at the Deauville Hotel on Miami Beach. Former U.S. Senator William Knowland, publisher of the *Oakland Tribune*, announced that the caucus had voted to "recognize Governor Reagan in fact is a leading and bona fide candidate for President."

Reagan, who was present, got a laugh from the reporters when he shook his head and smiled: "Gosh, I was surprised. It all came out of the blue."

Then I led him away to our communications trailer to meet

117

some more delegates. I was amused that year because all three of the major candidates had communications trailers. The use of the trailer as a communications command post was an innovation I had introduced at the 1964 GOP convention in San Francisco and it has been standard equipment at both Republican and Democratic conventions ever since. Apparently all recent presidential candidates have felt the trailer is an absolute necessity in order to keep in electronic contact with their people on the convention floor. In 1968, however, the current emanating from the Reagan trailer was more than just the wattage needed to keep in touch with the walkie–talkies carried by our people on the floor. It was the psychological electricity Harry Dent had felt so sharply on Monday.

Actually, the electricity had been building for some days in Miami before Reagan's formal announcement of his candidacy. He had come to Miami Beach for a day to give testimony before the platform committee at the Fountainbleau the previous Wednesday. The committee, which was being chaired by Senator Everett Dirksen of Illinois, had been in a somewhat somnolent mood before Reagan woke them up with his testimony. He ranged across the whole spectrum of issues, from Vietnam and the campus riots to the growth of the welfare state. Several times the audience, and even the committee members, broke into applause and cheers. A team of observers from *The Times* of London wrote later that "it was the only spontaneous display of emotion for a witness throughout four days of public hearings."

When Reagan returned to Miami on Saturday from his final round of visits to delegates meeting in their home states, the air was highly charged with rumors of his impending announcement. Privately, dozens of Nixon delegates were urging me to have the Governor make it official so they could go all–out in their efforts for him. The favorite–son role had inhibited them somewhat and they needed the public announcement to help them work on the other members of their delegations who were holding fast for Nixon. There were a few things we had to do first, however.

At noon on Monday the Governor and I had lunch with Harry Dent and his two friends, Bill Murfin of Florida and Clarke Reed of Mississippi. We wanted to give them advance notice of the announcement. The three of them actually seemed to be in favor of Reagan's candidacy, but I knew better, of course. Beneath their feigned enthusiasm I could see they were deeply worried we might beat their real candidate, Nixon. And in the end it was this trio, using Senator Thurmond as their spokesman, who kept us from breaking through.

It was a courtesy to Dent and the others that we let them know before the formal announcement of Reagan's candidacy was made. But we were also tacitly putting them on notice that we would now be fighting them all the way down to the balloting and that it would be wise for them to reassess their positions in light of the real desires of their own delegations.

All three of them knew I had secret pledges from people within virtually all of the Southern delegations, including one from Bill Murfin himself, though his pledge ultimately proved worthless. Before the convention I had a private meeting with Murfin and I told him it was obvious that Governor Reagan had a substantial bloc within his 34–member Florida delegation. Governor Claude Kirk, a professional maverick, was for Rockefeller, so that left 33 divided between Reagan and Nixon.

"If I get sixteen of these thirty–three, will you make it seventeen?" I asked Murfin.

He thought it over for a minute and then said, "Yes. I'll do that." We both knew this meant that under the unit rule the entire delegation, with the exception of Claude Kirk, who was refusing to abide by the rule, would vote for Reagan if I got sixteen delegates from Florida. Of course, Murfin didn't think I could get the sixteen or he would not have given me his pledge so readily.

I then went to Paula Hawkins, who was to become, in 1980, the first woman elected to the United States Senate from Florida. I asked Paula, a good conservative who, like so many, was philosophically committed to Nixon, that if I could get fifteen votes in Florida, would *she* make it sixteen. She gave me her word she would.

I had made similar agreements with delegates in a number of other delegations. However, neither Ronald Reagan nor I intended to turn the convention into a Republican blood letting. We were not going to ask our friends to go to the wall for us and get themselves shot out of politics. We had promised to call their pledges *only* if we had a real chance of stopping Nixon on the first ballot. These people I knew I could count upon. (My pre–ballot projection in 1964 had been off by only one vote.) And they knew Reagan and I would never call on them unless we were sure we could win.

You see, I knew Richard Nixon as well, or better, than anyone in that convention. And I knew if we called our pledges in from the swelling ranks of Republicans who were doubtful about him, and then *failed* to stop him, Nixon would go to any lengths to get back at these people afterward. I had no intention of turning them into kamikaze pilots for a hopeless cause.

One of my pledges was right in Senator Thurmond's own South Carolina delegation. He was Jim Edwards and he was prepared to lead the charge for Reagan if I could see we were ready to break through. But neither Jim nor I wanted to embarrass Senator Thurmond with a useless gesture and the correctness of this approach was later demonstrated when Jim Edwards went on to become Governor of South Carolina with Thurmond's backing. Today, Jim is Secretary of Energy and a respected member of President Reagan's cabinet.

I think it is fair to say that, in similar manner, the political careers of many other conservative Republicans were preserved in 1968, including, perhaps, Ronald Reagan's. No one wants to follow a leader who is not a realist, and Governor Reagan demon-strated at this convention that he had a firm grip on the most essential political realities and that he really cared for other people's careers as much as his own.

When Dent, Murfin and Reed left after our lunch on Monday in Miami Beach they knew they had a fight on their hands. I'm sure they went straight to Strom Thurmond with the news of Reagan's candidacy because soon after I heard the Senator was making the rounds of the Southern delegations, urging them to hold fast for Nixon. The alternative, he said, would be Rockefel-ler. The specter of Nelson's candidacy was enough to keep them in line.

About this time Bill Rusher got me on the phone. He had been trying to get through our security screen on the seventeenth floor of the Deauville Hotel where Governor Reagan and I had adjoin-ing suites.

"What the devil do I have to do to get up there?" Rusher asked.

"Work," I said. "If you want to help out, I'll give you a badge." He agreed and I put him to work immediately. His assignment was to visit the delegations that were being kept in line for Nixon by his good friends, Senators Thurmond and Tower, and outline the reasons why he thought Ronald Reagan would make the better candidate.

Rusher worked hard, as did all our team, including the people the Governor had brought in from California, among them Wil-liam Clarke, now Undersecretary of State, Ed Meese, counsellor to the President, Mike Deaver, Lyn Nofziger, and, of course, Tom Reed, who served as Reagan's ex officio chief-of-staff.

But no one worked harder than Ronald Reagan in the days before and just after that announcement in Miami. No matter what time of the day or night I needed him, he was always available. The meetings in our trailer and in our suites at the Deauville became an almost around-the-clock marathon. My friends in Young Americans for Freedom, capably directed by

David Jones, fanned out all over the convention floor and brought the delegates to the trailer to meet the candidate. Governor Reagan had a smile and warm welcome for every one of them and I don't know how many of them said, "We *really* want to go with you, Governor, but. . . . "

The biggest "but" of all was the unit rule, under which delegations agreed to vote as a bloc, at least on the first ballot. It was the strict enforcement of the unit rule in the key Southern delegations that kept us from stopping Nixon.

There were 1,333 delegates to the convention. Nixon had to get a simple majority, 667, to win. Actually, we came within a handful of votes in four Southern delegations from breaking the unit rule impasse and blocking him. The four delegations were Florida, Georgia, Louisiana and Mississippi.

Throughout the convention there were ostensible Nixon delegations just waiting and hoping for us to crack that impenetrable Southern line. Governor Nunn of Kentucky told one of my floor men he would bring in all 24 of his delegates for Reagan if we could get to the second ballot. Butch Butler, who had come out openly as our man in Texas, assured me he could get at least 40 of his state's 56 delegates to go for Reagan on the second round. Alfred Goldthwaite, the Republican chairman in Alabama, thought he had a good chance of bringing his whole delegation over to Reagan. And I knew we could get at least 25 of Florida's 34 delegates if they could just break the unit rule which their chairman, Bill Murfin, was rigidly enforcing. There were others from whom I'd received firm assurances of support once we got beyond that magic first ballot.

About 10 o'clock Monday night I was informed that Senator Thurmond and Harry Dent had gone to meet with Nixon and his campaign manager, John Mitchell. It is perhaps a measure of Nixon's perception that both he and Mitchell had not taken Reagan's candidacy seriously until that meeting because they regarded Rockefeller as their only threat.

The thing that had exercised Thurmond and Dent was a news report that Nixon would pick Senator Mark Hatfield of Oregon, a dedicated liberal, as his running mate. By the time they left the meeting with Nixon and Mitchell, however, they had a firm commitment Nixon would not give the Vice–Presidential nod to anyone who was not acceptable to "all sections of the party." Senator Thurmond interpreted this as giving him veto power over the vice presidential selection and, armed with that most reassuring of all news for the Southerners, he left to begin his successful defense of Nixon's candidacy.

The next morning Reagan went to see Senator Thurmond at his hotel. They spent nearly an hour together and the Senator expressed his high admiration for Governor Reagan—but he had given his word to Nixon. It was that iron–clad commitment that was keeping the Southern delegations in line. The high respect in which Strom Thurmond was held throughout the South made him the real power at this convention.

One of the most damaging rumors that spread through the convention hall was a report that Reagan would be Nixon's choice for Vice President. Many of the delegates visiting us in the trailer on Tuesday and Wednesday kept bringing this up. It seemed to satisfy them in their desire to have Reagan on the ticket and it weakened our position considerably. The Governor denied, as adamantly as he could, that he would even consider the Vice-Presidential spot. He then came up with a one liner that tickled all of us, the delegates included.

"Even if they tied and gagged me," Reagan told them, "I would find a way to signal 'no' by wiggling my ears."

I thought we had a good chance of cracking the Florida delegation and to this day I believe most of the Florida people were for us. I did get the sixteen votes we needed for Bill Murfin to make the seventeen. But instead Murfin threatened to resign as state chairman if the delegation refused to hold for Nixon. They reaffirmed the unit rule by the margin of a few votes and it was really on that action that our chances were lost.

Clarke Reed played a similarly efficient role as the enforcer in the Mississippi delegation and Bo Callaway in Georgia. The Louisiana delegates also stayed in line. Senator Thurmond had been making the rounds, assuring them he had veto power over the Vice-Presidential choice, which, in effect, he did have.

The tip as to whom that choice would be came when Governor Spiro Agnew of Maryland came out in support of Nixon. He may not have had a commitment from Nixon when he did this, but Agnew certainly saw an opportunity and he was not slow to grab it.

I must say that the Nixon forces had done a superlative job of organizing the convention. Rogers Morton, their floor manager, and Bill Timmons, the overall convention manager, had instituted a "buddy system" so that no delegate could leave the floor without someone going with him. Gerald Ford, then the House minority leader, was the permanent chairman of the convention and he ran it with an iron gavel. Ray Bliss, who was then Republican national chairman, had been around a long time in politics and he had good lines into every delegation. Nixon had rounded up a well–tailored regiment of young lawyers from his New York firm and elsewhere. And, most telling of all, there were all the members of my old cadre working for Nixon and capably led by Strom Thurmond and John Tower and others who had been with me four years before.

The Times of London team later wrote: "White was one man against a small army." They did not mean that literally, of course, for I did have a lot of help from the hard core members of my cadre who stuck with me, from the Young Americans for Freedom, from the American Conservative Union people, and most notably from our candidate and his California associates. Nonetheless, with our national cadre split, and so many of them working for Nixon, the cards *were* stacked against us.

The Florida vote on Wednesday afternoon really sank the 1968 Reagan ship, as I've noted. Buz Lukens, who had a lot of friends in Florida, had sat up almost all night Tuesday with some of the Florida delegates trying to persuade them to vote for Reagan. And the Governor had a number of meetings with the delegates himself. About half of the Florida delegation were women and many of them broke into tears in our trailer because they were so torn between voting for the Governor and supporting their state chairman, Bill Murfin.

Finally, at 5 o'clock on Wednesday afternoon, I called my regional directors to a meeting in the trailer for a final count. We had picked up some votes, but nowhere near enough to slow the Nixon tide. The Rockefeller forces had failed to add very many to their pre-convention count. It was obvious Richard Nixon would win the nomination.

I met with Ronald Reagan in the trailer and laid it out for him. "We have only one option left," I told him. "We can fold the tent now. Or we can keep working and hope for a break."

"Well," he said, "that's what we're here for, isn't it? Let's get back to work."

For the rest of the evening he kept meeting with the delegates; my regional directors and their Young Americans for Freedom allies kept bringing in a steady stream to the trailer. Some of our people had already tossed in the towel, but not Ronald Reagan. He is a born fighter and he was not going to go down without exploring every possible opening, every conceivable chance that we might have to reverse the tide.

For a fleeting hour on Wednesday night I thought we might at last be getting the opening we had been trying so hard to find. The *Miami Herald* came out with a story by Don Oberdorfer, now with the *Washington Post*, claiming that Nixon *would* name Mark Hatfield as his vice presidential choice. I ordered two thousand copies of the *Herald* and the Young Americans for Freedom and our other stalwarts delivered them to every delegate and alternate they could find.

The Southern delegations began to waver under this news that contradicted Strom Thurmond's firm assurances of the day before. But Harry Dent got hold of Don Oberdorfer and almost literally dragged him before the Louisiana delegation. Dent offered to bet him $500 his story was wrong, but Oberdorfer was unwilling to put his money where his story was and the Louisiana delegation fell back into line. The tale of Oberdorfer's doubt about his own story was spread through all the other Southern delegations and that, really, was our last gasp.

However, Ronald Reagan never quit. He was still meeting with members of the Mississippi delegation when the roll call began at 1:19 a.m. We didn't start off badly on the roll: Alabama came in with 12 for Reagan as against 14 for Nixon. California's 86 votes held solid for Reagan. But when the roll reached Florida the unit rule dictated 32 votes for Nixon. Only the Governor, Claude Kirk, went against his delegation and voted for Rockefeller while one other Florida delegate abstained. Mississippi went the same way, only more so—all 20 votes for Nixon under the unit rule. The favorite sons who came after that held most of their delegations, except for Senator Clifford Case of New Jersey, who lost 18 of his votes to Nixon because of the efforts of my old friend Frank Farley. But Nelson Rockefeller held New York and Governor John Rhodes kept a firm hand on Ohio, where Nixon was able to take only two votes from Ohio's 58. Reagan got only 15 votes out of Texas, in spite of Butch Butler's best efforts. Wisconsin's 30 votes for Nixon gave him the nomination.

In the end, Nixon had 692 votes, 25 more than he needed but far less than the margin of 228 Barry Goldwater won by on the first ballot in San Francisco four years before. However, he had the nomination and with it, that year, went the Presidency.

There is no doubt in my mind that many, if not most, of the delegates who voted for Nixon at Miami Beach in 1968 soon realized they had been the victims of a monumental confidence game. Richard Nixon had posed as a conservative to win the nomination. But it very quickly became apparent after he moved into the White House that he was not a conservative at all.

Ron Reagan was with me in the trailer during the balloting. When Wisconsin put Nixon over the top I asked him if he wanted to go to the rostrum and make the nomination unanimous. Reagan knew it was a necessary gesture to unite the party and he said he would do it.

We went into the convention hall together and made our way to the rostrum. But we were stopped just behind the platform. Ray Bliss was throwing his vaunted power around that night and he didn't want Reagan stealing the show.

Roger Allen Moore, the GOP's expert on convention rules, was there and I told him to inform Bliss that if he didn't let Governor Reagan speak he would go down to the floor and make his announcement from there. Bliss finally relented and Reagan touched off the most delirious demonstration of the convention when he went to the rostrum and moved that the nomination of Richard Nixon be declared unanimous.

When it was all over Ron and I went back to the hotel. Our team was waiting for us in my suite next door to his. Reagan got up on the staircase leading to the duplex rooms above and gave a short, but very gracious, little speech, thanking the people who had worked so hard for him for all their efforts. He got off a couple of jokes and the heavy atmosphere that had prevailed moments before seemed almost tangibly to lift. Then he and I went next door.

It was a sad and tired little group in the Governor's suite. Reagan sat down in a chair and Nancy came over and hugged him. Then, very tenderly, she took off his shoes and began massaging his shoulders to relieve the fatigue and tension after the eighteen-hour day he had just put in. The only other people in the suite were Dr. Davis, Nancy's father, and his wife. We chatted a little while and I then got up to leave. Just outside the door my 15-year-old daughter, Carole, was coming down the corridor. Tears were streaming down her face and I put my arms around her and tried to comfort her. But Carole was inconsolable and she kept crying because her father and his candidate had lost.

I went back into the Reagan suite and told the Governor about Carole. He came out with me and put his arms around my still tearful daughter.

"Carole," he said, "the good Lord knows what He is doing. This wasn't our turn."

The next day I talked with Governor Reagan about the Vice-Presidential nomination. I had learned that Governor Agnew of Maryland was to be Nixon's choice, with Strom Thurmond's blessing. Neither of us knew Agnew very well but we had heard nothing against him. Both of us felt it was wise to accept Nixon's selection. Reagan had made it very plain to me all along that he would not accept second place on the ticket if it were offered him and he reaffirmed this position during our conversation.

Later, as the delegates were gathering in the convention hall, I started my rounds of the floor, as I always do before each convention session. The first person who came up to me was Bill Timmons, carrying his Nixon walkie-talkie.

"Tell me what you're going to do about the Vice-Presidential nomination," Timmons smiled.

I laughed and shook my head. "You can put that thing away," I said, pointing at his walkie-talkie. "You won't need it tonight. Reagan isn't running."

However, when I got to our communications trailer outside the hall there was Tom Reed conferring with a Virginia delegate who wanted to place Ronald Reagan's name in nomination for Vice President if the Alabama delegation would yield to Virginia. The Alabamans were willing to do it and one of them was on Tom's line waiting for the word to go ahead.

On our TV monitors behind Tom I could see Mrs. Consuela

Bailey, the gracious lady who called the rolls at Republican conventions for many years. She was just about to start the roll call for the balloting on the Vice–Presidential candidate. Alabama came first on the roll and I knew if the delegation yielded to our Virginia friend the convention would stampede to Reagan should his name be placed in nomination by the Virginians. Tom Reed looked as though he was about to give the signal to our Alabama friends.

"Tom, if you pick up that phone, I'll shoot you," I said. "I promised Ronald Reagan he will not be nominated tonight and we can't let him down."

Reed smiled and the Alabama delegation passed. Spiro Agnew was soon nominated and the convention was unaware it might have had a choice to name Ronald Reagan instead. The balloting was soon over and Nixon came down and greeted his running mate before delivering his formal acceptance address to the convention.

In later years I occasionally wondered what would have happened if Tom Reed had let the Alabama delegation yield to Virginia and Reagan had been nominated. Would Reagan have rejected the nomination after it was tendered? Probably. But if he had not, the country may have been spared the Watergate crisis because as long as Ronald Reagan was Vice President he would have been the best insurance policy Richard Nixon ever had for finishing out both his terms. On such slender threads history often hangs.

12

The Outcasts

When Ronald Reagan returned to Sacramento after the 1968 Republican national convention he was asked at a press conference: "Is the Presidential bug finally out of your system?"

"There never was a Presidential bug in my system," Reagan replied.

I can testify that this was true. He had fought for the nomination only because so many of us wanted him to run and because he felt it was his duty to do so. When I got back home after the Miami convention I wrote him a report analyzing our effort. A few days later I got the following letter back from him:

"You beat me to it. I'm sure both of us have been sitting with the idea of what we would say to each other. You found the words first.

"Judging from the words you found, I sense that perhaps you, too, have been bothered by a small feeling that perhaps someplace along the line you didn't do all that should have been done. I say this because I have been nursing that nagging guilt feeling that perhaps I let you down by not being a more open or aggressive candidate, and yet, like you, my mind keeps coming back to the surrounding circumstances, and over and over again I arrive at the same conclusion—there wasn't anything we should have or could have changed.

"Stan Evans, in the National Review Bulletin, has summed up our effort and has been extremely kind to both of us. He says, and frankly I think he assesses it properly, that we, with our effort, preserved our candidate from moving, as he very well might have, to the left. He says that we have shaped policy, and if he [Nixon] becomes President, the policy of our government [will have been shaped] perhaps as much as we could have even holding the nomination ourselves.

"Let me just say to you that I have no regrets whatsoever, and no feeling that any of us fell short of what could be done, and I want you to know if I had it to do over again starting tomorrow on the basis of all that I now know, I would come running to one Clif White to ask his help.

"This has been a great experience for me, and I hope our paths not only cross, but run closely parallel for many years to come. Nancy joins me in this, and it is our hope that this friendship goes on as long as the time allotted us."

Alas, we did not keep Nixon from moving to the left, although in the fall campaign of 1968 no one campaigned harder for Richard Nixon than Ronald Reagan. Some of the other Republican presidential hopefuls may have held back a bit, hoping a Nixon loss might set the stage for their entry to the White House four years later. But not Reagan. He travelled some 30,000 miles urging voters in 21 states to cast their ballots for Nixon.

Nixon's own campaign was not a very good one. He started out with high ratings in the polls but by the time of the November election he had almost blown his once comfortable lead. The Vietnam bombing halt President Johnson announced the Friday before election gave Humphrey a final spurt that almost carried him to victory. Indeed, there are those who believe that if the bombing halt had been announced even a few days earlier the voters, believing in this illusion of peace, would have given Humphrey the Presidency.

Actually, Lyndon Johnson planned to announce a halt to the U.S. Air Force's bombing of North Vietnamese military targets nearly two weeks before he did. He delayed because he and several members of his Cabinet spent those two weeks trying to track down a "leak" to the effect that Johnson was planning the bombing halt in order to get Vice President Humphrey elected.

As it was, the last–minute surge to Humphrey turned the election into the closest cliff–hanger since Woodrow Wilson's narrow 1912 victory over President William Howard Taft and former President Theodore Roosevelt, the Bull Moose Party candidate. In fact, the 1968 results were not completed until Illinois' 26 electoral votes were firmly counted in Nixon's column the day after the election.

Nixon received 31,304,992 votes to 30,994,354 for Humphrey, a margin of only 310,638. This was some 3,000,000 votes less than Nixon had received in his 1960 race against John Kennedy. But he captured 302 electoral votes to 191 for Humphrey and 45 for Governor George Wallace of Alabama. Wallace's third party, variously named in different states, garnered 9,825,459 popular votes, the largest ever for a third party.

Many editorial writers correctly added the Wallace vote to Nixon's to arrive at the conclusion that 1968 had been a landslide year for conservatives, or what were perceived to be conservative candidates. Nixon apparently failed to reach that same valid conclusion, or if he did it was not reflected in his appointments.

A few conservatives were named to posts in the Nixon adminstration, almost all in the lower echelons. But for the most part conservatives remained political outcasts during the Nixon years. And the few who did succeed in obtaining responsible positions soon found themselves boxed in on all sides by liberal holdovers from the Kennedy–Johnson administrations or by Nixon's own liberal appointees. Richard Allen, for instance, wound up working under Henry Kissinger in the National Security Council and, after a frustrating tenure, felt compelled to resign.

Nixon even appointed a number of Democrats to key posts. One of them, John Connally, was a solid conservative and as Secretary of the Treasury he tried to represent the conservative viewpoint in the Cabinet. But other Nixon Democrats made no attempt to conceal their inherent liberalism. Daniel Patrick Moynihan, presently the Democratic Senator from New York, had held posts in the Kennedy–Johnson regime and supported Bobby Kennedy in 1968. Yet Nixon named him to the White House staff. Pat Moynihan's main contribution to the Nixon era was the formulation of a plan for a guaranteed annual income for all citizens, whether they worked or not, a plan that even the Democrat–controlled Congress gagged on.

Other patently socialist schemes were promulgated under Nixon. His wage–and–price control agency, the first such agency in peacetime, not only failed to slow inflation, it actually heated it up more and when the controls came off the inflation rate shot up sharply.

In foreign policy, Nixon adopted the essence of the liberal position by permitting Kissinger to concoct *detente*, which was accompanied by a further weakening of America's strategic defense system as the administration strove to bless *detente* with the Salt I treaty. Moreover, the Nixon-Kissinger axis almost immediately began to reduce American troops in Vietnam, at a time when the enemy was hanging on the ropes. Ultimately, they engineered our retreat from Vietnam with the predictable result that, following the false truce of 1973, within two years the North Vietnamese again invaded the south and annexed it to their Communist dictatorship, throwing virtually all of Southeast Asia into an ongoing reign of terror.

These and other actions of the Nixon administration angered conservatives and they naturally began thinking in terms of an alternative to Nixon for 1972. Their thoughts almost always gravitated to Ronald Reagan, whose role as the opponent of Nixon at the 1968 convention had projected him firmly into the leadership of the conservative movement nationally.

I saw Reagan fairly frequently during this period. In the spring of 1969 I visited Nancy and Ron at their home in Sacramento and had dinner with them there. We talked politics, of course. Both the Governor and I expressed disappointment at some of Nixon's appointments and the direction his foreign policy was already taking the nation, particularly in Vietnam. But it was still too early in the Nixon experience for either of us to be thinking in terms of an alternative to the incumbent President.

The Governor had his hands full in Sacramento. The campus disturbances did not let up with the election of Richard Nixon and in some cases they appeared to escalate. After one particularly bloody confrontation in May 1969 between the police and alleged student groups at Berkeley, the site of the University of California's central campus, Reagan held a press conference in which he made it plain he was not going to back down before the rioters. One newsman reminded him that "demands are growing that police be forbidden the use of firearms in situations like this." Then the reporter asked, "What are your specific views about the use of firearms?"

Reagan replied that "the police of this country traditionally have been allowed the use of weapons that are believed to be necessary, not only in the prevention of crime, but the apprehension of criminals, in the defense of individuals, private citizens and property. . . ."

"It would seem to me," he added, "that when you are faced

with a mob that goes on the offensive . . . that was attacking, that hospitalized a half a hundred of your police before shots were fired, and they are going at you from rooftops and fire escapes with huge chunks of broken concrete, with . . . construction steel cut into short pieces, and many of them with sharpened ends, and you are being assaulted with those kind of weapons, I think it is being very naive to assume that you should send anyone into that kind of conflict with a fly swatter. He's got to have an appropriate weapon."

The shooting of President Reagan on March 30, 1981 was not the first attempt on his life. Ever since he entered politics he has been a target for potential assassins.

The prior attempts on Reagan's life were thwarted, thanks to alert security work like that of the Secret Service agent who drove off the two arsonists who tried to burn down the Reagan home in Sacramento in July 1980. Edward Hickey, Reagan's security chief when he was Governor and later in his 1980 presidential campaign, kept most of the would-be assassins at bay and their plots seldom were carried out.

In the spring of 1969, however, no less than five fires were set in closets at the Biltmore Hotel in Los Angeles one night when Governor Reagan was speaking there. My old friend Travis Cross, who was then at the University of California's Berkeley campus in an executive position, wrote me about what he called this "act of fantastic violence." Travis added that the Governor was the "focal point for hatreds" and strongly urged more stringent security for him, something that is very difficult to implement in our open society.

Reagan's firm stand against the anti-Vietnam War protesters was only one reason for his becoming such a favorite target of the crazies. Almost everything he did and said angered them. He upset a good many other people who were not disposed toward violence, of course. If a man is to stand for anything in politics, he must expect to make enemies. Here are a few of the positions Reagan took that drew fire, though I believe his remarks accurately reflect the way most Americans feel about these issues:

On Crime: "There is no single reason why the crime rate keeps rising in America. But up near the top of the list must be the sad fact that so much of our criminal justice system has become a technical game between lawyers, without regard for guilt or innocence."

On Gun Control: "God help us if a burglar prowling the street at night has a government guarantee that there is no gun in any home he may choose to enter."

On Environmentalism: "Hysterical pollution leads to political pollution with the result that all too often little or nothing gets done about actual pollution."

On Welfare: "A man may choose to sit and fish instead of working—that's his pursuit of happiness. He does not have the right to force his neighbors to support him."

On Food Stamps: "A multi-million dollar administrative nightmare, a staggering financial burden at the federal level and the newest nesting place for welfare abuse and fraud."

On Big Government: "If you look back you find that those great social reforms really didn't work. They didn't cure unemployment. They didn't solve social problems. What came from them was a group of people who became entrenched in Government, who wanted social reforms just for the sake of social reforms."

On the Vietnam War: "When 50,000 Americans make the ultimate sacrifice to defend the people of a small, defenseless country in Southeast Asia from Communist tyranny, that, my friends, is a collective act of moral courage, not an example of moral poverty."

Probably no issue worried Ronald Reagan more during the last decade than the weakening of our national defense. In the spring of 1969 Tom Reed sent me a copy of a speech Governor Reagan gave at a dinner in Rhode Island in honor of John Chafee, who had then recently become Secretary of the Navy. I still have the typed copy of this speech with Reagan's notes and changes in his own handwriting. The speech got little attention at the time but the points he made in this important address are still valid today and may help explain why President Reagan has given such high priority to restoring America's defenses.

He noted in the Rhode Island speech that the Institute for Strategic Studies in London had three weeks before that released its latest strategic survey. "It said, in unequivocal terms," Reagan stated, "that the United States has now *lost* the ability to be the dominant power in the world. They point out that the Soviet Union has now become the full equal of the U.S. in military and political power and will likely surpass the U.S. in missile capacity this year."

Reagan pointed out that "practically all of the truly commanding weapons systems" then in the American inventory "were brought forward during the Eisenhower years and there has been no comparable contribution since." By inference he attacked the policies of the prior Kennedy–Johnson administration. "Eight years of neglect," he said, "have taken their toll."

Referring again to the study of the Institute for Strategic Studies, he said its survey had shown that "Even worse than the ability, they point out that the United States has lost the *desire* to be the dominant power in the world."

"By accident?" he asked. "A corrosion of the will by forces beyond our control? I think not.

"Firm Soviet military pressure from the outside has been accompanied by a steady subversion of our will to be free," he said.

He deplored the protests against the Vietnam War with "parades honoring the flag of North Viet Nam" while Americans were dying in defense of South Vietnam's independence.

"Right now we have demonstrations and disturbances attempting to divorce our academic communities from the defense of our country," he continued. "We see the organization of sabotage teams and anti–war 'coffee houses' operating adjacent to our forts, bases and naval stations.

"And who organizes these? And for what purposes?"

He then named a half-dozen anti-war activists and cited their links to Communist governments in North Vietnam, Cuba, China and the Soviet Union.

Reagan emphasized that the people involved in these activities were a small minority but they were alienating many youths from our society.

"The youth of America, whose fathers went ashore at Anzio and Guadalcanal, and whose grandfathers fought at Bellieu Wood and Chateau Thierry, these young Americans must realize that freedom is always one generation away from extinction. . . . The desire to remain free is under steady, sophisticated attack."

At another point in this address, he quoted Arthur Krock, for many years the top Washington correspondent for the *New York Times:* "I have contracted a visceral fear," Krock said. "It is that the tenure of the United States as the first power in the world may be one of the briefest in history."

Obviously, Ronald Reagan shared that fear. So did millions of other Americans. It is my view that this is the principal reason Ronald Reagan is President today.

As Governor of California, Ronald Reagan was on the front line fighting the revolution that was attempting to overthrow our democratic system in the 1960's and 1970's. For a time the action centered on San Francisco State College, where the anti-war protests had blended with the violence of a group of black activists. Reagan vigorously supported S.I. Hayakawa's successful efforts to restore order to the college. When revolutionaries from the Third World Liberation Front beat up students who continued to attend classes at San Francisco State, Reagan sent in the State Police in February 1969.

"Students have been assaulted," the Governor said in informing the public as to why he took this action. "Arsons and fire bombings have occurred and the university property has been destroyed."

A year later, in May 1970, another outburst of rioting hit the nation's campuses in the wake of the protests over the brief American foray into Cambodia. The deaths of four students during a riot at Kent State University in Ohio escalated the violence and Governor Reagan ordered all twenty–eight campuses of the University of California and state colleges closed for four days. He also asked private colleges and universities and the state's ninety–two locally controlled two–year community colleges to suspend classes for the same period.

"I hope that this period will allow time for rational reflection away from the emotional turmoil and encourage all to disavow violence and mob action," Reagan said in making the announcement.

Reagan took this action in an election year when he was getting ready to seek reelection. Many other governors were tip–toeing among the political tulips that spring, reluctant to undertake any measures against the rioters lest it lose them votes. But Reagan's firm stand did little damage to his popularity and he won the 1970 election by a half–million votes over Jesse Unruh, the very popular Democratic leader of the California legislature. Although this was a reduction of Reagan's margin over Pat Brown, it was no small accomplishment. Jesse Unruh was a legend in California and had powerful friends in both the Democratic and Republican parties as well as a huge following among voters up and down the state.

After this election, Governor Reagan went to work in earnest to reform the state's welfare system. By this time there were more than 2,200,000 people on welfare in California, fully 10 percent of the state's population. Exclusive of medical programs, the welfare costs were running at $2.5 billion per year. But by cracking down on welfare fraud, tightening up on eligibility standards, and requiring that all welfare recipients who were able had to try to find work, the welfare budget in California. was significantly reduced.

The welfare reduction did not come in California without a fight, however. In a struggle with the Democrat majority in the legislature reminiscent of his 1981 duel with the Democrat–controlled U.S. House of Representatives, Reagan finally won out. He was willing to negotiate with the Democratic leaders of the California legislature. But they found, as Speaker O'Neill and others in the Congress have found in more recent times, that Reagan may bend a little, but he doesn't break.

Robert B. Carleson, director of California's Department of Social Welfare, was the author of the successful plan to cut the welfare roles and he bore the brunt, with Reagan, of the often vituperative attacks against the legislation. During one set of hearings when Democrat opponents of the cut-backs became particularly obstreperous, the Governor told Carleson, "When they get abusive again, you just get up and leave. Tell 'em I told you to leave."

Although Carleson never did leave, he was deeply grateful for the way Ronald Reagan "hung in there when most politicians would have caved in or compromised or fired some scapegoats." Carleson, who later became U.S. Commissioner of Welfare, says the Reagan administration in Sacramento prevented the welfare rolls from growing by 500,000 during the 1970's, as the experts had predicted. And in 1980, nearly a decade after the reforms went into effect, he could count 300,000 fewer welfare recipients in California than when the reforms went into effect in the spring of 1971.

Dealing with a Democrat–controlled legislature was not always easy. Reagan was often forced to veto spending measures the legislature passed and sent to him. California law gives the Governor authority to reduce specific appropriations as well as eliminating them entirely. Invoking this "line item" method of cutting spending, Reagan used his veto power nearly a thousand times during his eight years as Governor.

Although he saved California taxpayers billions of dollars, inflation kept increasing both the state's costs and its tax income, the latter because individual income kept rising. Reagan managed to give the taxpayers back nearly $6 billion in rebates before he left Sacramento but he still left the state with a healthy surplus.

Today, most state governors are following the Reagan example and trying to cut back or hold down expenditures. But when Ronald Reagan became Governor in 1966, and even during his second term beginning in 1970, serious cost-cutting was a pioneering innovation. I believe that Reagan's political instincts were far ahead of his time. He could see then that the people were already getting disenchanted with government spending programs and during his second term he anticipated Proposition 13 by seven years when he advocated a similar measure limiting property taxes. The voters, confused by an expensive propaganda campaign waged by state and local employees against the measure, turned it down, only to approve Proposition 13 some years later.

Even many of Reagan's political opponents in California acknowledge that he was a good administrator. He put in a full nine–hour day at the Governor's office, but he believed in delegating authority and he tried not to second–guess his cabinet and staff once a decision was made. Often his recommendations were based upon information he got from his staff's "mini–memos"—brief, three–or–four–paragraph summaries of an issue or pending legislation. This led his critics to label him as a "chairman of the board" governor. But I say that is the *only* way the chief executive of a state, and more especially of a nation, can govern in today's complex world. If he attempts to become an expert on everything, as I think President Carter tried to do, he will end up losing sight of the wood for the trees and he will go to sleep at night counting the trees while the forest is being burned down.

At any rate, the proof of Reagan's success as governor is that he restored California bonds to a Moody's Triple A rating for the first time in some thirty years. And this was a state that very clearly was on the road to bankruptcy when he took the helm in Sacramento.

13

The Changing Scene

Ronald Reagan and I saw a good bit of each other and corresponded frequently in the years immediately following Richard Nixon's election to the Presidency. We never missed getting together at the semi–annual National Governors Conferences and at the separate meetings of the Republican governors. I remember one night during the reception before dinner at a gathering of the GOP governors in Hot Springs, Arkansas, when he, Governor John Love of Colorado and I were standing together in a corner of the room swapping jokes. People kept coming up to say hello but they would hesitate and then shy away. After a number of these near-greetings Reagan asked what was the matter. "They all think we're having a high–level political conference here," I said. And the three of us got another laugh out of that.

I had helped Reagan get elected chairman of the Republican Governors Conference after the 1968 election and had given him a hand with his re-election to that post two years later. This helped broaden his national political base and I thought it would prove to be an asset for him if he did decide to make another run for the Presidency in the future. Meanwhile, he continued making speeches around the country at Republican fund–raisers, occa-

143

sionally on university campuses, and frequently before conservative groups like Young Americans for Freedom. In the summer of 1970, shortly after I had visited with him again in Sacramento, the Governor sent me the following letter:

> Randal Teague, Executive Director of Young Americans for Freedom, has written to invite me to Sharon, Connecticut, in September to receive an award along with Bill Buckley and Senator Barry Goldwater.
>
> As you may know, YAF is celebrating its tenth anniversary this year. Because of the campaign [he was running for reelection as Governor that year] and state business, it will be impossible for me to attend and I would sincerely appreciate your attending and accepting my award. I will send a message to you to be read that evening if Mr. Teague feels that it would be appropriate.

I was happy to fill in for the Governor, though I was heavily involved in a campaign myself that year as manager of James Buckley's successful race for the United States Senate seat held by Charles Goodell of New York. Goodell had been appointed to the Senate by Governor Rockefeller when Senator Kenneth Keating resigned to become U.S. Ambassador to Israel.

Charlie Goodell had been elected to a House seat from a Western New York state district by running as a conservative Republican. But when he was named to the Senate he took a sharp turn to the left and many people in New York were upset with him.

Leaders of both the Republican Party and the Conservative Party approached me about running against Senator Goodell. But I told them I had made a firm decision early in my political career that my vocation lay in helping other people get elected to office, not in running myself.

Jim Buckley called some weeks later and when we met he told me he had been asked to run against Goodell. Jim had been a candidate for the Senate in 1968 when he ran on the Conservative line against the incumbent, Jacob Javits. The Conservative Party, founded in the early 1960's, did not run candidates in those days with much hope of electing them. They were in politics to exert leverage on both the Republican and Democrat parties in order to shift them to the right, in much the same fashion the Liberal Party in New York had moved both major parties to the left. Under the skillful leadership of its state chairman, G. Daniel Mahoney, and his brother–in–law, Kieran O'Doherty, the Conservative Party was already moving ahead of the Liberal Party in New York. In 1966, for instance, it fielded an unknown gubernatorial candidate named Paul Adams who surprised everyone by running neck–and–neck with the Liberal Party candidate, Franklin Roosevelt, Jr. Governor Rockefeller won the election, of course, but the Conservative Party had established itself as a force to be reckoned with.

However, Jim Buckley made it plain to me he did not want to run again on either the Conservative or Republican lines unless he had a real chance of winning. I suggested we commission a survey to see if he could win and Jim agreed. When it was completed the survey showed James Buckley had a recognition factor among New York voters of only 16 per cent. Nonetheless, I could see from the survey that the necessary elements for a Buckley victory existed, provided he waged an effective campaign. I passed this appraisal on to Jim Buckley and he said he would think it over.

A few days later he called and said, "You have a candidate." At first I was reluctant to serve as his full-time campaign manager because I was in the process of building a new public affairs business. But I finally did get involved full–time in managing Jim Buckley's Senate race and I brought in David Jones, the former executive director of Young Americans for Freedom, as campaign director. We tried to get Buckley on the Republican primary ballot but the GOP state committee turned us down and we had to run Jim on the Conservative Party line exclusively.

Despite his innate shyness, Jim Buckley made a magnificent candidate. When he spoke no one doubted his sincerity and his very warm human qualities came through even when he wasn't saying anything, but just listening to others.

The key to his victory was a series of television debates Jim Buckley engaged in with Charlie Goodell and Richard Ottinger, the Democratic candidate. We had several meetings with our opponents' campaign managers and it became apparent Ottinger did not want to debate, having established himself as the front-runner through an expensive primary campaign. But I was determined to get him in a TV face-off with Buckley and Goodell.

Early in September I called Goodell's manager, and asked if his candidate would debate. Since Goodell's recognition factor wasn't much better than Buckley's, he agreed to the idea.

Next, I called the station public affairs manager at WABC in New York City and told him we were prepared to debate.

"But what about Ottinger?" he asked.

"I think we should offer him the same privilege," I said.

"I don't know if we can do it that way," the WABC man hedged.

"Well, I don't know if you can either," I replied, "but if you don't, I will issue a press release and say that we made you the offer but you turned us down."

"I've got to talk with David Garth," he said. Garth was Ottinger's campaign manager and in recent times he has been a campaign consultant to Governor Hugh Carey of New York and to Prime Minister Menachem Begin of Israel.

I suggested to the WABC man he tell Dave Garth what I had just told him.

The result was that we got a debate.

Jim Buckley handled himself exceedingly well on television and he won the debate by articulating the conservative position on the issues while Ottinger and Goodell were forced to defend their liberal stands in the naked light of the experience the voters of New York had had with liberal programs and public officials. But most important, Buckley established himself as a serious candidate and he showed that he was not just a third party gadfly.

After the WABC debate, both the CBS and NBC outlets in New York City felt they had to have the Senate campaign debates, too, so we got two more debates on television, and each time Jim Buckley went up in the polls.

One night late in the campaign I flew to Rochester when Jim became ill there and I had an informal briefing with a half-dozen reporters in my hotel room. I told them we were going to win and one of them asked if I would predict how much of the vote Buckley would get.

"We are going to get 38.7 per cent of the total vote," I said.

Most of them obviously didn't believe me because they didn't write stories about my prediction. Only Woody Frichette of the Gannett Binghamton paper filed a story. And he wrote another one the day after the election, which James Buckley won by 38.5 per cent of the vote.

Buckley became the first third party candidate in the history of New York to be elected in state-wide balloting. Although he lost in his 1976 reelection bid running on both the Republican and Conservative Party tickets, a campaign that I was not deeply involved with, Jim Buckley certainly paved the way for greater voter acceptance of conservative positions in New York as evidenced by the election of Al D'Amato, who beat Jacob Javits in the Republican primary and went on, with Conservative Party support, to win election to the U.S. Senate from New York in 1980.

In 1972 I served as a consultant to Jesse Helms in his first run for the U.S. Senate in North Carolina. Jesse had been the general manager of WRAL, a television station in Raleigh and he was well known and liked in his state. Tom Ellis was his very capable campaign manager and I have seldom worked with a more dedicated group than Jesse Helms' team in North Carolina.

The only problem I ever had with Jesse, if it can be called a problem, was talking him into supporting Richard Nixon, who was running for reelection that year. But when Nixon came to North Carolina Jesse Helms was there with him on the platform. Jesse won the election and became the first Republican Senator from North Carolina since Reconstruction.

I was in North Carolina on election day but had to fly back home to vote later in the day. Before I left I said goodbye to Jesse Helms.

"Now," he smiled, "can I go back to being a conservative after you've made a liberal out of me?"

I laughed. "Jesse," I said, "after today you had *better* be a conservative." Needless to say, I never had any doubts about what Jesse Helms would be when he got to the United States Senate. He was reelected handily in 1978 and I certainly would not want to bet against him if he runs for his third term in 1984.

The Helms and Buckley elections were only two of a number of significant victories chalked up by conservatives in Senate, House and gubernatorial races in the early 1970's. We were gaining strength in spite of—and probably *because* of—the liberal policies pursued by President Nixon in the guise of conservatism. The Committee for the Survival of a Free Congress, founded by Paul Weyrich with Robert Casey as its first chairman, helped elect a number of conservatives to Congress, thereby contributing to the legislative branch's gradual shift from liberal to conservative.

Two veteran Republican Senators from Nebraska, Carl Curtis and Roman Hruska, played important parts in this change. With Senator Gordon Allott of Colorado they helped form the Senate Republican Steering Committee, which was capably staffed by Richard Thompson, James Streeter and others who had worked with me in the Goldwater campaign. Senator James McClure of Idaho was eventually named chairman of the Steering Committee and under his aegis it became a powerful conservative force in the Senate. Senator McClure was first elected to the Senate in 1972, a year full of foreboding for the Republican Party and for the nation.

As I noted earlier, many conservatives were unhappy with President Nixon in 1972. But there was little serious discussion about Ronald Reagan trying for the Republican nomination against Nixon. A number of people sounded me out about my thoughts on Reagan's chances. I told them all the same thing: I don't believe you can beat an incumbent President for the nomination. But if you do, you will probably be beaten yourself in November, and what's more, you will do your party serious damage.

Ronald Reagan, then in his second term as Governor of California, shared my feelings. However, you could not keep people from speculating on the possibility of his taking another crack at the nomination in 1972 or, more likely, in 1976. As early as January 1971 the press tried to get him to reveal his plans for '76.

At a luncheon for him at the National Press Club I had been invited to sit at the head table with Governor Reagan and several members of his Sacramento staff who had come east with him. I was a bit embarrassed, albeit somewhat amused, by two of the questions thrown at the Governor after his speech.

The first was: "Governor, is it true that F. Clifton White is seeking to put you on the Republican ticket in 1972 in place of Spiro Agnew?" Reagan laughed and bucked the question down the table to me. I denied it, of course.

The second question looked a bit farther down the road: "Governor, is it true that Clif White is putting together a campaign team for you for President in 1976?" That was one Ronald Reagan could easily deny himself, though I will admit now that I did have some plans. As for the campaign team, I always had my cadre in reserve.

In those years I was traveling a good deal on business, as I still do, and whenever I read a news article I thought Governor Reagan might be interested in, I would mail it to him. In the notes and letters I got back from him, the Reagan wit was often in evidence. For example, in 1971 I sent him a series of articles on California published in a British newspaper and received the following reply:

> It was good to hear from you and thanks for the tear sheets from our English brother. I appreciate having them, although in some parts of the series on California they reminded me of the old stories about New Yorkers who thought Chicago was in Indian country.
>
> One line in particular referred to our one-time redwood forested hills, now "nude and barren". How about that—I finally got rid of all those trees! [California probably has more forests, and certainly more redwoods, than any other state.]
>
> Nancy sends her best and we'll look forward to seeing you soon.

After the 1972 election, however, many of Ronald Reagan's letters were in a more serious vein as the country moved into one of the most traumatic internal crises of this century. Governor Reagan was not personally involved in the Watergate controversy, but like most Americans he could not help but be saddened by the damage it inflicted upon the nation.

14

Time of Trauma

Richard Nixon was reelected President in 1972 by the biggest popular vote in the history of the Republic. He received 47,165,234 votes to 29,168,110 for his liberal Democrat opponent, Senator George McGovern. Only one state, Massachusetts, cast its 17 electoral votes for McGovern. All the rest, 49 states with a total of 520 electoral votes, went to Nixon.

Yet within a matter of months President Nixon was hanging on the ropes, waiting to be knocked out of the political ring.

It has always been something of a mystery to me why the Watergate scandal, which broke in June 1972 but remained quiescent all during the presidential campaign, should suddenly be revived *after* Nixon's reelection. No President since Franklin Roosevelt had enjoyed a more overwhelming mandate than Richard Nixon. But his enemies were determined not to let him enjoy the fruits of that mandate. Was this because they interpreted the election as a *conservative* mandate? If so, they were entirely correct because Nixon was perceived to be a conservative President, even though he was not.

My role in the 1972 presidential campaign was a very limited one. I was retained as a consultant by the Committee to Re–Elect the President for the sole purpose of making sure that the Republican Party in New York State stayed solidly behind Nixon. This meant that I had to keep Governor Nelson Rockefeller and Senators Buckley and Javits all happy with the President. This was not too difficult since their only alternative would have been to support George McGovern, something neither Rockefeller nor Javits were prepared to do, let alone Jim Buckley.

The Committee provided me with an office and telephone whenever I was in Washington that year but I was not invited to participate in any of their policy sessions.

One night, not long after the Watergate break-in, I was leaving the Committee's office at the end of the day and I ran into Jeb Magruder, the assistant to John Mitchell. He asked me to come into his office for a chat and when we had made ourselves comfortable he asked me what I would do about "this Watergate thing."

"I'd find the guy who was responsible for the break–in and fire him," I said.

"At about what level would that have to be in order to make it credible?" Magruder asked.

I laughed. "I guess that would be about your level, Jeb."

It was meant as a joke, of course. I had no idea Jeb Magruder or John Mitchell were implicated in any way in Watergate.

However, it was not until the end of the year that the serious questions began to be raised in the press about Watergate. J. Fred Buzhardt, who left his post as chief counsel of the Department of Defense to become the President's counsel at the height of the scandal, later told my co-author, William J. Gill, that Nixon "didn't take Watergate seriously at first because the whole business of wire tapping was just part of the Washington scene," something all of his presidential predecessors had done in the post World War II era, something that presidents just did to protect themselves and the national security.*

*For documentation of this see Victor Lasky's It Didn't Start with Watergate.

Nonetheless, Nixon had gone his predecessors one better. None of them, to my knowledge, had wire tapped the conversations of their Oval Office visitors as Richard Nixon had done. And it was this activity that ultimately brought Nixon down as the court and the Congressional committee began asking questions about this practice, and specifically about the missing section of tape that may have implicated the President more directly in the cover–up.

In retrospect, we can now see Watergate as primarily a media event, a three–ring circus that unfolded every night for a year–and–a–half on our television screens and all day, everyday, in our newspapers. No President had ever been subjected to such saturation tactics by the media, and I hope no President ever will be again. *

Five or six times a day, and some times more, I would get calls from my friends in the media asking me about the latest Watergate development. I knew very little about the matter except what I read in the papers and saw on television but because I had been a consultant to the Committee to Re–Elect the President I was considered a news source on Watergate. I'm afraid there wasn't much I could tell my journalist friends but I'm not sure they were after hard news so much as the reaction of another anonymous "Republican Party source."

"Don't you think Nixon will have to resign now?" they would ask me, referring to whatever new development had been revealed that particular day. Actually, right up until the end I did not think Nixon would resign. But I suppose no man could withstand

---

*George Washington, in his second term as President, was the target of a sustained and vituperative attack by the press because he had fired his Secretary of State, Edmund Randolph, whom he had good reason to believe had indulged in high treason by feeding confidential information to the Revolutionary French minister to the United States in Randolph's effort to thwart the Jay Treaty. The Treaty, entered into with Great Britain, was designed to keep us from going to war on the side of France and its Revolutionary regime against England and its allies.

However, mass communications was in its infancy in the 1790's and the newspaper attacks on Washington could not reach the level of intensity they did during Watergate, although the language used against Washington was much more vituperative. President Washington's stature was such that he never deigned to answer the press attacks and he rode out the storm in silence.

the barrage of charges, proven and unproven, that were leveled at Richard Nixon for nearly twenty months.

It was the most agonizing domestic scandal in our nation's history. Day after day, month after month, it tore our country asunder. It shook the faith of our people in their government as nothing had ever done in the past and yet, when it was all over, most of us realized that none of the critical issues confronting the nation had been resolved by Nixon's resignation. Indeed, they were still there, as they had been before, waiting to be treated, waiting for solution.

I was managing a campaign for Charles Sandman, the Republican gubernatorial candidate in New Jersey, when Spiro Agnew resigned as Vice President in the middle of Watergate, though his resignation came about on other grounds. I believe Sandman would have won that fall if it hadn't been for the one–two punch of Watergate–Agnew that knocked out our campaign. All my workers simply went home. And most of them didn't even bother to come out again for the election.

In general, the conservatives held up better under the twin scandals involving the President and Vice President than other Republicans. For the most part, they were able to see Watergate and Agnew in a more broad perspective. They understood that all the other problems facing the nation would still be there after Nixon and Agnew were gone. Although many of them were understandably discouraged, conservatives had no intention of surrendering. In fact, after Watergate most of them were more determined than ever to bring about a real conservative victory, not merely the pale imitation Nixon had offered them and the nation.

Gerald Ford was regarded by many conservatives as an inter-regnum President. He had never been a Presidential contender and when Nixon appointed him as Vice President, Ford had made it plain during his Congressional confirmation hearings that he would not try for election in 1976.

Most conservatives looked to Ronald Reagan as the man they wanted to lead the Republican Party to victory in 1976, although some felt John Connally would make a good President. The liberals still had Nelson Rockefeller, of course. But after Ford's appointment as President he, in turn, appointed Nelson as his Vice President and Jerry was surprised to find that Rockefeller was more a political liability than an asset. Not only wasn't Nelson seriously considered for the Presidential nomination in 1976, Ford soon knew that he would have to dump Rockefeller as Vice President if he hoped to get the nomination for the top spot himself.

Long before Ford became President in August 1974 there had been speculation about Reagan trying again. Paul Hope of the *Washington Star* wrote one of the earliest stories on this possibility in June 1973. After an interview with Reagan in Sacramento, Hope reported that the Governor was "itching" to get out and "sell his conservative philosophy to the country." He said Reagan had "implied that if the voters are in a buying mood, he wouldn't mind going to the White House."

"I don't think you could walk away from this and go back to the ranch and ride horses," Hope quoted Reagan as saying. He did rule out running for Governor again in 1974. But when Paul Hope pressed him about when he might make a formal decision to run for the nomination, Reagan replied: "I don't think an individual makes that decision. I think the people make that determination."

As for Watergate, Reagan said: "Admittedly it was a mess, but it was a mess on the part of a handful of individuals. It would be a terrible guilt–by–association thing" if Watergate should reflect on all Republicans.

About this time several of my friends gave a testimonial dinner for me at the Plaza in New York. The Buckley Clan was out in strength that night, led by Bill and Jim's mother, Mrs. William F.

Buckley, Sr. Bill Rusher presided as master of ceremonies and Bill Buckley gave the principal address. Tom Reed, who was still on Governor Reagan's Sacramento team then, was at the head table, as was Dan Mahoney, the chairman of the Conservative Party in New York.

My pastor, the Rev. Joseph P. Bishop, of the Presbyterian Church in Rye, New York, had just given the invocation when we learned that two other expected guests, Senators James Buckley and Barry Goldwater, could not make it because the Senate had been called into a night session. However, both of them were piped in by telephone over the public address system from the Senate cloak room.

Then, much to my surprise, Governor Ronald Reagan's voice came over the sound system, too. He was calling from California and after extending his greetings he said, "Hang on just a second, Clif, I've got someone else here who wants to talk with you." The "someone else" was Nancy Reagan, who transmitted her very special glow from the Reagan home in Sacramento to the Plaza Ballroom via Ma Bell's telephone lines. It was a wonderful evening, one my wife and I will always remember.

In July 1973 several members of our *Hard Core* group from the 1964 campaign met in Chicago. I'd had a hand-written note from Governor Reagan about 10 days before suggesting we get together there since he was to speak at a dinner I was attending. When I saw him at the dinner I asked if I could bring along the members of my group who wanted to get to know him better. He said fine, bring them to his room at the Chicago Hilton at 8:00 the next morning. This was cutting things a little close because I had to catch a plane back to New York about 9:30 but I thought we could wind up our meeting in about a half–hour and give me just enough time to get to the airport.

At 7:30 I met Frank Whetstone, Andy Carter, Tom Van Sickle and John Kerwitz for a quick breakfast in the Hilton dining room and then we went up to the Governor's room. A security guard stopped us in the corridor and said he had orders not to let anyone in until 8:30. I told him the Governor and I had set the time at 8 o'clock but the guard insisted he was under direct orders from Robert C. Walker, Reagan's special assistant, not to let anyone in. I asked if I could see Mr. Walker and was told he was down in the dining room.

When I found Walker I told him the Governor was expecting us at 8 o'clock and we were already fifteen minutes late because of the security guard blocking the door. Walker just smiled and said we could not go in until 8:30. I reminded him that the Governor had set the time with me himself but Walker just shrugged.

I suggested to my friends that they go to the meeting at 8:30 and explain to the Governor what had happened. It was nearly that now and I had just enough time to catch a cab to the airport.

About a week later I got a note from Ron Reagan saying that he had been sitting in the room waiting for me at 8:00 and he was sorry about the mixup.

It wasn't until early in 1974 that I learned that Bob Walker had sold John P. Sears III to Ronald Reagan to plan the 1976 campaign for the nomination. Apparently some members of the Governor's staff in Sacramento had persuaded him that "Clif White has enemies." When I was told that Ron had said this about me I just laughed and said, "Well, I hope so. If you've been in politics as long as I have, and you *don't* have enemies, then you haven't stood for very much or accomplished very much."

I didn't take any of this very seriously at the time, but the truth is that a wedge had been driven between Ronald Reagan and me and it would be some years before it was finally removed. In fact, it was not until John Sears was fired by Reagan after the New Hampshire primary in 1980 that I again was invited to become a member of his team.

I must confess I was unaware of the wedge for nearly two years.

Reagan and I continued to correspond and we saw each other at the Governors Conference meetings and elsewhere. He was always very friendly and I don't think there was any lessening in our *personal* relationship. But when Ronald Reagan started his campaign for the 1976 nomination with Sears as his manager, I knew that something had happened to our *political* relationship.

Ironically, my *Hard Core* cadre had begun laying plans to get Reagan the 1976 nomination during an August 1973 meeting at Charlie Barr's home in Matteson, Illinois. Indeed, one of the people who had attended the meeting was Paul Haerle, who had been on the Governor's staff in Sacramento and had later become the California Republican Chairman. Moreover, several of my group who were at this meeting, including Andy Carter and Frank Whetstone, wound up working for Reagan in 1976 and stayed with him right through the 1980 campaign.

In these meetings we always reviewed the potential presidential candidates of both parties. In leading off, I noted that Ronald Reagan had said he will not run again for governor but I emphasized that "he had better elect the next governor if he is going to control the California delegation in 1976." Unfortunately, this was not done. In the 1974 election the governorship went to Pat Brown's son, Jerry, much to the sorrow of the whole state of California. However, I don't think Jerry Brown's victory was a reflection on Ronald Reagan. In 1974 *all* Republicans were having great difficulty getting elected in the wake of Watergate and Nixon's resignation in August.

The other Republican presidential possibilities we discussed at our Illinois meeting were John Connally, Howard Baker, Charles Percy, James Buckley and Melvin Laird. Connally already had Strom Thurmond's support, though I wasn't so sure that would be as decisive as it had been in 1968 because of the Nixon record. Baker was getting a good press and I mentioned that Senator Buckley considered Baker to be very smart and well organized.

Percy had hired a campaign consultant and a poll in the Northeast had shown he had some support there, although I doubted he would find much anywhere else, including his own state of Illinois. I thought Mel Laird, who was then Secretary of Defense, would do well in the Wisconsin primary but it was doubtful if he could extend his base much beyond that. And James Buckley had to run for reelection to the Senate in 1976. "That," I emphasized, "must be his Number One Concern."

Paul Haerle told us at the meeting that Ronald Reagan "wants to run" but, unlike most people who actively seek the Presidency, he said his boss "does not thrive on politics, he thrives on issues." Haerle frankly felt that the Republicans would have a difficult time electing a new governor because of Watergate, a prediction that unfortunately came to pass.

Tom van Sickle reported on the meeting with Reagan in Chicago a month earlier after I'd had to make my dash for the airport because of the time mixup with Bob Walker. Tom said he, Frank Whetstone and John Kerwitz had spent about 45 minutes with the Governor and had told him we were prepared to present him with a list of our friends in every state if he decided to seek the nomination.

Although our group decided not to make a commitment to any candidate until after the New Year, it was obvious where the sentiments of my cadre lay. I had a date to see Reagan in San Francisco the following month and I told the group I'd report back to them on it afterward.

Reagan and I did have a cordial meeting in San Francisco that September. He had interrupted his annual vacation at the beach to address the Young Americans for Freedom and also to speak at the Bohemian Grove. We got together for an hour before the YAF dinner and had a good talk. By this time Gerald Ford had taken over as President and I told the Governor I thought that would complicate things in 1976 in spite of Ford's commitment not to run.

At the time, I never dreamed I would be working for anyone else except Ronald Reagan in the 1976 race for the nomination. But politics, like life, is often unpredictable and it can take us down byways we never expect to travel.

15

The Split

The preparations for the 1976 Presidential campaign began early. Potential Democratic candidates, sensing Richard Nixon's impending fall, were already maneuvering for position in the spring of 1973. Ultimately there were to be nearly a dozen announced presidential candidates among the Democrats, with as many more unannounced waiting coyly in the wings.* No political party in all our history had ever had such a plethora of people who were deemed to be, or deemed themselves to be, qualified for the nation's highest office.

The Republicans had a much smaller field. Almost from the beginning there were only two candidates—Gerald Ford and Ronald Reagan. And once more, as in 1968, conservatives were divided. Most of them wanted Governor Reagan. But there were substantial numbers who thought the country needed the continuity of a full term for the incumbent President. There were

*The announced Democrat candidates were: Senator Lloyd M. Bentsen of Texas; Governor Edmund G. Brown of California; Senate Majority Leader Robert Byrd of West Virginia; Governor Jimmy Carter of Georgia; Senator Frank Church·of Idaho; former Senator Fred Harris of Oklahoma; Senator Henry M. Jackson of Washington; Governor Milton J. Shapp of Pennsylvania; Sargent Shriver of Maryland; Congressman Morris Udall of Arizona; and Governor George Wallace of Alabama.

other factors at work, as we shall see. But the Ford–Reagan struggle was more in the nature of a family argument, with conservatives lined up fairly evenly on both sides.

I continued to consult with Ronald Reagan in 1974 and I assumed I would be part of his team in 1976 if he tried again for the nomination. In the spring of that year I had a letter from Bob Walker, Reagan's political man in Sacramento, saying he was "working on the Governor's fall schedule" and requesting "guidance" on Congressional candidates in New York who needed help. Reagan was willing to do a fund-raiser for one and I wrote back suggesting he do it for Jack Kemp in the 38th District (Buffalo).

In September I sent Reagan an article regarding the seriousness of the world situation and got this note back from him:

> Just a quick line to say thanks for the article, although I must say it was not one to cause dancing in the streets. Do you have a well-furnished cave in mind? Seriously, it does point out the situation as I believe it is in the world and makes us realize how much depends on this country. I pray to God we are going to have the strength we need.
>
> I hope to see you soon.

We got together at a Governors Conference meeting later on but somehow we never seemed to talk much after that about his coming campaign. By this time I had learned that a young Washington lawyer, John Sears, was advising Reagan on 1976 and since Sears seemed to be the Governor's choice there wasn't much I could do for him from then on.

John Sears and I are from very different political schools. I don't mean this in the sense of the difference in our ages. There are literally thousands of young men and women in politics today, people much younger than John Sears, who belong to essentially the same school I do. And there are others, most notably among my colleagues in the professional political consulting field, who belong to John's school of "pragmatic" politics.

Richard Nixon is, or was, the great patron and leading example of this school. John Kennedy and Lyndon Johnson were also among its exponents. The pragmatists believed, and many still believe, that ideology has no real place in politics. It should be manipulated and used but it should never be *adopted* as one's *raison d'être*. For the pragmatists, power is the only goal worth achieving.

My school of politics believes that ideology is important, that unless one believes in a philosophy of government, then one must become a puppet of the polls, swaying and bending with every errant and conflicting wind that wafts across the political landscape. This is not to say that one's political philosophy should not be tempered with realism. In all my years in politics, I don't think anyone has ever seriously charged me with being anything other than a realist. I learned how to count very early in the game and whether I'm counting delegates at a convention or potential votes for an election I have never tried to delude myself. I can face reality as well as the next person, and I have had to face it more frequently than most, in both victory and defeat.

In political usage, however, pragmatism and realism are not necessarily the same thing. In fact, they are not often the same any longer. The conservative revolution may yet be thwarted by the pragmatists. But if it is, they, the pragmatists, will be contributing further to the disenchantment of the people in their government by proving to all Americans the one thing we never want to believe, i.e., that our system can no longer work. Even the more enlightened liberals recognize this and several of them, including Hodding Carter, III, made this point in their writings after the 1980 election.

It is one of the great political ironies of the past decade that Ronald Reagan, who I believe is a dedicated and committed conservative, should fall into the hands of the pragmatists in 1974. Their influence with him, although never total, lasted for nearly six years.

Strangely, the two people who led Reagan down the pragmatist path the first time were men who had fought us at the 1968 convention. Indeed, they epitomized the "Nixon men" who were running around Miami in their vested suits and button–down shirts carrying messages for the people who were really running the convention for Nixon. I was unable to discern that they exerted any real influence in Miami, but they were there in great numbers and, as we know, most of them moved into the White House or other administration posts with Nixon.

The two Nixon men who temporarily captivated Ronald Reagan were John Sears and Robert Walker. I have already told how Walker recruited Sears for Reagan in 1974. They had worked together in setting up a Nixon for President office in 1967, although Walker later worked for Reagan in 1968 and became his political advisor in Sacramento.

Sears bounced in and out of Nixon's White House in almost record time, thanks to his penchant for talking incessantly to the press, a penchant he has never lost. I think people in politics *should* talk with the press, incidentally, and I've always tried to keep my channels of communication open to the media. But you have to be aware when you are talking with the press that *everything* you say is subject to winding up in the news and it is prudent to demonstrate some restraint.

Jules Witcover, in his book *Marathon*, the story of the lengthy 1976 presidential campaign, tells how reluctant John Sears was to become involved with Ronald Reagan.

"Reagan was probably not the kind of candidate Sears would have picked had he had a wide choice," Witcover writes. "But in the reality of the party and the time, it was Ford or Reagan, and Sears knew he would never be in command of a Ford campaign."

This was not a supposition of Witcover's. John Sears had spelled it out for him in intricate detail:

To Sears, a Reagan nomination was, in the political jargon, do–able. Yet he was troubled about an alliance with Reagan because as a pragmatic political operative he did not want to be tagged as an ultra–ideologue of the right; he did not want Reagan's right–wing label to rub off on himself. And, beyond that, Sears' association with members of the Washington political press corps was more to him than a marriage of convenience; he wanted them to understand and accept his move to Reagan.

A more vivid picture of the pragmatist is difficult to envision. But John Sears apparently wanted his self–portrait to be painted in the boldest hues that day at Harvey's. And Jules Witcover was, understandably, willing to oblige.

"Most important," Witcover said in reporting Sears' conversation in his book several years later, "Reagan was malleable: the man could be educated on the issues, and could be moved more to the center of the political spectrum if handled correctly. As an actor, Sears said frankly, Reagan was accustomed to direction: he could keep the True Believers in the ranks while altering his rhetoric to broaden his appeal."

For Witcover this was "an optimistic outlook," but, he added, "Sears obviously needed to believe that he could succeed in this remaking of Ronald Reagan if he were going to undertake direction of his candidacy and live with himself and his friends."

But even Sears, with his cynically pragmatic view of Reagan, saw one great obstacle to his plans: "The patriotism the man wore so transparently on his sleeve really did seem to beat intensely in his breast as well; he seemed to aides sincerely to want the new President, Jerry Ford, to be successful."

In that one respect, I am certain John was correct. And nothing could better illustrate the difference between the pragmatist and my school of political philosophy than this. I believe that every member of my school, which includes patriotic liberals as well as conservatives, *wanted* President Ford to lead the country out of the quagmire of Watergate and up onto higher ground.

Moreover, Gerald Ford did just that. When he took over the helm from Nixon the ship of state was foundering and the confidence of Americans in their government was at the lowest point in history. We were in an economic recession that was accompanied by accelerating inflation, a phenomenon seldom experienced before. By using the Presidential veto to halt the Democratic Congress's wildest spending programs, Ford got inflation under reasonable control and by mid–1975 the worst unemployment in three decades was behind us and we were emerging from the recession.

There wasn't much President Ford could do about Vietnam, given the mood of the country and the complexion of the Congress. The North Vietnamese Army, spearheaded by Russian-built tanks, came back across the DMZ in force early in 1975 and by April Saigon had fallen just hours after we evacuated the last of our troops via helicopter.

Two weeks later, however, when Cambodian gunboats seized the U.S. container ship Mayaguez and its crew, Ford called it an "act of piracy" and sent the Navy and Marines after the captured ship. Three Cambodian gunboats were sunk and the Marines took an island where the Mayaguez crew was reported in captivity. There were casualties, but we got the ship and its crew back and, with it, some of our national self–respect.

The Democratic Congress tied President Ford's hands firmly behind his back when he tried to aid the anti–Communist forces in Angola, however. The result was that the Cuban expeditionary force, armed with Russian weapons, captured Angola's cities, though the fighting continues to this day in the jungles. The Communists, seeing that the Congress would not permit Ford to intervene in any areas of conflict, expanded their aggression in Africa and Central America, and began the systematic genocide of the Cambodian people.

Unfortunately, Ford gave his Secretary of State, Henry Kissinger, a free hand in dealing with the Soviet Union and the Communist aggression was inexplicably rewarded by our entering into a number of new agreements with the Russians, including the Salt I Treaty Ford was talked into before and during the summit conference with Brezhnev in Vladivostok.

Meanwhile, it had become apparent that Jerry Ford would run for a full term. Many conservatives were unhappy with him, primarily on the basis of his foreign policy, and there were a number of meetings early in 1975 to discuss alternatives to a Ford candidacy.

One alternative was put forward by my friend William A. Rusher in his book, *The Making of the New Majority Party*. In his lucid prose, Rusher advocated the formation of a Third Party that would eclipse both the Republican and Democrat parties because, in his view, they had outlived their usefulness and, indeed, no longer reflected the will of the people. Although I did not agree with Rusher that the usefulness of the existing major parties was at an end, I did find it hard to debate him on whether they were actually doing what the people expected them to do, at least at this time. The pragmatists in both parties were in ascendancy and they had so distorted and blurred the issues that the body politic naturally felt confused and frustrated.

Nonetheless, I believed Bill Rusher's thesis deserved a thorough hearing and debate. And that is just what it got at the annual Conservative Political Action Conference in Washington in February 1975. Two of the speakers at this conference, Ronald Reagan and Senator James L. Buckley, tried to discourage the Third Party move.

Reagan, in his speech, asked: "Is it a third party we need, or is it a new and revitalized second party, raising a banner of no pale pastels, but bold colors which makes it unmistakably clear where we stand on all of the issues troubling the people?"

This was not the end of the Third Party movement, however.

The conference, which is sponsored annually by the American Conservative Union, Young Americans for Freedom, *Human Events* and *National Review*, named Senator Jesse Helms to head a committee to explore the idea further in the context of the 1976 election.

Several people on this committee wanted Ronald Reagan to run on a Third Party ticket with George Wallace as his Vice-Presidential running mate. Reagan said he did not want to do this on the grounds that Wallace was a Democrat and also that he didn't agree with the Alabama governor on a number of things.

Without Reagan it was obvious the Third Party movement wasn't going to get very far and it soon exhausted itself as both Reagan and Wallace began to actively seek the nomination of their own separate parties.

Before this, or at least before Ronald Reagan officially announced, there were more meetings of conservatives in which the Third Party idea was debated. Not long after the Washington conference, there was a more informal meeting at St. Michaels on Maryland's Eastern Shore. Senator Buckley was the ex–officio chairman of this meeting and he invited me to attend. I had dinner there with Senator Helms and his wife and I hope made my position clear to the Senator: I am opposed to third parties. It is my belief that there is enough room in both the Republican and Democrat parties to accomodate all but the most extreme elements of our society. Besides, I felt that we had proved rather conclusively in 1964 that the conservatives were the majority within the Republican party and it was my belief a decade later that we were well on the way to becoming the preponderant majority in the country.

It was about this time that I had my last private, or I should say, semi–private, meeting with Ronald Reagan for several years. Mike Deaver arranged for me to have dinner with the Governor in his suite at the Madison Hotel in Washington. I thought it would be just the two of us, with perhaps Mike sitting in, too. But shortly after I arrived there was a knock on the door and John Sears came in. After a little while, Mike Deaver left and Reagan, Sears and I sat down to dinner. I must confess I'm not sure what this meeting was supposed to be about. Sears seemed to be subtly preaching the pragmatist gospel and, if I understood him correctly, his lesson for that day was that pragmatism was the only way to go. At any rate, I went away more convinced than ever that modern political pragmatism is often totally divorced from political reality.

I kept in touch with Ronald Reagan after that. My business commitments would have made it impossible for me to become a full-time campaign manager but if he had asked me to serve in a consultant capacity I would have been glad to do it. But the invitation never was made.

Toward the end of 1975 it had become completely apparent to me that I was not going to be asked to become a part of the Reagan team again. The Ford people had been making overtures for more than a year, almost from the time Gerald Ford became President.

Jerry Ford and I were old friends. We had appeared on many platforms together over the years and I had always known Ford to be a conservative. I liked him as a person and thought he was doing a good job as President under very difficult circumstances.

Donald Rumsfeld, then on the President's staff, invited me to the White House several times and on one occasion I brought a half-dozen members of my *Hard Core* group and we had a meeting in the Cabinet Room with Don and Richard Cheney, now a Congressman from Wyoming and at that time the White House chief-of-staff. I told them our group would wait a while before we supported either candidate. Several of my old group were already involved with Reagan and would continue to be right through the primary campaigns the following year. Others had been preempted by the President. But most of us were simply marking time.

Early in November 1975 Ford reshuffled his Cabinet and at the same time it was made clear that Nelson Rockefeller would not be his running mate in '76. Don Rumsfeld became Secretary of Defense, replacing James Schlesinger. The press reported Schlesinger was fired because he was too much of a hawk for President Ford and this incensed many conservatives. However, some defense experts believe Schlesinger had placed the United States in a very dangerous position by theorizing openly about a "limited nuclear war"—a theory that appeared to be almost an invitation to the Soviet Union to push the button because they no longer had to fear the massive retaliation which had been the basis of our policy of deterrence since the administrations of Presidents Truman and Eisenhower. Moreover, Schlesinger had begun to carry his theory into actual practice and the U.S. Strategic Air Command had been ordered to eliminate Russian population centers as targets, thereby assuring the Soviets that they could hit our cities without fear of losing their own.

Obviously, this theory of a "limited nuclear war" represented a radical and exceedingly precarious departure from past policy, a departure that threatened world peace and endangered the very existence of the United States and the Free World.

President Ford did not spell out his reasons for replacing Schlesinger with Don Rumsfeld. He simply asked Schlesinger to the White House and informed him that he was appointing someone else to command the Pentagon. Schlesinger later became Secretary of Energy in Jimmy Carter's Cabinet.

Ford's other new Cabinet appointments did not attract quite as much attention as Rumsfeld's. But conservatives were unhappy about Elliott Richardson being named Secretary of Commerce to succeed Rogers C.B. Morton, who became the President's chief political advisor. George Bush was brought back from his post as our representative in Peiping and put in charge of the Central Intelligence Agency, replacing William Colby who, many people felt, had all but dismantled the CIA.

Four months earlier, on July 8, 1975, Gerald Ford had formally announced that he would seek the Republican nomination the following year. Several weeks before he had named Dean Burch, the former Republican National Chairman during the Goldwater campaign, to head his Advisory Committee. Indeed, a good many members of the committee were old friends of mine from the Goldwater movement and the President's campaign chairman, Howard H. (Bo) Callaway, had been one of our original cadre members in Georgia. Bill Timmons, with whom I had worked in the Young Republicans years before, was to run the convention for Ford.

I knew there was a lot of pressure on Ronald Reagan to announce that summer, too. But he seemed to be holding back, pretty much as he had in 1967–68. My friend, Senator Paul Laxalt of Nevada, had quietly put together an ad hoc group to explore the situation for Reagan and we talked several times about the lay of the land for 1976.

Frank Walton, who had been on Reagan's staff in Sacramento, was now in Washington as president of the newly–formed Heritage Foundation and he also talked with me about the outlook for '76, as did a number of other Reagan supporters. But nothing was ever said about my personally playing a role in Ronald Reagan's coming campaign if he did decide to run.

I knew that President Ford had offered Reagan a Cabinet post after Ron retired as Governor of California early in 1975, and I understood the offer had been repeated at least once. Reagan realized his acceptance would make it difficult, if not impossible, for him to take on Ford for the nomination and he had declined with thanks both times.

Reagan's position was, quite properly, that Gerald Ford had been chosen by Nixon, not by the Republican Party, and the party ought to have a chance to decide for itself whom it wanted for its nominee. Thus, when the Ford people appealed to his patriotism and to his party loyalty, his two most susceptible points, they found that Reagan had already innoculated himself against their persuasive arguments.

Finally, on November 21, 1975, Reagan made it official. He told reporters at a Washington press conference that he would run against President Ford for the nomination. In doing so, he fired off the following broadside: "Our nation's capital has become the seat of a buddy system that functions for its own benefit, increasingly insensitive to the needs of the American worker who supports it with his taxes. Today it is difficult to find leaders who are independent of the forces that have brought us our problems: the Congress, the bureaucracy, the lobbyists, big business, and big labor."

Typically, Ronald Reagan refused to identify Gerald Ford as part of the Washington "buddy system", nor did he indulge in any harsh criticism of the President. When the reporters tried to trap him into lashing out at Ford, he invoked the "Eleventh Commandment" he had used so effectively in California: "Thou shalt not speak ill of any fellow Republican."

Reagan emphasized that he was running on the issues, not because of any personal animosity for Jerry Ford.

Meanwhile, my old friends on President Ford's Advisory Committee, including Dean Burch and Bill Timmons, were urging me to join them. Henry Salvatori, a key member of our California cadre and one of the people who had persuaded Ronald Reagan to run for governor, had already come aboard the presidential express, as had Paul Haerle, the state Republican chairman in California, and many other old political associates of mine. Jerry Ford talked with me several times and shortly before the convention I agreed to join the Ford committee and support the President. I wound up running his delegate communications and the roll call for him at the 1976 convention, and it was the closest—and the toughest—count of my whole career.

16

The Long Battle

The running battle between Gerald Ford and Ronald Reagan for the Republican Presidential nomination in America's bicentennial year was very probably the most exciting, and certainly the closest, contest of its kind either major party has witnessed in more than a half–century. Not since former President Theodore Roosevelt came out of retirement in 1912 to challenge his successor, President William Howard Taft, had the Republican Party experienced such a nip–and–tuck struggle. By comparison, Barry Goldwater's victory over Nelson Rockefeller, William Scranton, and the other liberal candidates who came and went in 1964, was an organizational cake walk.

Reagan started the campaign with an amazing lead over Ford in the polls. Indeed, in one month he had come from 23 percentage points *behind* the President to a dozen points *ahead* of him, according to George Gallup's survey. For a while it looked as though the Reagan rocket would leave Gerald Ford's candidacy mired in the marshy ground of Washington. Then came New Hampshire.

In my view, the Presidential preference primary in New Hampshire ought to be outlawed. It gives a grand total of less than

200,000 voters in *both* parties in that small state the power to virtually dictate the Republican and Democrat candidates to the rest of the nation. Less than 60,000 votes were cast for two candidates in the Democratic primary in New Hampshire in 1968, with 28,791 of them for Senator Eugene McCarthy against a little more than 29,000 for Lyndon Johnson. Yet that relative handful of votes was enough to persuade the incumbent President to end his candidacy for reelection. Similarly, in 1976 a virtually unknown former governor of Georgia squeezed about 23,000 votes out of less than 80,000 for several candidates in the Democrat primary that year. But those 23,000 votes sent Jimmy Carter on his way to the White House, with sad results for the whole country and, in fact, for the world.

The voters of New Hampshire have become so spoiled, so pampered by Presidential candidates begging for their votes, that they now accept it as an article of faith that they should choose the nation's chief executive for the rest of us. In reality, it is the media that has puffed up the New Hampshire primary out of all proportion to what should be its actual importance. By focusing almost exclusively on the political scene in that state for the first two months of every Presidential election year, the media has elevated New Hampshire to the status of a David knocking out an army of political Goliaths, and many a candidate who deserved more serious consideration by his party has been consigned to oblivion by a relative handful of voters in this sparsely populated state.

The New Hampshire primary contest between Gerald Ford and Ronald Reagan in 1976 was a hard–fought, almost bitter battle, not so much because of anything either of the candidates did or said, but because of the way some of the differences between them were reported. The biggest issue in the campaign was Reagan's so–called "$90 billion mistake." During the summer of 1975 he had made a speech in Chicago saying that $90 billion could be carved from the Federal budget by cutting federal programs and turning many of them over to the states, which could then decide for themselves whether they wanted to continue the programs or let them expire.

The research for this speech, and the first draft, had been done by conservative columnist Jeffrey Bell. It had been gone over by Reagan's staff and they all gave it the green light. The speech did not get too much attention when it was originally delivered. But some of Gerald Ford's more diligent pragmatists spotted the $90 billion figure and they got their friends in the media to start cross–examining Reagan about it in New Hampshire. The passage they zeroed in on is particularly interesting to me, since it contained a central idea Ronald Reagan and I have discussed a number of times over the years.

"What I propose," Reagan stated, "is nothing less than a systematic transfer of authority and resources to the states, a program of creative federalism for America's third century. Federal authority has clearly failed to do the job. Indeed, it has created more problems in welfare, education, housing, food stamps, Medicaid, community and regional development, and revenue sharing, to name a few. . . . Transfer of authority in whole or part in all these areas would reduce the outlay of the federal government by more than $90 billion, using the spending levels of fiscal 1976."

He said such a step would eventually make it possible to balance the budget, begin paying off the national debt, and cut personal income taxes an average of 23 per cent. And, he added, it would "quickly liberate much of our economy and political system from the dead hand of federal interference, with beneficial impact on every aspect of our daily lives."

When the New Hampshire campaign started Democrat Jimmy Carter called Reagan's plan "ridiculous" and it was obvious the press almost unanimously agreed with him. Reagan was painted as a fiscal idiot, advocating unrealistic measures that could never be taken if he became President.

In light of what has transpired in the first year of Ronald

Reagan's Presidency I would suggest a good many journalists and politicians, including, I am sorry to say, Gerald Ford, ought to eat an awful lot of crow. None of them could see in 1976 *how* Reagan could accomplish his budget cuts and transfer of federal authority to the states. But in 1981 I think they would agree he has found a way. All of his suggestions cannot be implemented at once, of course. But by slashing the budget early in his first year, and getting the Congress to approve most of his cuts, he has, in one brilliant stroke, set his plan in motion.

As for his program of "creative federalism" to transfer former federal functions to the states, it too is on the way to fruition. The President and I have discussed this many times in the past and we talked about it again after his election. I suggested he establish a Presidential Commission on Federalism and he has done just that, naming our mutual friend Senator Paul Laxalt as chairman. I am presently serving as a member of this Commission and we met with President Reagan at the White House in June 1981 to formulate our plans for restoring the federal system created by the constitution.

There is, I think, a lesson in this for all of us. Too great a skepticism about proposals made in the heat of a political campaign leads to downright cynicism, and no government can operate indefinitely on a steady diet of cynicism. We should have sufficient confidence in our leaders to at least give them a chance to carry out their proposals, without prejudging and condemning them as was Ronald Reagan's federalism idea in New Hampshire in 1976.

The doubts that were created about Reagan in this instance very probably cost him the primary election in New Hampshire and perhaps the presidential nomination and the Presidency itself that year. He lost New Hampshire to Gerald Ford by 1,317 votes out of a total of a little over 108,000 cast for both candidates in the Republican primary. This paved the way for a string of Ford primary victories in Massachusetts, Illinois and Florida and for a time it looked as though Reagan was finished for '76.

As I have pointed out before, however, Ronald Reagan is a fighter, and these losses only made him fight all the harder. He scored a resounding victory over President Ford in North Carolina, thanks in large part to the very efficient organization forged in that state by Senator Jesse Helms and Tom Ellis but also to a half–hour television speech given by Reagan only because Jesse and Tom insisted on it against John Sears's advice.

After North Carolina, there was a succession of stunning Reagan wins, most notably on May 1 in Texas, where he beat the President two–to–one. Significantly, he was aided in this by a large number of Democrat crossovers, as he was three days later in Indiana. By early May he was ahead of Ford in the delegate count and every time I came by the White House during this period the gloom was almost palpable.

But Jerry Ford is a fighter too and he bounced back on May 25 with primary victories in Kentucky, Tennessee and Oregon. That same day Reagan won Arkansas, Idaho and Nevada, but Ford had surged ahead and he now had 771 delegates to 643 for Reagan.

The delegate count continued to be close right up to the convention. Early in June Ford won Ohio and Rhode Island and later in the month Reagan swept Montana, South Dakota and his own state of California, where he defeated the President by a large margin.

I had become more active in the Ford campaign during the latter stages of the primary trail and if I had been pressed hard after Reagan's impressive California victory I probably would have said Ron had the nomination all but sewed up.

On July the Fourth, 1976, the whole nation took time out to celebrate our 200th birthday. It was a grand and glorious day and I don't think any American could have helped but be stirred by our bicentennial observance. It was more than just the fireworks and the flotilla of tall sailing ships sent by a number of foreign countries to help us celebrate as we watched the festivities on television. It was a day that helped bring us all together for the first time in many years. Not since V-J day when World War II ended had we experienced anything quite like it. I think a lot of the credit for making the Bicentennial such a remarkable day should go to President Ford. He had helped restore our confidence in ourselves and I don't believe the same kind of proud feeling could have prevailed in the country a few years earlier during Watergate or a few years later under his immediate successor.

While we were all still basking in the glow of that glorious Fourth, those of us associated with President Ford's campaign were counting delegates and becoming more concerned that our candidate would fall short. On July 26, however, John Sears delivered his masterstroke—and handed the nomination to Gerald Ford.

Sears talked Reagan into naming Senator Richard Schweiker of Pennsylvania as his vice-presidential choice should he win the presidential nomination himself. Schweiker had exceedingly good liberal credentials in those days and Sears rationale was that this would attract liberals to Reagan's banner and bring him a sizeable bloc of convention votes from Pennsylvania, which has the third largest number of delegates.

It was a pragmatist's masterpiece. The only problem was that it ignored the ideological realities not only within the Republican Party, but, increasingly, in the country at large. The conservatives in the Reagan camp were horrified and this action cut the heart out of some of Ronald Reagan's most loyal supporters. In Pennsylvania, for instance, an operation was to begin that very day with every prospect of winning Reagan a fairly substantial number of delegates from that state. When he named Schweiker the operation was called off. Ultimately, Reagan was to receive only a handful of Pennsylvania's votes so even this element of the grand strategy backfired badly when Drew Lewis, now the Secretary of Transportation, held Pennsylvania's delegation in line for Ford.

We had our problems within the Ford camp too, of course. Some of his staff people had been urging the President from the beginning to conduct a blood–and–guts campaign and ignore Reagan's Eleventh Commandment about refraining from personal attacks on other Republicans. Among these were Stuart Spencer and Peter Kaye, who were largely responsible for the press, and for Ford, making a big issue out of what they regarded as Reagan's $90 billion blooper.

After Reagan's victory in Texas, many of Ford's advisors wanted him to go after his opponent on the national defense issue, one that Reagan had made hay out of in the Lone Star state. The only problem was that Reagan was *right* about this issue—our defenses were in sad condition *vis à vis* the Soviet Union, and the President knew it. Fortunately, cooler heads prevailed in this instance and Ford did not engage Reagan in a running debate on the defense issue, an issue in which I believe they were essentially in agreement.

I was constantly cautioning the pragmatists in the Ford campaign committee about going after Reagan too hard. My reasoning was that the Republican Party was going to be in for a very tough general election campaign in the fall and we could not afford to go into it with the party divided. But my suggestions were naturally suspect, since everyone knew I had worked for Reagan in 1968 and had continued to have a good relationship with him.

Luckily for Ford, his own good sense kept his criticism of Reagan within reasonable bounds, though every once in a while he would get impatient and let loose a blast that made the press jump for joy but made me wince. For some strange reason, one of the people urging Jerry Ford to take a harder line was Howard H. Callaway, the President's campaign manager in the early part of the primary campaigns. However, charges were made in the press that Bo Callaway had used his position as Secretary of the Army in the development of a Colorado ski resort and he resigned from the Ford campaign.

Nonetheless, there were plenty of others left in the Ford camp who wanted him to come out swinging against Reagan. One of them, I recall, was James Baker, now the White House Chief-of-Staff and then an Assistant Secretary of Commerce. Rogers Morton arranged a meeting with Jim Baker and me during the pre–convention period in 1976 and I spent the better part of a day briefing Baker on how we were going to run the convention for the President.

This was one convention I did not look forward to with a great deal of relish. But President Ford had given me a job to do and I certainly was going to do the best I could.

17

Convention '76

Gerald Ford and Ronald Reagan went into the Republican national convention at Kansas City in 1976 virtually tied for the nomination. With 1,130 votes needed to win, each of them had over 1,000, but there seemed to be enough undecided votes to make the contest go either way.

In the preliminary rounds, the debates over the key planks in the party platform, the Reagan forces had the upper hand. Led by Senator Jesse Helms, they practically rewrote the platform that had been previously drafted by the White House staff, particularly the passages pertaining to foreign policy.

On Monday, August 16, however, the ground gained in the platform skirmishes the week before was all lost in another masterstroke by Reagan's managers. John Sears went before the convention rules committee with a proposal for a new rule, 16-C. This would have required President Ford to name his Vice–Presidential choice before the balloting began for the presidential nominee. Reagan had already named his choice, Senator Schweiker, several weeks earlier so it seemed he had nothing to lose. Actually, he had the nomination itself to lose and as soon as I learned of the move I knew he was finished. The delegates were not about to stampede to Reagan on an issue like this that broke with all past tradition.

I ran the roll call for the Ford forces the following night when the vote was taken on Rule 16–C. It was a strange sensation, I must admit. Although most of the people working with me in the Ford trailer command post were old friends from the 1964 Goldwater campaign, and from the 1968 Reagan effort, so were most of those laboring in the Reagan trailer right next door. I knew that several members of my *Hard Core* cadre were struggling against me in the Reagan trailer that night, including Andy Carter, Roger Allen Moore, and Frank Whetstone. I also knew that most of the Reagan people working the convention floor were also old friends, among them Senators Laxalt and Helms.

But there is no room for nostalgia when a roll call is being taken and I flashed the word to all the Ford people that we could not afford any backsliding among our delegates on 16–C. The vote would be interpreted as *the* great test of the President's strength and if he did not win this one he stood a good chance of losing the nomination the following night. But I was confident that we had an issue we could win on.

The Ford forces had given way on the Panama Canal treaty and all the other volatile issues which could have broken the President's political back in the platform fights. But a vote on a procedural issue that defied tradition made no sense at all to either the Ford delegates or the relative handful of uncommitted delegates, who ultimately would decide the outcome of the convention.

The roll call on 16–C began quite late Tuesday night. In my pre–vote count in the trailer I had Ford winning by 110 votes. There was only one weak spot I could see, and that was the Mississippi delegation, where Clarke Reed was again the chairman as he had been eight years earlier. I never really knew what Clarke Reed was going to do and I don't think he did either. He had started off strong for Reagan in 1976 but when Schweiker was announced as Reagan's Vice-Presidential choice, Reed came over to Ford, as did a number of other delegates, and not just in the South but in the West, Midwest and Northeast as well. However, this time I had Harry Dent on my side, and he undertook to keep Clarke Reed in line for Ford.

Nonetheless, Dick Cheney, Jim Baker and some of the other people working the Ford office at the hotel were exceedingly nervous about Reed, and they had reason to be. Reed had already voted for 16–C in the rules committee on Saturday and our Ford group within the Mississippi delegation had barely held the unit rule intact during a caucus Sunday night.

Before the vote on Tuesday night copies of a newspaper with a banner headline proclaiming that "Ford would write off the South" started circulating in the Kemper Arena where the convention was being held. The story was based on a comment by Rogers Morton that the Ford campaign would focus on the industrial states of the Northeast and Midwest, thereby, in effect, conceding the South to Jimmy Carter, who had been nominated by the Democrats a month earlier in New York.

I hit all the buttons in the trailer when I heard about this headline and told our floor people to insist, in as strong terms as they could, that this was *not* Gerald Ford's strategy. But it had already shaken the Mississippi delegation, which has become to our Republican conventions what New Hampshire is to the primaries, the state that gets all the media attention while the real action is taking place elsewhere. In this case, the decision was being made in the Florida delegation and several others which held fast for Ford.

When the roll call came to Mississippi, Clarke Reed passed. To his surprise he was booed by the convention, having failed the hopes of both the Reagan *and* Ford people. Florida had also passed, giving us a nervous moment in the Ford trailer. But when Florida's turn came again it cast the decisive vote against Rule 16–C and the Mississippi delegation's vote had become superfluous.

The final vote on 16–C was 1,180 against the rule and for Ford; 1,069 for the rule and for Reagan. I had missed the margin of victory by one vote. It was a respectable showing for Reagan, but not enough to change the course of the convention.

Although it was after midnight by the time this roll call was completed, another fight was shaping up on a platform provision calling for "morality in foreign policy." Nelson Rockefeller and several others interpreted the plank as a slap at Henry Kissinger, which indeed it was designed to be. Nelson tried to persuade Jerry Ford to go for a roll call on this plank, now that he knew he had the votes to win. But as I looked at our television monitors inside the trailer I could see that many of the delegates were already leaving the arena, obviously thinking the night's action was over and done. Immediately, I got word to our floor people to keep the delegates in place. If there was going to be another fight, we could not afford to lose it. Then I called the President's suite and urged him to let the foreign policy plank stand as it had come out of the platform committee.

"After all," I told him, "you certainly aren't *against* morality in foreign policy. None of us are. Let our friends have their plank."

The President agreed and the plank was hammered into the platform with the approval of *both* the Ford and Reagan forces on a voice vote. Jesse Helms and Tom Ellis had done their best to get a roll call on the foreign policy provision, but John Rhodes, who was serving as convention chairman, gavelled the plank into place when the "Yea's" drowned out the "Nay's."

By that time, everyone was so tired we just wanted to go back to our hotels and go to bed. But I called Roger Allen Moore in the Reagan trailer and suggested we "wrap the whole thing up" by getting Reagan to make the nomination unanimous for Gerald Ford the following night.

Roger laughed. "You know the Governor better than that," he said.

I had to smile. The truth was I *did* know Ronald Reagan better than that. He would never quit until the final roll was taken. But we were all so bone tired by then I didn't relish the thought of running another roll call the next evening.

Somewhat earlier in the convention I had played a part in squelching a last-minute boomlet for Jim Buckley. After Reagan had announced he would run with Senator Schweiker, Jesse Helms and several others felt, quite correctly, that Ford was going to win on the first ballot. Casting about for a way to halt Ford, Helms urged his Senate colleague, Jim Buckley, to run in order to get the convention into extra ballots. Congressman Philip Crane resigned from the Reagan team and on the Saturday before the convention formally opened he announced he was starting a Draft Buckley Committee.

A reporter told me about this move as I was walking through the lobby of the hotel in Kansas City. I confess I was surprised. When I got up to the floor where President Ford was staying Rogers Morton cornered me. "What the devil is Buckley doing?" he asked with some agitation. I said I didn't know but I would find out.

I reached Senator Buckley on the phone and asked why he was letting his name be used as a candidate. He explained that many of the delegates in the North Carolina delegation, and perhaps some others, wanted an alternative so they could "vote their conscience."

"I don't know whether they are voting their conscience," I said, "but I do know they will have to vote the way the laws and voters of North Carolina have instructed them to vote." As a result of the Reagan victory in the primary, the North Carolina delegation was committed to split its vote between Reagan and Ford on the first ballot.

There was another point I raised with Senator Buckley. He had promised Howard Baker to place the Tennessee Senator's name in nomination for temporary chairman of the convention but there was a rule that no one candidate could himself address the convention before the balloting.

"I think you owe it to Senator Baker to let him know you won't be nominating him," I said. I gave him Baker's phone number in Kansas City and suggested he call him.

Others have written that Jim Buckley pulled out because he was "ordered" to by Richard Rosenbaum, the New York state Republican chairman. I don't think either the people who wrote this, or Mr. Rosenbaum, knew Senator Buckley very well. He is a quiet, unassuming man, but he would not take "orders" from any politician. Jim Buckley got out, in my view, because he could not break his promise to Howard Baker, which he obviously did not know was in conflict with convention rules until I informed him of it.

The short–lived Buckley for President campaign did not, however, help him in his Senate race against Daniel Patrick Moynihan that fall in New York. The boomlet lasted only a few hours, but it gave some liberal Republicans an excuse to sabotage Buckley in the Senate campaign after Labor Day.

On Wednesday, the day of the balloting for the Presidential nominee, both the Ford and Reagan camps were busy making preparations. Ronald Reagan visited a number of delegations where he had been led to believe he might pry loose some votes. But the Ford people were holding firm. I had to admire the way Reagan refused to give up, just as he had refused to surrender to Nixon in Miami eight years before. But after the 16–C vote there was no doubt of the outcome.

I was told that Reagan had promised every delegation he visited that under no circumstances would he accept the Vice–Presidential nomination if Jerry Ford offered it to him. I wished later, and I think Ron did too, that he might have been just a little less adamant about this.

Before the balloting, I called in the Ford regional directors and went through my final "head count." No delegates had budged since the previous evening. I called President Ford and advised him to relax.

Some time later Senator Laxalt told me that Dick Schweiker had come to Reagan's suite that day and offered to withdraw as his Vice–Presidential candidate. "The Governor just looked at him and said, Senator, we came to Kansas City together and we're going to leave together," Paul Laxalt told me. We both agreed that there weren't many politicians who would have taken that position.

When the convention was called back into session Wednesday night the Reagan forces staged a demonstration that just wouldn't stop. After nearly an hour, Richard Cheney called me from President Ford's suite and asked if I didn't think it was time to call it off.

"These people are totally charged up, Dick," I said. "They've been looking toward this moment for eight years, since Miami in '68. I'd let them run it out. Besides, they'll be so tired they won't have a boo left in them when we get to the roll call."

Cheney agreed and the demonstration went on for another hour. Some of the Reagan people were so hoarse they couldn't speak for several days.

The balloting for the top prize went almost exactly the way the vote had gone on Rule 16–C the night before, only we didn't have to go back to Florida because practically nobody wanted to pass that night. The result was that President Ford was nominated by the time we got to West Virginia. The final vote was Ford, 1,187 and Reagan, 1,070. Reagan had picked up only one vote since the ballot on 16–C and Ford had gained seven. It was one of the closest nominating votes in any convention in this century.

After the balloting, the door to the Ford trailer burst open and in came Andy Carter and Frank Whetstone. They congratulated me on the Ford nomination. Frank said, "It was tough to lose, but if we had to be beaten, I'm glad we were beaten by you." I laughed and suggested we all go and have a drink some place.

Before I could leave the trailer, however, I got another call from the President's suite. They wanted to know if I thought Reagan would accept the Vice-Presidential nomination.

"I don't think he'll take it," I said. "But it would certainly be a good idea to ask him."

Unfortunately, no one did ask him and I still think Ford lost the election because of that. I'm not sure what the reasoning was, but I think it was probably that Ronald Reagan had been too persuasive in convincing people he did not want the nomination. This was the proper posture *before* the ballot for the Presidential nominee, and I believe Reagan meant it. But he had been so adamant he had convinced everyone in the Ford camp, including me, that he would not accept under any circumstances.

Although it was after midnight when the balloting was finished, President Ford rode over to the Alameda Plaza where the Reagans were staying. He had sent word he was coming, of course, but the Reagan people let it be known that the Governor did not want to entertain any offer for the Vice–Presidential spot. Reagan congratulated Ford and the President commended his rival on putting up such a good fight. Then Ford consulted with Reagan about Vice–Presidential possibilities and out of this conversation, I was later told, came the selection of Senator Robert Dole of Kansas as the President's running mate, although the final decision wasn't made by Ford until hours later. Dole was known as a conservative and had done a good job as chairman of the Republican National Committee several years earlier, keeping the committee divorced from Watergate and establishing generally good relations with the press.

The next day President Ford's staff called and asked me to invite Nancy and Ronald Reagan to share the platform with him and Betty Ford when he gave his acceptance address to the convention that night. I phoned the Reagan suite and conveyed the invitation to Michael Deaver. A little later Deaver called back and told me, "The Governor feels this is Jerry Ford's night."

The implication was that Ron did not want to divert attention from the President's candidacy, now that it had been approved by the convention. I relayed this to Ford and he was genuinely disappointed.

That night Gerald Ford gave, in his acceptance address, the best speech of his long career in politics. He threw out a challenge to the Democrat candidate, Jimmy Carter, to debate him on television, a gesture I felt was not only unnecessary but fraught with danger, but which the Republican convention obviously approved. Speaking directly to the millions of citizens watching on television, the President reminded them, "You are the people who make our system work. You are the people who make America what it is. It is from your ranks that I come, and on your side that I stand."

The crowd broke into prolonged cheers, and for once I did not have to give any signals from the trailer for a "spontaneous" demonstration. When the President finished his speech he turned to the gallery where Nancy and Ronald Reagan were seated and waved at them to come down, reinforcing his gesture with a spoken invitation over the public address system.

When the Reagans reached the platform, the crowd went wild. Shouting "Viva! Ole!", the clarion call of the California delegation, the whole convention joined in cheering the man who had been the leader and chief spokesman of the conservative cause in America for the decade past. They wouldn't shut up until Reagan agreed to speak, something I know he had not planned to do. But his brief, yet eloquent, plea for party unity just set the demonstration off again. Betty and Jerry Ford, Liddy and Bob Dole, Nancy and Ron Reagan waved happily at the delegates and gallery while a parade of other distinguished Republicans kept mounting the platform to take brief bows with the President on this, the final night of the 1976 national convention.

"Ronald Reagan could get a standing ovation in a graveyard,"

H.L. Richardson, a California state senator, was later quoted as saying.

The following day Reagan said goodbye to his campaign workers at his hotel. "We lost, but the cause, the cause goes on," he said. Then he dredged up a few lines from an ancient Scottish ballad:

I'll lay me down and bleed awhile;
Though I am wounded, I am not slain.
I shall rise and fight again.

"It's just one more battle in a long war and it's going to go on as long as we all live," Reagan told his people. "Nancy and I, we aren't going to go back and sit in a rocking chair and say, 'Well, that's all for us.' "

I don't think many people took Reagan's hint of another try for the Presidency very seriously at the time. He was already of an age when most men in our society are forced into mandatory retirement, a silly custom foisted upon us by the social security system and the insurance company actuaries. But I knew Ronald Reagan well enough to realize that he really would "rise and fight again."

18

Between Battles

Gerald Ford lost the Presidency to Jimmy Carter in 1976 by a narrow margin in both popular and electoral votes. The former Georgia governor received 40,276,040 individual votes and 297 electoral ballots to 38,532,630 and 241 for Ford. The shift of a few thousand votes in just two states, Ohio and Mississippi, would have given Ford a majority in the Electoral College.*

It is my judgment that President Ford lost the election in his first television debate with Governor Carter. His attempt to classify Poland as something less than a puppet of the Soviet Union was at best premature and made people think Jerry Ford was rather naive about foreign policy. Jimmy Carter took full advantage of this and came through in the debate as a more sophisticated and more hard-line anti-Communist. The next four years were to prove that Carter was not at all sophisticated about foreign policy and his open surprise at the Soviet invasion of Afghanistan betrayed a degree of naiveté that Gerald Ford at his

*The margin separating Carter and Ford in Ohio was 7,575 votes out of nearly 4,000,000 cast, meaning that a shift of 3,788 votes would have given Ford Ohio's 25 electoral ballots. In Mississippi, the margin for Carter was 11,861 and a shift of 5,982 votes there would have added seven more electoral votes for Ford and this would have given him 271 votes in the Electoral College to 265 for Carter.

most charitable could not have approached. Nonetheless, the damage was done during the election debates and Ford never recovered from this unforeseen setback.

Presidential debates are at once a refreshing democratic innovation and a very dangerous device. Although the American people have come to regard them as something to which the electorate is historically and traditionally entitled, the fact is they are a recent development. The first nationally televised debates were between John F. Kennedy and Richard Nixon in 1960 and there is no doubt Kennedy won his close election in the opening debate of that series. Lyndon Johnson was too smart to get into a TV debate with Barry Goldwater in 1964, and Nixon, the second time he ran for President in 1968, managed to escape debating Hubert Humphrey, who probably would have beaten him. There was no question of Nixon elevating George McGovern's candidacy with a debate in 1972, and Gerald Ford would have been well advised to have taken the same tack in 1976. But he obviously felt confident he could win the debates with his far less experienced opponent.

Debates are essentially theater, and they do not necessarily bring out the best in a candidate. The television viewers get a very superficial impression of the relative merits of the contenders and a person's capabilities and experience may actually prove to be a handicap. Moreover, by their very nature, debates favor the underdog. And Americans, throughout our history, have been susceptible to underdogs, not just in politics, but in virtually every other facet of our lives. This is both a strength and a weakness and it would be well if we began to recognize more clearly the dual nature of this aspect of our national character.

In spite of Jimmy Carter's victory, there was virtually no change in the composition in either house of the Congress. The Republicans had a net gain of one seat in the Senate and managed to hold their own in the House, where the majority continued to be heavily Democratic.

Nonetheless, conservatives generally fared quite well, particularly in Senate races. Orrin Hatch won in Utah; Malcolm Wallop in Wyoming, where he beat the redoubtable Gale McGee; Harrison (Jack) Schmitt in New Mexico; William V. Roth in Delaware; and Richard G. Lugar scored an impressive win over incumbent Senator Vance Hartke in Indiana. Harry F. Byrd, running as independent, but known to be one of the most consistently conservative members of the Senate, sank retired Admiral E.R. Zumwalt in Virginia by a wide margin. And S.I. Hayakawa, Ronald Reagan's close friend, ousted incumbent Senator John V. Tunney in California.

There were several other new faces in the Republican lineup in the Senate after the election, most prominently John Heinz of Pennsylvania and John Chaffee of Rhode Island, both of whom tended to vote with conservatives, at least on national defense issues. However, one honored Republican name was missing from the Senate roster in the 95th Congress. Robert Taft, Jr., was edged out of his Ohio Senate seat by millionaire Democrat Howard M. Metzenbaum.

All in all, there was a discernible advance for conservatives in the 1976 elections, the Carter victory notwithstanding. In fact, as I noted earlier, even Governor Carter was regarded as something of a conservative by the nation's voters, and he was careful not to dispel that impression during the campaign.

Moreover, Ronald Reagan, in campaigning that autumn for Gerald Ford, drew large crowds everywhere he went. Indeed, more enthusiasm was shown for Reagan in some cities than for President Ford, much to the embarrassment of local Republican officials.

The election results also made it embarrassingly apparent that if Ford had only had Reagan as his running mate he would almost certainly have won the election. With Reagan the Republicans would surely have captured more of the Southern states, but as it was Carter took the entire South with the sole exception of

Virginia. Further, I had the feeling Reagan would have drawn enough votes in Ohio to shift that state and its 25 electoral votes into the Ford column.

Yet I understand Jerry Ford was upset with Reagan after the election, believing Reagan had damaged his chances in the primary campaigns the previous spring. Personally I don't believe that was the case. Reagan had fought a good clean campaign against Ford and he had every right to contest the nomination, especially in view of the fact Ford had not been elected either Vice President or President. In addition, Ford had never been elected by a larger constituency than his home Congressional district in Michigan, whereas Reagan had twice been elected governor of the nation's most populous state, and his efforts had most assuredly helped put California's big bloc of electoral votes in the Ford column.

Further, Reagan was right in pointing out after the election that the Republicans were well on the way toward becoming the nucleus for the new conservative coalition that had been building in the country since 1964. With only about 20 percent of the registered voters in America, the GOP had attracted almost 50 percent of the national vote, which meant that it was bringing in substantial numbers of Democrats and Independents. Reagan underlined this in a comment he made after the election.

"Our party wasn't quite ready this year to rechristen itself and to offer a permanent home to conservative independents and Democrats," he stated. "But it did take a big first step when its rank–and–file hammered out a platform which recognizes that a majority of Americans, according to public opinion polls, today consider themselves conservatives."

Ronald Reagan didn't put himself forward as the leader of the effort to continue forging the conservative coalition. But he did say that the message he got out on the campaign trail that fall was that the Republican Party "should reshape itself into a clear–cut alternative to the Democrats." And he added, "I intend to be in the thick of that effort."

He didn't waste any time getting into the thick of it either. On January 15, 1977, while Washington was filling up with Democrats for Jimmy Carter's inauguration, Ron Reagan came to town and addressed a dinner of Victor Milione's Intercollegiate Studies Institute at the Mayflower Hotel. Reagan stressed on this occasion, as he did on many more occasions following, that conservatives were no longer a minority within the minority party. Indeed, he said, conservatives had been a majority in the Republican Party since before 1964 and we had the potential for making the GOP the new majority party by bringing conservative Democrat and Independent voters into a new coalition. This was a plan he and I had discussed many times over the years and the thesis upon which I had predicated the creation of our conservative cadres in the early 1960s. However, in this speech to the ISI, Ronald Reagan went me one better.

"The New Republican Party I envision will not, and cannot, be limited to the country club–Big Business image that for reasons both fair and unfair it is burdened with today," he said. "It is going to have room for the man and woman in the factories, for the farmer, for the cop on the beat, and for the millions of Americans who may never have thought of joining our party before. If we are to attract more working men and women, we must welcome them, not only as rank–and–file members but as leaders and as candidates."

"I refuse to believe that the Good Lord divided this world into Republicans, who defend basic values, and Democrats who win elections," Reagan continued. "We have to find the tough, bright young men and women who are tired of the cliches and the pomposity and the mind–numbing economic idiocy of the liberals in Washington."

He pointed out that only "a little more than a decade ago more than two thirds of all Americans believed the federal government could solve all our problems with its multitude of bureaus, agencies, and programs, without restricting our freedom or bankrupting the nation. . . .

"Today more than two thirds of our citizens are telling us, and each other, that social engineering by the federal government has failed. The Great Society is great only in power, in size, and in cost. Freedom has been diminished and we stand on the brink of economic ruin."

I doubt if even Governor Reagan knew that night how prophetic his words were. Before the next four years were finished, the United States would witness the worst inflation in its history, with interest rates reaching 20 percent and more, while millions of factory workers were thrown out of jobs and construction tradesmen swelled the ranks of the unemployed. The price of gold soared to all-time highs as the dollar plummeted in value on world currency markets.

Reagan's speech to the Intercollegiate Studies Institute also brought a reaffirmation of his deeply held belief in what the conservative movement really stands for in America.

"Concern for the people is at the very heart of conservatism," he said. "Concern for the dignity of all men—that those in need shall be helped to become independent, not lifetime recipients of a dole. Concern that those who labor and produce will not be robbed of the fruit of their toil or their liberty. Concern that we shall not forfeit the dream that gave birth to this nation—the dream that we can be as a shining city upon a hill. . . .

"Believing in that dream, I became a Republican and because of that dream, I am a conservative," Reagan declared, raising aloft the standard that millions of Americans would rally to in 1980.

Actually, millions of people had already followed Ronald Reagan's lead out of the Democrat Party in the years since he had dropped his Democratic registration to work in the U.S. Senate campaign in California of the distinguished Republican lawyer, Lloyd Wright, in 1960. Nowhere is this massive shift away from the Democrat Party better seen than in the Commonwealth of Virginia, once the most Democratic state in the Union, and today probably the most Republican, and certainly the most conservative.

The turnaround in Virginia was engineered by a group of people who worked closely with me in the early days of the conservative political resurgence. Among them were Richard D. Obershain, Caldwell Butler, J.D. Stetson Coleman, John Dalton, James M. Day, and Mills Godwin. There were others, too numerous to name, but these were the people I knew best. Jim Day, then a young lawyer, worked with me at the Draft Goldwater headquarters in Washington in 1963–64 and the late Stets Coleman was one of the most active and effective fund raisers we had then, and put up substantial sums himself as well.

Jim Day became the Republican chairman of Arlington County, just across the Potomac from Washington, and with the aid of Stets Coleman, James Olmstead, and a nucleus of other conservatives they transformed this populous county from a Democratic fortress into a Republican stronghold. By dint of hard work and intelligent planning Jim Day and his friends got control of the County Board for the Republicans and by 1969 they had helped elect Republicans to all of Arlington County's four seats in the Virginia House of Delegates as well as the state Senate seat.

Meanwhile, other counties in Virginia were discovering that it no longer was considered heretical to vote Republican. In 1969 Lynwood Holton was elected as the first Republican Governor in this century, and he was succeeded by Mills Godwin in 1973 and John Dalton in 1977. (Virginia permits only one four–year term for its governors.)

The Republican Party won a lot of new friends in Virginia in 1968 when it supported conservative Senator Harry Byrd for reelection. The Senator, and his famous father before him, had been powers in the Democratic Party for nearly a half century. The senior Harry Byrd, brother of the famed Polar explorer

Admiral Richard E. Byrd, had fought a rear–guard battle against federal spending all during the Roosevelt–Truman years and on into the Kennedy Administration. It is not too much to say that the Byrds were, and are, the most highly respected political family in Virginia. Although Harry Byrd, Jr., has not, as of this writing, seen fit to register as a Republican, he did divorce himself from the Democrat Party and continued to win as an Independent. By supporting him, the Republican Party picked up a good deal of support itself.

After the 1980 presidential campaign I was visiting one day with Governor John Dalton of Virginia and I congratulated him on helping bring his state into the Republican fold. "Clif, you just don't know the half of it," Governor Dalton said. "Virginia *is* a Republican state now."

In 1980, nine out of ten of Virginia's Congressional seats went to Republicans, and the other seat, held by Dan Daniel of Danville, was unopposed because Dan is considered too conservative to field a Republican against him. The late Richard Obershain, who played such a major role in Virginia's Republican Reformation and served as GOP state chairman, was killed in a plane crash after winning nomination for the U.S. Senate in 1978. But even this tragedy failed to slow the Republican tide that has swept Virginia. John Warner, former Secretary of the Navy, was nominated and elected in Dick Obershain's place and he has turned out to be one of the most conservative members of the United States Senate when it comes to national defense measures.

In 1978, the year John Warner was elected to the Senate, no less than 9,600 delegates attended the Republican state convention in Richmond, making it, according to Jim Day, "the largest political convention in the history of the United States." By contrast, the Democrats were lucky to turn out 1,000 for their state convention the same year.

Similar, if less complete, GOP Reformations have taken place in Florida, Oklahoma, North Carolina, Texas and other states which were traditionally Democratic territory. Nor is the swing away from the Democratic Party limited to the Sun Belt. It can be seen in Ohio, Pennsylvania, New York and other Northern industrial states where the Democrats had dominated since the days of Franklin Roosevelt.

Because of business commitments, I did not participate very actively in the 1978 election races. However, my old friend, former Senator William Brock of Tennessee, had been named chairman of the Republican National Committee after the 1976 election and he invited me to serve on the Committee's advisory board.

The 1978 elections proved to be another step forward for the conservative movement. This was especially apparent in the U.S. Senate races, as a whole squadron of new Republican Senators came flying into Washington. Among them were William L. Armstrong of Colorado; Roger W. Jepson of Iowa, who defeated one of the most liberal Democrats in the Senate, Dick Clark; Ted Cochran of Mississippi; Gordon J. Humphrey of New Hampshire; Ted Stevens of Alaska; and Alan Simpson of Wyoming.

Moreover, almost all of the conservatives running for reelection to the Senate emerged victorious, including Strom Thurmond of South Carolina and John Tower of Texas, two of the men who have come to symbolize the conservative surge in America.

For some reason, Republicans did not do as well as expected in the 1978 House races, although we did pick up fifteen more seats. And the GOP staged a good comeback in the gubernatorial races, electing a number of promising future leaders of the party, including James R. Thompson in Illinois; Robert D. Ray in Iowa; William G. Milliken in Michigan; Albert H. Quie in Minnesota; my old friend Charles Thone in Nebraska; another old friend, Robert List in Nevada; William Janklaw in South Dakota; Lamar Alexander in Tennessee; William P. Clements, Jr. in Texas; Richard A. Snelling in Vermont; and Lee Dreyfus in Wisconsin. In addition, James A. Rhodes won in Ohio, Richard Thornburg in Pennsylvania, and Victor Atiyeh in Oregon. Not all of these governors were conservative. Indeed, several, like Dick Thornburg and Al Quie, were liberals. But again, they were almost all more conservative than their Democratic opponents.

Following the 1978 election I went to the Mayo Clinic in Rochester, Minnesota, for a medical checkup. I didn't think there was anything wrong with me but it was time for a thorough examination just to make sure. While at Mayo I suffered a massive heart attack and was immediately placed in an oxygen tent.

After a few days I was let out of the tent but was kept in intensive care and the nurses refused to let any phone calls come through unless my wife was there to take them, as she almost always was. One day Bunny had gone out for a brief spell and she turned off the phone in my room before she left. A nurse came in to give me a pill and told me someone had called while I was asleep. I asked who it was.

"It was a governor or something," the nurse said.

"It wouldn't have been Ronald Reagan?" I smiled.

"Reagan? Yes. That sounds like the name. I told him he wasn't supposed to be calling you but he said he'd call back to find out how you are doing."

I thought afterward that the reaction of this nurse was somehow typically American. She was so busy doing her job—and doing it very capably, I should add—that she was not at all impressed by receiving a call from a former governor, who just happened to have been twice a Presidential candidate and would be elected President of the United States in less than two years. I know Ronald Reagan would agree with me that my nurse is the kind of person who keeps this country going, paying more attention to her job than to politics, which is the way it should be, though I'm grateful for the people who get involved in politics, too.

The next day Ronald Reagan called again and this time he somehow got through, although there was still supposed to be security on my phone. His was the only non–family call that I received while in intensive care. He wished me a speedy recovery and said that he and Nancy were praying for me.

"My brother Neil had a bad heart attack some years ago, but now he can play eighteen holes of golf and I'm sure you'll be doing the same," Ron assured me. Then he put Nancy on for a minute and she seconded her husband's wishes for my recovery.

Although I didn't tell anyone at the time, I made a little private vow that day: If I had my health back in 1980, I would do what I could to help elect Ronald Reagan to the Presidency of the United States, even if I had to do it as a precinct worker in my town, Greenwich, Connecticut.

19

Comeback

In September 1979 I spoke before a group of political scientists at the University of California's Long Beach campus, and said that the 1980 presidential nomination and election would be Ronald Reagan's to lose. There was a high degree of skepticism among members of the audience which became apparent during the question–and–answer period. But I stuck to my guns, not out of stubbornness, but because that was the way I read the coming campaign.

Reagan had started early enough this time and he had certain advantages which he had lacked in his previous attempts. For one thing, it appeared as though his chief opponent for the Republican nomination would be George Bush, a liberal. This meant that the conservatives probably would unite behind Reagan. Although John Connally was receiving a lot of support from the business community, Reagan had the rank–and–file conservatives behind him and, in terms of delegates and votes, that was what counted.

Actually, I think Reagan started running the day after Jimmy Carter's election, whether he admitted it to himself or not. He stepped up his schedule of speaking engagements and he had two other pretty good pulpits from which to preach his conservative message—his radio program and his newspaper column. He also organized his Citizens for the Republic as a follow-up to the 1976 campaign's Citizens for Reagan. In short, it was apparent that Reagan was planning a comeback.

However, at a quite early stage Reagan became angry with the Republican National Committee when it cancelled a campaign to oppose the Panama Canal Treaties after raising a substantial sum of money with the mass mailing of a letter Reagan had signed calling for a fight against the treaties.

Senator Paul Laxalt was representing Reagan's interests in Washington between the 1976 and 1980 elections and he regarded Jerry Ford as the main reason for the Republican National Committee's differences with Reagan. Ford threw himself actively into the battle for Senate ratification of the Canal treaties, even meeting with other treaty supporters at the Georgetown home of Averell Harriman, the mentor of the most liberal wing of the Democratic Party.

Like Reagan, most conservatives were strongly opposed to giving up American authority over the Panama Canal. It was a very emotional issue, and although the treaties transferring jurisdiction of the Canal Zone to the government of Panama were eventually approved by the Senate, President Carter and most of the Senators who supported him on the treaties suffered considerable political damage. In fact, Howard Baker, the majority leader of the Senate, severely hurt his chances for the 1980 Republican Presidential nomination by voting for the Canal treaties.

Later, Reagan took an active part in the fight against Salt II, the Strategic Arms Limitation Treaty. This agreement with the Soviet Union had originally been concocted by Kissinger during the Ford Administration but was reinforced and pushed hard by President Carter, although the wind went out of Salt's sails after the Soviet invasion of Afghanistan in December 1979.

Salt II, which conservatives said would have given the Russians an irretrievable advantage over the United States in strategic nuclear weapons, was stopped dead in its tracks even before the Afghanistan incursion. The Coalition for Peace through Strength, organized by John Fisher and the American Security Council, became one of the largest caucus groups on Capitol Hill, numbering some 200 members of the House and Senate in its camp. Working with a number of independent associations and groups interested in national security, the Congressional Coalition killed Salt in the face of an all–out press campaign by the Carter Administration for its ratification by the Senate. Ronald Reagan joined Barry Goldwater, John Tower, Strom Thurmond and other Republican leaders in the fight against Salt II, and he helped sound the alarm nationwide on the dangers of this treaty.

The risky moves by the Carter Administration on foreign and defense policy no doubt did much to confirm Reagan's decision to run for President again. To get the Republican nomination, however, he had to go into the convention with the conservatives solidly behind him and not split between him and other candidates as they had been in 1968 and in 1976.

Since Reagan would be 69 in 1980, the age issue seemed to act against him, although his relatively youthful appearance and obvious good health helped offset this handicap. Nonetheless, he found Republicans looking over a field of younger potential candidates, including Senator Baker, the minority leader of the U.S. Senate; Senator Dole, the 1976 vice-presidential nominee; Congressman Philip Crane of Illinois, who had a large following among conservatives; and Congressman Jack Kemp of New York. Moreover, John Connally, who was closer to Reagan's age, was siphoning off some financial support, though Reagan had never had the substantial help from big business that Connally had.

In the summer of 1978 Reagan met in Washington with members of the Kingston Group, a committee of what the press called

"New Right" leaders, although both Ronald Reagan and I could identify some of our old friends from the Goldwater campaign among them. I was told later Reagan had promised this group that John Sears would not be his campaign manager in 1980. Several of Reagan's close friends sounded me out on running his next campaign but I made it clear that I had made a conscious decision before 1976 that I would never again actively manage a presidential nominating or election campaign. "I've paid my dues," I told them. "But I'm available for consultation if Ron needs me." In November 1978 my heart attack underlined my decision and convinced my friends that I really meant it.

Meanwhile, Philip Crane formally announced his candidacy for President in August 1978, thereby becoming the first Republican to toss his hat in the 1980 ring. Congressman Crane had been a strong Reagan supporter in both 1968 and 1976 but at this time no one could be sure Reagan would run again and, even if he did, Crane felt it would be well for the conservatives to have a backup candidate.

Crane had been chairman of the American Conservative Union and he was a very articulate spokesman for conservative causes. He also had strong support from the "New Right" and Richard A. Viguerie, the direct mail czar, agreed to handle Crane's fund–raising mail campaign.

Although Crane obviously had quite substantial support, I did not think he could go the distance against Reagan. For one thing, Ronald Reagan had built a very large national constituency in his two previous campaigns for the GOP nomination, and in addition he had literally hundreds of Republican officials across the country indebted to him because of his successful fund–raising appearances in their behalf or in their communities.

This broad base of Reagan support was obvious when my friend Paul Laxalt announced the Reagan for President Committee in the Eisenhower Lounge of Washington's Capitol Hill Club on

March 5, 1979. Standing behind Senator Laxalt were about fifteen of his Senate and House colleagues and the list of more than 300 Reagan supporters he released was very impressive. In fact, it included several members of Gerald Ford's cabinet, among them former Secretary of the Treasury William Simon; former Secretary of Health, Education and Welfare Caspar Weinberger; and former Secretary of the Interior Stanley Hathaway.

Incredibly, however, Paul Laxalt announced that John Sears would be Executive Vice-Chairman of the Reagan for President Committee and, although Paul was chairman, this meant that John would be the working campaign manager. I felt much better about the rest of the working group, which included Michael Deaver, Edwin Meese, Lyn Nofziger, Charles Black, Jim Lake and Martin Anderson. Most of them were old friends of mine and I knew they were professionals. But I was frankly worried about Sears, who, in my opinion, had cost Reagan the 1976 nomination with his Schweiker ploy, the futile fight over Rule 16–C at the convention, and other actions.

Although Reagan had not himself formally announced for the Presidency, the unveiling of the Laxalt committee was the public signal that he would definitely run. Within a few months after that there was a whole platoon of announced Republican candidates, yet still not nearly as many as the regiment of Democrats who had made the bold try in '76. The Republicans openly seeking the nomination for 1980 included, in addition to Reagan, Connally and Crane, George Bush, Howard Baker, Bob Dole, and John Anderson. There were also some "favorite sons" among the governors, hoping lightning might strike when the convention rolled around.

In the early fall of 1980 I got a note from Ronald Reagan inviting me to attend the formal opening of his campaign at a dinner at the Hilton Hotel in New York on November 13. It was a fundraiser for his campaign, but Ron knew I must have had heavy medical expenses since my heart attack, which also prevented me from conducting my business for over a year, and it was typical of him to ask me to come as his personal guest so I would not have to make the heavy contribution for the dinner.

I met a lot of members of our original conservative cadre at this dinner and I could see that, for the first time since 1964, we were going to be together going into 1980. It was significant that Governor Reagan had selected New York as his official launching site for his comeback campaign. It showed he intended to make a strenuous effort to capture the Northeastern states in both the primary and general election campaigns. And his speech that evening reflected his concern for the increasing problems faced by the industrial sector of the country.

"The great productivity of our industry is surpassed by virtually all the major nations who compete with us for world markets, and our currency is no longer the stable measure of value it once was," he told us.

With the dollar diving to new lows on world currency markets this audience knew that Reagan wasn't just indulging in campaign rhetoric. The crisis he and our whole conservative movement had been predicting for more than a decade was upon us in 1979. Moreover, Reagan showed that night he understood, and probably better than most of the economists in Wall Street, that the value of any currency is merely a reflection of the confidence people have in their government and the confidence other nations place in the strength and stability of that government.

"The confidence we have lost is confidence in our government's policies," he emphasized. "Our unease can almost be called bewilderment at how our defense strength has deteriorated."

But Reagan also made it clear that he was not going to tailor his appeal to suit the sophisticates of Park Avenue or Wall Street, as so many other presidential candidates have done in the past. "I believe this nation hungers for a spiritual revival," he declared, "hungers to once again see honor placed above political expediency; to see government once again the protector of our liberties, not the distributor of gifts and privilege. Government should uphold and not undermine those institutions which are custodians of the very values upon which civilization is founded—religion, education, and, above all, the family."

The chairman of this dinner, William J. Casey, and his wife Sophia had also invited me soon after I'd received the note from Ronald Reagan. Bill had been a law partner of the late Leonard Hall, another close friend of mine, and we had been getting together for lunch once or twice a month to talk politics. Casey was on the Reagan for President Committee but I don't think either of us could foresee then that he would wind up as Reagan's campaign director.

The first tentative test of Reagan's strength came within a few days after the New York kick–off for his campaign. There was a straw vote in the Florida Republican Party to make a preliminary determination of the party's presidential preference in that state and Reagan won hands down over John Connally with George Bush a distant third.

However, through my many friends in the Reagan committee I kept hearing about the dissensions among members of the candidate's staff. After Thanksgiving, the staff feuding broke into the open when Michael Deaver resigned. It seems there had been a meeting at the Reagan home on Pacific Palisades above Los Angeles and John Sears deliberately provoked a confrontation, giving Reagan the uncomfortable choice of accepting his resignation, along with that of Charlie Black and Jim Lake, who were also present, or firing Deaver. The press later reported that Mike Deaver, who had been with Reagan since his Sacramento days, tendered his resignation rather than see the entire team broken up on the eve of the primary campaigns. *Newsday* later quoted Reagan as telling Sears and the others after Deaver had left: "You were not big enough to give in. Mike was the only guy big enough to walk away."

I suspect this was the real beginning of the end for John Sears' association with Ronald Reagan. But Ron is not a man to do things precipitously and he bided his time until the day of the New Hampshire primary before firing Sears. I was informed that Sears was in trouble just after the Iowa caucuses on January 21, 1980, so I sensed well beforehand that Sears would be going. I think it would have happened even if Reagan had won in Iowa but his loss there certainly made it easier for him to resist the pleas of the pragmatists who wanted Sears to stay.

There was absolutely no reason for Reagan to lose the Iowa caucuses. The sentiment of the state was decidedly conservative, as recently demonstrated by the 1978 Senate victory of Roger Jepson and the gubernatorial win of Robert D. Ray. But the Sears team had the idea they had to "protect" Reagan from the people and the press and they scheduled him into Iowa for only a few brief visits. Indeed, Reagan was more than conspicuous by his absence at the nationally televised debate arranged by the *Des Moines Register & Tribune*. All the other Republican candidates were there—George Bush, Howard Baker, John Connally, Phil Crane and Bob Dole—but not Ronald Reagan. It was obvious to me, and I'm sure to most other people, that Reagan's team just didn't have enough confidence in him to let him take on his opponents in open debate. The irony was that Reagan was easily the best speaker and debater of the bunch and the campaign team's low estimate of his talents only proved their own lack of political perception.

The result of Reagan's absence was that George Bush, who had campaigned exhaustively in Iowa, narrowly won the state caucus and gave the all–but–defunct liberal wing of the Republican Party their first real glimmer of hope in sixteen years. The media built up the Bush victory to a point where many newspaper readers and television viewers must have thought George had the nomination in the bag. This notion was undoubtedly reinforced by John Sears, who had made himself, in effect, Ronald Reagan's mouth-piece. Instead of seeing the candidate on TV, making his own statements on the issues, television audiences were constantly treated to John Sears delivering his latest pragmatic prognosis of the campaign.

I cautioned Bill Casey and others in the Reagan committee that unless Reagan rectified the situation with an impressive victory in New Hampshire he could be in trouble in his third drive for the nomination. I urged them to "take the wraps off Reagan" and let him go out and face the people. Fortunately, the opportunity for letting him face the voters nationwide soon pre-sented itself. It turned out to be quite an event.

Reagan and Bush had agreed to debate at the high school in Nashua, New Hampshire, toward the end of the primary campaign in that state. For some reason, Bush refused to split the cost of the debate and Gerald Carmen, a former Republican state chair-man who was directing Reagan's volunteers in New Hampshire, very wisely decided that the Reagan committee should absorb the entire cost, which was $3,500. The other candidates, meanwhile, were demanding that they be included in the debate and Reagan, having picked up the tab, invited them to participate.

The night of the debate all the candidates except John Connally, who was campaigning in South Carolina, showed up at the Nashua high school. But George Bush sulked in one class room while Reagan and the others waited in another to be called on stage. Bush and his campaign director, Jim Baker, kept insisting on the one–on–one debate with Reagan and refused to let the others take part. After a considerable delay, Bush finally came out and sat in one of the two chairs on the stage while Reagan came on, followed by Baker, Dole, Crane and Anderson, who were forced to stand behind him.

The local newspaper had been the original sponsor of the debate and its editor was acting as moderator. But he overstepped his authority when he ordered the sound man to turn off Ronald Reagan's microphone as the Governor tried to explain to the audience just what had happened. Now, Ronald Reagan is a mild–mannered man but he, like any honorable person, does have limits as to what he will take. When the editor tried to silence him, he shouted into the mike, "I'm paying for this microphone!" and the crowd, booing the editor's boorishness a moment before, now broke into loud cheers. In that one instant, Reagan had won the debate with an instinctive reaction of the kind that has become too rare in politics and, in fact, in American life.

However, neither Bush nor the editor of the Nashua paper seemed to get the message. They still refused to let the other candidates participate and the audience was treated to the spectacle of two United States Senators and two Congressmen forced to leave the stage.

Reagan won the debate easily and the Bush boom, so enthusiastically promoted by the media since the Iowa caucuses, was considerably deflated. This was soon confirmed by the results of the New Hampshire primary. Reagan walked off with more than 50 per cent of the vote, no small feat in such a crowded field. Bush received 22 per cent; Baker, 13 per cent; Anderson 10 per cent; and Connally, Crane and Dole divided the remainder.

I was informed on the day of the New Hampshire primary that Reagan had fired John Sears, along with Charlie Black and Jim Lake, and named Bill Casey as his campaign manager. He took this action before the election returns were reported but, as I mentioned, I had known it was coming for weeks.

Apparently Sears had tried to get Reagan to fire Ed Meese and people thought this was the straw that finally broke the camel's back. But by this time I think Reagan knew he could not continue with Sears for a whole lot of reasons, and the attempt to sabotage Meese was just one. Another was the perilous condition of the Reagan campaign's finances. Sears and his crew had been spending money hand over fist without any recognition that the new election law restrictions on campaign contributions would soon leave the Reagan campaign with no funds.

Bill Casey's main task was to cut back drastically on the spending in order to save enough money to get the campaign all the way to the convention in July. It was no easy job, but Bill did it with great efficiency and effectiveness and, in so doing, kept the Reagan bandwagon rolling in high gear all the way to Detroit.

The day before the New Hampshire primary Bill Casey called and told me he was going to be announced as Reagan's campaign director. We had discussed this more than a month earlier after the Iowa caucuses when Reagan had first sounded out Casey about managing the campaign. He asked me at the time what I thought. I reminded Bill that he and I had agreed some time ago that we would spend the rest of our lives doing only what we most wanted to do in politics. "Do what you want to do on this one," I told him, knowing full well what his decision would be.

Casey had told me he was scheduled to meet with Reagan's regional political directors right after New Hampshire. The RPD's numbered mostly people from our early conservative cadres and from my *Hard Core* group, including Andy Carter and Frank Whetstone. Andy and Frank called me a little later to size up the new campaign manager. I told them frankly that "Bill Casey has been in politics a lot longer than any of us and he knows an awful lot about the political scene." In my opinion, I said, "Ronald Reagan couldn't have a better manager. Bill will do what needs to be done."

A day or two later Bill Casey called me after his meeting with the Reagan regional directors. "Thanks for clearing me with your guys," he said. I laughed and congratulated him on passing muster with this segment of the cadre. Bill asked me to ride down to Washington with him on a plane the following day and we arranged to meet at La Guardia Airport. On the way to Washington, he asked me to join the Reagan campaign to help him out.

"Ron wants you back," he said. I reminded Bill that I was still under doctor's orders to look after my heart and that I could not take on any operational responsibilities. He promised that I would not have to become involved in operations, only strategy. On that basis, I agreed to come into the campaign. Actually, wild horses probably couldn't have kept me out once I knew both Ronald Reagan and Bill Casey wanted me in. Having come this far with the conservative movement in America I wanted to be there for this, the most crucial and clear–cut test we had faced since the movement began.

20

Roundup

There were a number of hurdles after New Hampshire that Ronald Reagan had to scale before he could claim the 1980 Republican Presidential nomination. But he took them all in good stride and the few setbacks he encountered along the way proved to be transitory.

The first obstacle he was confronted with, following his stunning victory in New Hampshire, was Gerald Ford. The very next Sunday *The New York Times* carried an interview with the former President in which he issued an open invitation to the Republican Party to draft him.

Jerry Ford's thesis, and old hangup with many Republicans, was that "a very conservative Republican can't win in a national election" and Ronald Reagan was "perceived as a most conservative Republican."

Ford gave the interview to the *Times* at his home in Rancho Mirage near Palm Springs, California. For the next few days there was a steady stream of pilgrims to Rancho Mirage, all urging Ford to run for "the good of the party." One of the first, not surprisingly, was John Sears, fresh from receiving his discharge papers from Ronald Reagan and now full of advice for Jerry Ford. He was followed by Henry Kissinger, who wanted Ford to come out swinging on foreign policy, an area where he and Ford thought Reagan was vulnerable. Meanwhile, a Draft Ford Committee surfaced and its chairman was an old mutual friend of Ronald Reagan's and mine, Tom Reed. However, the "draft" didn't get very far.

On March 8, 1980 Reagan scored another impressive primary win, this time in South Carolina. He soundly defeated John Connally, who had had the backing of that state's long–time political hero, Strom Thurmond. Reagan chalked up 54 percent of the vote in this primary to 30 percent for Connally and only 15 percent for George Bush. Connally decided to pull out of the race entirely because of this defeat. He had spent some $10 million in quest of the nomination and had only one delegate to show for it. He retired in good grace, calling Reagan "the champ" and indicating he would support him wholeheartedly in the general election, which he did.

Three days later, Reagan took the primaries in Florida, Georgia and Alabama, racking up a healthy 57 percent of the vote in Florida, while Bush was lucky to get a little more than half that and John Anderson was left with less than 10 percent. I marked this as Reagan's red letter day on my calendar—the day he put the nomination in his pocket, although he still had the Ford hurdle and a few others to surmount.

Jerry Ford came to Washington in the middle of March to speak at a Republican fundraiser. He got a rousing reception, but when he took soundings among his former colleagues on Capitol Hill Jerry was surprised to find there was very little support for him in the Congress. Senator Laxalt had done a good job for Reagan on the Senate side, aided by Senators Helms, Hatch and some others; Congressman Thomas Evans of Delaware, a former Co-Chairman of the Republican National Committee, had done an equally good job on the House side, as had Jack Kemp of New York and a number of the conservative Congressmen.

At the dinner where Jerry Ford spoke I had a chance to talk with Tom Reed, Dick Cheney, Jack Marsh and Stu Spencer, all of whom were working for Ford. I told them Ford just did not have the votes and he was going to be embarrassed if he persisted.

Back at Rancho Mirage, Ford called a meeting of his people on March 15, discussed the situation further, and then announced that he was not a candidate. "I will not become a candidate," he said. "I will support the nominee of my party with all the energy I have. America is in deep, deep trouble and needs the help of all of us."

It was a wise decision on the former President's part. He could see that Republican sentiment was running strong for Reagan and he would have divided the party deeply if he had become an active candidate. It was the kind of decision, however, that I would have expected of Jerry Ford. I believe he has always put the party and the country before personal considerations and, though I haven't agreed with his positions on some issues, I feel he has been a good conservative as well as a good Republican.

The same day Ford held his meeting in California Bob Dole announced he was ending his candidacy, too. That left Reagan, Bush, Crane and Anderson in the race. All four were entered in the Illinois primary on March 18 and Reagan won this, his home state, with 48 percent of the vote, against 37 percent for Anderson and only 11 percent for Bush and 2 percent for Crane, who was tacitly supporting Reagan.

The Illinois campaign was the occasion for another television debate in which Reagan came off very well. John Anderson had said he would rather have Senator Edward Kennedy, an announced Democratic candidate, as President than Ronald Reagan. Reagan, with an obvious twinkle in his eye, asked Anderson: "John, would you really find Teddy Kennedy preferable to me?" John Anderson huffed and puffed as the audience laughed uproariously. Then Phil Crane pulled a letter out of his pocket which Anderson had signed in a fundraising mailer for four of the most liberal

Democrats in the Senate—George McGovern of South Dakota, John Culver of Iowa, Birch Bayh of Indiana and Frank Church of Idaho.

Phil Crane pretty well proved with this action that John Anderson had already pushed himself out of the Republican Party and a month later John made it official that he was ending his candidacy as a Republican but would run as an independent. Significantly, all four of the Democrats Anderson signed the letter for were beaten in their Senate races in November. And John Anderson received less than seven percent of the total votes cast in the Presidential election.

An old political associate of mine, Don Totten, ran the Reagan campaign in Illinois and did an excellent job. In fact, by this time the whole Reagan effort was clicking along with great efficiency, thanks to our candidate's leadership and to Bill Casey's management.

On March 25, Reagan took almost all of New York state's big bloc of convention delegates in a contest in which George Clark, now the state Republican chairman, worked hard to rally New York behind Reagan. Many people in the Reagan camp were amazed at this victory, but it proved what I have contended for a long time, namely that New York state is much more conservative than people think it is. Even New York City is growing more conservative as the fallacies of the liberal theories become more and more apparent to the voters there.

On the day Reagan took New York, George Bush captured Connecticut, his home state. But Reagan got more than a third of the vote in the three–way race with Bush and Anderson, and came in a very respectable second. Two weeks later Bush also won in Pennsylvania, where he received 53 percent of the total vote to 46 percent for Reagan. Bush had all–out support from the Republican state administration in Pennsylvania, which is headed by one of the party's most liberal governors, Richard Thornburg. This proved to be George's highwater mark, although he also won

the Michigan primary with the backing of another liberal Republican governor, William Milliken. In addition, Bush turned in a
quite respectable showing in Texas, his adopted state, although
Reagan walked off with a majority of the votes and most of the
delegates.

On the night of the Michigan primary, May 20, the news
media announced that Ronald Reagan appeared to have enough
votes to give him a majority of the delegates in the Republican
convention, although there were still several big primaries to
go—California, Ohio, and New Jersey. On May 26 George Bush
faced up to the reality of Reagan's triumph and formally withdrew
from the race at a press conference in Houston. Bush went out
with a very sportsmanlike gesture, requesting all the delegates
pledged to him to switch their votes to Governor Reagan at the
convention. He had put up a good campaign, much better than
many political pundits had thought he would in the early stages.

There were a number of issues which helped Ronald Reagan's
successful campaign for the Republican nomination in 1980. I
have already touched on some of these, including growing public
dissatisfaction with our existing foreign and defense policies, and
deepening concern about inflation and the future of the economy. These all contributed to the darkening mood of the nation as
people became more and more worried about the future of the
country. This concern was not limited to conservatives, as it
primarily had been in the past. It now extended to all Americans
and even the liberals could see that the country could not continue on the uncertain course we had been following, although
many liberals still were stubbornly clinging to their disproven
theories.

In 1980, moreover, there were several other elements that
aided Ronald Reagan and the conservative cause he represented.
There was a growing concern for the obvious moral decline of our
society and this was manifested in a number of ways, most
apparently in the success of the so-called "single interest groups,"

particularly those which had mobilized against legal and federally–funded abortions and the Equal Rights Amendment.

The Right–to–Life and anti–ERA groups had been in existence for some time, but they attracted more adherents in 1980 and were much better organized. Only four years earlier ERA had seemed to be an issue which no national politician dared oppose, and President Carter was still espousing it in 1980. But the defeats and rollbacks of ERA in a succession of state legislatures showed that the grassroots were up in arms against it, although the Congress failed to heed that message when it extended the ratification period for this constitutional amendment in an unprecedented and, constitutionally, very questionable action.

Ronald Reagan's strong opposition to both legalized abortion and the Equal Rights Amendment won him dedicated support from people across the land. His firm stand with the Right–to–Life people earned him support not only among Roman Catholics, but among the many other Christian groups who had coalesced with the Catholics into the "Moral Majority."

There has been a good deal of criticism in the press of the "Moral Majority" and the single–issue groups. However, these groups have every right to express their views and work within the political process to change laws they find abhorrent or which go against their religious beliefs. They are not throwing bombs or advocating violent overthrow of the government as many members of the New Left (and the Old) did not too long ago. Moreover, their critics seem to have forgotten that the Pilgrims first came to America not only to escape religious persecution in Britain, but to establish a healthier moral climate to raise their families in the New World than they had found in Holland, where they first had settled.

Ronald Reagan, speaking before a Religious Roundtable conference in Dallas in 1980, told the Moral Majority groups assembled there that he did not expect their endorsement, because he knew the conference could not issue explicit political endorsements of any candidate. "But," he said, "I want you to know that I endorse you and what you are trying to do."

I believe more and more people in America feel the same way and these groups will continue to be a political force to be reckoned with, even though their primary thrust is religious and moral. Nonetheless, if they are to achieve their maximum potential in the political arena, they will have to take a more charitable view of their fellow citizens, many of whom resent being publicly, and sometimes too harshly, judged by other human beings. After all, the Bible is quite clear that only God will be our final judge.

Man is forced to make judgments about other people every day, of course, but we should be careful about reading others out of the human race because they do not measure up to our moral standards. We do not have to associate with them or approve of their conduct, but if we insist on absolute perfection we will soon be overwhelmingly outvoted because perfection is very rare indeed in this world.

The thought occurs to me that this same "sermon" might also apply to some elements of the press, even those who are so bent on "exposing" and condemning the Moral Majority.

After the primaries ended in June 1980 Bill Timmons and I flew to Los Angeles for a meeting with Ronald Reagan and the regional political directors to make plans for the convention, then only a month away. Timmons was appointed convention director for Reagan and I was named director of political operations. Paul Laxalt, as the Reagan for President Committee's National Chairman, was in overall command with Bill Casey, Reagan's campaign manager. Lyn Nofziger was in charge of the press operation; Peter Hannaford of research and writing; Chuck Tyson was director of convention operations; Keith Bulen was director of arrangements; and Peter Dailey of promotion and advertising.

The candidate's personal staff was headed by Ed Meese with

Mike Deaver and Dick Wirthlin as senior advisors and Ed Gray as press secretary.

As director of political operations I was to have charge of the communications trailer and the delegate roundup at the convention. I named Frank Whetstone as my deputy and Paul Manafort as trailer manager; Roger Allan Moore was my legal parliamentarian and Loren Smith worked with him. Congressman Bob Michel was our floor leader, assisted by Paul Russo and Ralph Vinovich. Keith Bulen looked after logistics for the trailer and Fred Biebel overseered our delegates' information desk.

While Timmons and I were in Los Angeles there was a strong move mounted to get rid of his old boss, Bill Brock, as Republican National Chairman. I had known Brock since our Draft Goldwater days, when he had been one of our earliest allies in Tennessee before he moved into the Congress, first in the House and later in the Senate. In addition, I had served as chairman of two advisory committees of the Republican National Committee since Brock took over the RNC in 1976 and I knew that he had done an outstanding job of revitalizing the National Committee, building a new, computerized communications–mail system and thus improving the RNC's fund-raising capacity. I felt that dumping Brock at this point, on the eve of the convention, could only serve to hurt the party and damage the candidate as he prepared to go into the fall campaign.

I talked with both Paul Laxalt and Bill Casey about Brock and urged them to keep him on as National Chairman. Senator Laxalt heard me out and said, "You present a very persuasive case. I have already made my case and I will say nothing more," meaning that henceforth he would keep hands off the campaign to oust Brock. Casey promised me he would talk further about it with Ronald Reagan and he subsequently went to California where he met with both Reagan and Brock. There were a lot of other people defending Brock, too, of course, and I think the combined effort persuaded Reagan to keep him on. He was reaffirmed as National Chairman with Drew Lewis, Reagan's man in Pennsylvania, named as his deputy.

However, Reagan rightly refused to compromise on Mary Crisp, the National Co–Chairman of the party. The acerbic Mrs. Crisp had been critical of Reagan for some time and she was a leading advocate of both the Equal Rights Amendment and legalized abortion measures. Moreover, she had publicly declared her admiration for John Anderson, who had now excommunicated himself from the Republican Party. Mrs. Crisp didn't want to leave the RNC and the press made much of her being forced out, but after she left she soon found a new home in John Anderson's campaign, where I'm sure she felt more comfortable.

The stage was now fully set for the 1980 Republican National Convention. It was to be the first convention since 1964 that the conservatives were, as I've said, completely united. There was no doubt about the outcome, at least for the Presidential nomination. Some people in the press were already commenting on what a boring convention it would be—"no drama, no suspense." But once again they reckoned without Ronald Reagan's talent for managing a crisis. And in Detroit in 1980 this talent elevated the Republican National Convention to the level of high drama.

In the opening chapter of this book I treated Reagan's selection of his Vice–Presidential running mate, which provided the central drama of the convention. There is no point in going into greater detail on the events in Detroit. The main issue, of Ronald Reagan's own candidacy, was never in doubt. The conservatives obviously remained united behind Reagan and they swept most of the remaining liberal elements of the party along with them. Conservatives also prevailed on the platform, and it was a refreshing change for them to prevail with the *support* of the candidate on most planks, rather than against him, as they had to do with Nixon and Ford.

Running the delegate count for Ronald Reagan in Detroit in 1980, as I had for him in Miami in 1968 and for Barry Goldwater in San Francisco in 1964, was for me the culmination of an effort that had consumed a good share of my life for the better part of twenty years. The conservative revolution in America had finally taken its second successful step on a nationwide scale, thanks to steps previously taken in hundreds of elections at all levels of government and to thousands of unheralded actions by so many individuals and organizations over a period of nearly four decades. The first national step, which had brought Ronald Reagan actively into politics, had been made with Barry Goldwater's nomination in 1964.

Now we were ready for the third step—Ronald Reagan's campaign against Jimmy Carter.

21

Election

Immediately after the Detroit convention a group of us flew to
Washington to get the Reagan campaign against the Democrats and
President Carter into high gear as soon as possible. Senator Paul
Laxalt and Ann Armstrong were cochairmen of the Reagan–Bush
Committee and William J. Casey was the overall campaign director.

Our strategy committee met every morning at 7:30 at the
campaign headquarters in Arlington, Virginia. The members of
the strategy group, in addition to Mrs. Armstrong, Senator Laxalt,
Bill Casey and myself, were Ed Meese, who served as Ronald
Reagan's chief of staff, Lyn Nofziger, Mike Deaver, Robert Gar-
rick, Peter Dailey, Bill Timmons, Jim Baker and Richard Wirthlin.
Most of these were deputy campaign chairmen, but Jim Baker and
I had the title of senior advisors.

On any given day one or more of these people might be
traveling with Reagan, especially Lyn Nofziger, who was in charge
of press relations, and Mike Deaver, who was the tour director.
Other regulars on the campaign jet were Martin Anderson, Reagan's
domestic issue advisor, and Richard Allen, his foreign policy
man. Jim Brady, who had worked in John Connally's campaign,
was also aboard the plane.

The Democratic convention opened in New York August 11, nearly four weeks after the Republicans ended theirs in Detroit.

Senator Edward M. Kennedy withdrew as a candidate on the first day of the New York convention, advising his delegates to "vote their conscience." In spite of this generous release of the Kennedy delegates, the Senator still received an impressive 1,146 votes on the first and only ballot of the convention, about one–third of the total votes. Moreover, Kennedy's supporters won a number of important platform fights, nailing in planks that were generally much more liberal than the Carter forces wanted.

Jimmy Carter came out swinging against Ronald Reagan in his acceptance address in New York and he never stopped until Election Day. This would have been fine, except that so many of Carter's punches were aimed below the belt. In his New York speech on August 14 at Madison Square Garden Carter claimed that Ronald Reagan was advocating a "radical and irresponsible" nuclear arms race that, he said, "could put the whole world in peril."

I thought we were hearing an almost verbatim replay of the broken record Lyndon Johnson's people had played against Barry Goldwater in 1964 when Carter declared, "The life of every human being on earth can depend on the experience and judgment and vigilance of the person in the Oval Office," clearly implying that Reagan could not be trusted with the awesome responsibility of commanding our deterrent forces. The difference between 1980 and 1964 was that President Johnson for the most part let his surrogates and Democrat television commercials crucify Goldwater on the flaming cross of war, whereas Jimmy Carter wanted to do the job himself on Ronald Reagan.

The Carter campaign against Reagan got more strident as the election neared and the President grew more visibly desperate. Nor was the stridency limited to the question of war and peace. Carter labeled Reagan's program to cut taxes and social services in the most extreme terms and in a speech in Atlanta he wildly charged that Reagan had introduced "hatred" and "racism" into the campaign and tried to paint the Republican candidate as a tool of the Ku Klux Klan.

Reagan could not really reply to this kind of flailing on the part of the President, although he had predicted even before the fall campaign that the Democrats would try to depict him as "a combination of Ebenezer Scrooge and the Mad Bomber." However, after one particularly virulent attack on him by Carter, Reagan said, "The President is reaching the point of hysteria." I believe he was only echoing the feelings of many Americans when he made this observation.

The press had begun, almost from the very start of Reagan's campaign, to cast him in the role of a bumbling old actor who was muffing his lines. Shortly after the Republican convention they hit him on his old position of restoring full diplomatic relations with the Republic of China on Taiwan, a position that did cause problems for George Bush on a trip he made to China.

Next, the press went after him for a statement he made on the Vietnam War in a speech before the Veterans of Foreign Wars convention in Chicago on August 18. Yet, again, he said nothing more nor less on Vietnam than he had said in the past, namely that the 58,000 Americans who had lost their lives in that war had died in "a noble cause" in defense of a small nation attacked by "a totalitarian neighbor."

A third press flap was brought on by a real mistake, but one that certainly was not very significant in the overall context of the major issues of the 1980 campaign. On Labor Day in Detroit, Reagan said in a remark to a person in the crowd that President Carter was "opening his campaign in the city that gave birth to, and is the parent body of, the Ku Klux Klan." However, the city in question, Tuscumbia, Alabama, was not the birthplace of the Klan, as one of Reagan's research people had told him.

The cumulative effect of these incidents was that Reagan began to slide a bit in the polls and the press predicted he was in trouble. By this time Nancy and Ron Reagan had moved to a home in Northern Virginia for the duration of the campaign and he called a meeting of our strategy committee there in September.

I made only one recommendation at this meeting and that was that Reagan be given enough time to absorb the speeches that were prepared for him and to work them over as thoroughly as in the past; in short, to make them his own speeches. The hectic schedule of a Presidential campaign affords the candidates very little time for thoughtful reflection, and although that was not entirely the problem in this case, it certainly was part of it. Reagan was handed a speech as he got on the plane and was expected to grasp every nuance by the time he gave the speech a short time later.

The strategy meeting went on most of the afternoon and there were a number of other things besides Reagan's speeches that we discussed. One of them was not the advertising campaign, but this was a subject that came up repeatedly at our regular strategy meetings. Our surveys had shown that although Reagan was widely recognized in the Far West as a successful former Governor of California, east of the Rockies his gubernatorial record was not at all well known. Thus, the Reagan television and radio commercials bore down on his record in Sacramento in the early stages of the campaign to reinforce Reagan's identity as a leader and able public official, although in the later stages the commercials would deal more extensively with his positions on national issues.

Peter Dailey was responsible for the campaign advertising and he was criticized for this strategy. However, Dick Wirthlin and I and some others supported Peter and it was decided to continue with this game plan which, at any rate, was only meant as an introduction.

I rode back in a car from the Virginia meeting with Jim Baker, Bill Timmons, and Dean Burch, who was George Bush's campaign manager. The others all seemed somewhat worried about the campaign and I think that was because at the time none of them knew Ronald Reagan as well as I did. I knew he was capable of conducting a great campaign, and I did not view the few kinks that had been blown up in the press as anything very serious.

We held an event on the steps of the Capitol in Washington about this time that got us a lot of press coverage throughout the country. Ronald Reagan appeared with several hundred Republican members of Congress and candidates for the House and Senate and they all entered into a pact with the American people to restore the federal government to the people. I was in charge of the planning for this event, the first of its kind in history, and I had very able help from Paul Russo, who did most of the work in rounding up the Congressmen and candidates. It was a successful event but some elements of the news media could not resist taking pot shots at "Reagan the Actor" for staging a play on the Capitol steps with a huge supporting cast.

The media's persistence, at least up through the 1980 campaign, in presenting Reagan as an aging actor who couldn't memorize his lines properly was one of the most shallow and superficial interpretations of any man in public life in this century. Yes, Ronald Reagan had been an actor, and quite a successful one. He had made a good living at this profession for nearly twenty years, less time out for service in an Army film–making unit during World War II. While pursuing his early profession, he had been president of his union, the Screen Actors Guild, for six terms, and for ten years was chairman of the Motion Picture Industry Council, which represents some 35,000 members.

In 1954, Reagan began another career when he went to work for the General Electric Company. Although he was host of television's highly successful *GE Theater* for the next eight years, he was also General Electric's goodwill ambassador to its 250,000 employees, a job that did much to prepare him for his success in public office. Reagan has estimated that he visited all of GE's 135 plants and installations during those years, and in one two–year period he was traveling almost constantly for his company.

In 1960 he began to edge into politics, serving as honorary campaign chairman for Lloyd Wright, a conservative lawyer who ran in the California Republican primary against liberal GOP Senator Thomas Kuchel. By 1964 he was deeply involved in the political arena when he worked as Co-Chairman of our Citizens for Goldwater Committee in California. In 1966 he was elected Governor of California, the nation's most populous state, and was reelected to a second four–year term in 1970, serving a total of eight years as chief executive of his state. After leaving the governorship in 1975 he obviously continued to be active in politics so by the time he was inaugurated as President he had a total of nearly two decades in public life, and for eight years before that had been with a major industrial corporation.

I repeat this resumé of Ronald Reagan's career because I think it should be cast in proper perspective. And I raise the question: how could the press continue to cast him as "an actor" after all those years in public service as governor, politician, industrial relations man, and union president? Robert Lindsey of *The New York Times* wrote in 1980: "Ronald Reagan is by profession a performer, and it is the single most important fact about him."

This is tantamount to taking a man who was, let us say, a newspaper reporter, who later moved into industry and politics and after more than twenty–five successful years away from his original profession, and still referring to him as "a reporter." And, moreover, that is judged to be "the single most important fact about him."

Contrary to the "actor" image projected by the press I have found in my long association with Ronald Reagan that he is one of the most genuine people I've ever met. And he is far from being a theatrical puppet willingly manipulated by others. He studies the issues, listens to all sides, and then makes up his own mind. One incident during the campaign illustrates this.

The media's obsession with Ronald Reagan "the actor" was so pervasive that it penetrated our strategy committee and created doubts about whether the candidate should debate Jimmy Carter. I was for the debates, as were most of the people who knew Reagan well, but those not so well acquainted with him were in opposition. Finally, at one of our morning strategy sessions Bill Casey called for a vote on the question of whether Reagan should debate Carter one–on–one and much to my dismay those of us who were for the debate lost.

However, at this point the telephone rang. It was one of the campaign people traveling with Reagan and he informed us that the candidate had just announced to the press that he was calling for a debate with *both* President Carter and John Anderson.

"Well," I said to the group, "I just won on a minority vote."

"Yes," retorted one of the others, "but it was a *weighted* vote."

There was no doubt that in the 1980 campaign Ronald Reagan called the shots, as he always has, for himself.

Jimmy Carter at first refused to debate on the grounds that John Anderson was not a major candidate and should not be included. Reagan's position was that in the interest of fair play the Illinois Congressman should have a chance to present his views. Carter was adamant and the first debate was between Reagan and Anderson, with the President embarrassingly conspicuous by his absence.

I don't think debates are won or lost so much on the basis of the substantive issues as on the demeanor and delivery of the debaters. In this instance, Ronald Reagan came off as a reasonable, thoughtful man, which he is, and John Anderson appeared as a rather excitable, very cocky fellow who, moreover, was in favor of such things as legalized abortion, the Equal Rights Amendment, and an additional 50 cent per–gallon tax on gasoline.

Reagan advocated cutting federal spending and taxes at the same time and Anderson went after him tooth and nail on that, though Reagan's program has now been enacted by the Congress. Anderson did get in some of the most telling points in the debate—against Jimmy Carter. Several times he referred to "the man who isn't here tonight" and the President, if he was watching, must have wished he had shown up. Indeed, Carter, *in absentia*, was the real loser of the Reagan–Anderson debate.

Before this debate we had a dry run in Washington and David Stockman played the part of John Anderson, whom he had once worked for before running for Congress himself. Stockman did so well debating Reagan that apparently it was this performance which projected him into his present job as director of the White House Office of Management and Budget.

After the rehearsal I told Reagan, "You've had a lot of information thrown at you, and you've received a lot of advice. It's important to master the information, as I know you have. But you got where you are by being Ronald Reagan, so be Ronald Reagan and you'll be OK."

Later I told Nancy to keep everyone away from Ron the next day while he was studying up for the debate and she promised to do her best.

Actually, I don't think there is a politician in the country today who could beat Ronald Reagan in open debate. For one thing, he has more "presence" than anyone else in politics, but that is only part of it. As I said before, he does his homework. And he prepares himself thoroughly before he appears in public.

After much negotiation, a Reagan–Carter debate was finally arranged very late in the campaign, on October 28. By this time Carter at last realized he was behind and he *needed* the debate to pull him out of the hole he had dug for himself over the previous four years. I believe he was desperate or he never would have consented to debate Ronald Reagan, although a *Washington Post* headline that morning informed the world, "CARTER GOES INTO DEBATE WITH LEAD IN NEW POLL."

The debate was held in Cleveland and I flew out on the plane with Nancy and Ron Reagan, Bill Casey and the other members of the campaign strategy committee and some advisory committee people, including Jeane Kirkpatrick, now Ambassador to the

United Nations, who sat next to me on the way out. When we got to the hall and were seated the candidates came out on the stage and I saw Ron wink at Nancy and she winked back. I knew then he was completely relaxed and in command.

Carter led off with a barrage on his favorite theme: Reagan, he said, was a "dangerous" warmonger who, moreover, would deliver nuclear weapons into the hands of terrorists. He overstepped the bounds even more when he injected his little daughter, Amy, into the debate, saying that he had asked Amy what she thought was the most important issue in the campaign and she had replied the nuclear arms issue.

Reagan kept his sense of humor and said Carter's distortion of his views on nuclear weapons and their proliferation was "like the witch doctor that gets mad when a good doctor comes along with a cure that will work."

On domestic issues, Carter characterized Reagan's programs as "heartless" and even implied that Reagan opposed disease prevention and outpatient care because he was against national health insurance.

Reagan shook his head and smiled, "There he goes again." And most of the people watching on their television screens must have felt the same way. Carter's excesses, one is tempted to say extremism, actually won the debate for Reagan, though I believe he would have won it even if Carter had appeared to be more reasonable.

As President, Reagan concluded, he would mount a crusade to "take the government off the backs of the great people of this country and turn you loose again to do those things that I know you can do so well, because you did them and made this country great."

When the debate was over, Robert Strauss, Carter's campaign manager, was running up and down the press area of the hall frantically trying to respond to the media's questions. But I had arranged to have a score of Reagan luminaries on hand who could cover all the media bases.

In the age of the instant reaction, the press had to have their story right away and no one man could handle all the demands for a reaction at once, as Bob Strauss was now trying to do. Even Henry Kissinger was on hand to back up Reagan, along with John Tower, Bill Simon, Tom Evans, Anne Armstrong, Jeane Kirkpatrick, Charles Schulz and others. The press was properly appreciative of our extra effort to accomodate them and I think our galaxy of stars shed a little more light on TV that night than Strauss and the one or two other people Carter had with him.

I believe Ronald Reagan had the election sewed up before his debate with Jimmy Carter but his clear–cut victory over the President in the October 28 exchange certainly added more impetus to his impending landslide. However, you can never afford to let down in any political campaign, and both Reagan and his campaign team kept working hard right down to the day of the election.

One of the operations we mounted in the latter part of the campaign was a Truth Squad, which preceded Jimmy Carter into the cities he visited, and another such squad to follow him. There was nothing new about Truth Squads, but this was the first time, to our knowledge, that they had been used to "bracket" a candidate, both before and after his appearances. I was in charge of this Truth Squad operation and some of the people who volunteered to serve on the squads were Alexander Haig, John Tower, Bill Simon, Charls E. Walker and Elizabeth Dole, wife of Senator Robert Dole and now the special assistant to the President for public affairs.

Reagan made a strenuous effort during the campaign to attract blue collar workers to the Republican standard. Most of them instinctively supported his positions on foreign and defense policy, but Reagan wanted to reassure them on domestic issues as well. He reminded workers that he had been president of his own union, an AFL–CIO affiliate, for six terms and he promised to build a "great coalition made up of the producers of America," an obvious slap at the non–producers riding the welfare rolls on taxes paid by working men and women.

Near the end of the campaign Carter bore down hard on his favorite theme that Reagan "just didn't understand" such things as foreign policy, the defense system and international economics. After one of these Carter sallies, Reagan responded: "I've heard that Mr. Carter assembled members of the press corps today to tell them that Ronald Reagan did not understand. Well, you know, for once I agree with him. He's hit it right on the nose. I don't understand why we have had inflation at the highest peacetime rates in history and I don't understand why his answer to inflation is to put two million people out of work."

On another occasion he took issue with Carter on the definition of a depression, when Carter tried to reassure the country that it was only suffering through a mild recession. "If it's a definition he wants," said Reagan, "I'll give him one. A recession is when your neighbor loses his job. A depression is when you lose yours. Recovery is when Jimmy Carter loses his."

Reagan returned to California for the wrap-up of his campaign, a rally in San Diego and a nationally televised address to the people of the United States. He urged them to go to the polls and show the world that "America is still united, still strong, still compassionate, still clinging fast to the dream of peace and freedom, still willing to stand by those who are persecuted and alone."

On election day most of our Reagan strategy group flew to Los Angeles to be with the candidate when the returns came in. However, I stayed behind in Arlington to man the national headquarters and to answer queries from the Washington press corps. About noon I had a call from one of the television networks informing me that Reagan had "the makings of a landslide." I told the reporter I'd check it out and see if we would have any comment. Then I called Dick Wirthlin, our survey chairman, and he verified the network's forecast. "In that case," I said, "we had better make sure no one on our team claims victory or people will stop going to the polls." Wirthlin and I got word to Bill Casey and Paul Laxalt and urged them to hold off on any victory statements. Then I spent the rest of the afternoon trying to persuade the networks and other media people that we were not making any claims just yet.

However, early in the evening the Los Angeles headquarters called to tell me that Jimmy Carter had just telephoned Ronald Reagan to concede the election. "Guess what," my caller informed me. "Reagan was in the shower when Jimmy called!" I laughed and said that I hope he had dried himself off before he got on the phone.

Nancy and Ron left their Pacific Palisades home a little while later to go out to a dinner at the home of Earle Jorgensen, another one of our cadre from the 1964 campaign. As they drove down the hill to Sunset Boulevard, people had lined the streets to cheer them on their way. When they reached the boulevard people in the cars started leaning on their horns and the Reagan's ride to the Jorgensens' must have been one of the noisiest triumphal processions of any presidential election in history.

After dinner, the Reagans went to the Century Plaza Hotel, in Los Angeles to watch the election coverage on television. Bill Brock, the Republican National Chairman, and I, with some others of the rear guard in Washington, assembled at the Washington Hilton, where the crowds became so great the fire marshals had to close off the grand ballroom fairly early.

The extent of the Reagan landslide exceeded even my expectations, and I had been predicting an overwhelming vote for him for some weeks. Reagan carried all but six states—Jimmy Carter's home state of Georgia, Hawaii, Maryland, Minnesota, Rhode Island and West Virginia, plus the District of Columbia.

Reagan swept *all* the big industrial states of the Northeast and

Midwest, burying, I hope forever, the old canard that no conservative presidential candidate could take these states. One after another they had fallen into the Reagan column on November 4—New York, Pennsylvania, Ohio, Illinois, Michigan, Missouri, New Jersey, Wisconsin, even Massachusetts, the lone state to go for George McGovern against Richard Nixon in 1972.

Some states Reagan took by margins of more than two–to–one over Carter, including Alaska, Arizona, Idaho, Nevada, New Hampshire, North Dakota and Wyoming. He overwhelmed Carter by better than three–to–one in Nebraska and more than that in Utah. And his margin of victory in California was a resounding 1,400,000; in Texas nearly 700,000, in Florida almost 600,000; in Ohio, 500,000, in Illinois, Indiana and Michigan, close to 400,000 each, and in New Jersey, Pennsylvania and Utah more than 300,000.

The final official returns gave Reagan 43,899,250 to Carter's 35,481,435. John Anderson received only 5,719,437, far less than the margin that separated Reagan and Carter in the popular vote. Even assuming that *all* of the Anderson votes would have gone to Jimmy Carter—a by no means safe assumption—this would *not* have affected the result. There were some states where Anderson polled enough votes to have given Carter their electoral votes, most noticeably New York and Wisconsin. But Reagan's landslide of 489 Electoral College votes to only 49 for Carter would easily have withstood a shift in these and even a number of other states.

In short, Ronald Reagan's was a complete and consummate victory, a clear mandate for the man who has been the leader of the conservative cause in American for fifteen years.

Moreover, Reagan helped carry with him enough Republicans to capture the United States Senate for the first time in nearly a quarter-century, and the GOP made impressive gains in the House, state legislatures, and local offices across the country.

Ronald Reagan made a moving victory statement after Jimmy

Carter publicly conceded defeat on election night. He came to the ballroom at the Century Plaza Hotel with Nancy and other members of their family and told his campaign workers, "There has never been a more humbling moment in my life." He thanked his campaign teams and workers in every state for their efforts on his behalf and promised to do his best to justify the faith of the voters.

It was typical of Ronald Reagan that he should give special recognition to his wife on this, the greatest moment of his life. "Nancy is going to have a new title soon," he said. "But it really isn't new, because she has been the First Lady in my house for a long time." Then he added:

"I'm not frightened by what lies ahead and I don't believe the American people are frightened. Together, we are going to do what has to be done."

22

A Look Ahead

After his election as President, Ronald Reagan wasted little time trying to get a handle on the Federal government he was to head. He held a series of informal meetings in California, Washington and New York to seek advice on future policy, personnel, and the nuts and bolts of putting together his administration.

When he came to New York for the first time as President–elect I went to see him at the Waldorf Towers. I found him in the presidential suite, where we had stayed during his first campaign for the Republican nomination a dozen years earlier. He welcomed me in his invariably warm and friendly manner and I remarked that he was now staying in the Presidential suite legitimately and not merely as a candidate, as in our previous stay there.

I told him that for the first time in many years I now felt that there was a real chance to halt the precipitous decline of Western civilization. The country, indeed the world, had been searching for both spiritual and temporal leadership for a long, long time. I felt the spiritual leadership was already being provided by the humble Polish priest who had become Pope John Paul II. And, I said, I believed he had the opportunity to provide the temporal leadership.

239

It was my suggestion that he focus on the truly big, important issues and leave the subidiary ones to his Cabinet. We both knew that some little issues would inevitably be blown up into big issues and come clamoring for his attention, But insofar as possible, it was my opinion that he should not permit himself to be tied down by the Lilliputian crises that had diverted so many of his predecessors from the really vital things that would decide the future course of the nation.

There were only two specific recommendations that I made during this meeting and I am pleased that President Reagan has acted on both of them. The first was an approach to the government that we had discussed and agreed upon in the past—the restoration of the federal system as intended by the Constitution. I thought it would be a good idea to appoint a Presidential Commission on Federalism, which, as I mentioned earlier, he followed through on shortly after he moved into the White House.

The other recommendation was one that I had made to several previous Republican Presidents, but which had never been fully or properly implemented, and that was the creation of the new post of national political director based in the White House.

"If you think it would be advisable, you could give the job the title of public affairs director," I said. "Just as long as you know the person you put in the job is minding the political store which seems to have had a habit of getting neglected in the past."

It was typical of Ronald Reagan that he should give the job its proper title and not attempt to camouflage it under a euphemism. Even before he took office he had already designated our old mutual friend, Lyn Nofziger, as the *political director* on his White House staff.

Toward the end of our nearly hour–long talk in New York, Mike Deaver joined us. I realized the President–elect probably had another appointment that afternoon, although, and again typically, Ronald Reagan had not mentioned it or let on in any way that we were under any time pressure. I rose to leave and he walked me to the door and thanked me for taking the time to come and talk with him. This was not merely a polite gesture. He was genuinely grateful, though, of course, it was I who was thankful for him so generously giving me his time.

On the way out I saw Edward Hickey, who had travelled with Reagan and me all over the country during the 1968 pre–convention campaign when he had been a Secret Service agent assigned to my candidate. Ed had left the Secret Service afterward to become the Governor's security chief in Sacramento and had stayed on with Reagan during the intervening years.

"Remember," I chided Ed, as I always do, "you have the second most important job around here." Ed laughed and I left the presidential suite and took the elevator down to the garage. Out in the busy Manhattan streets it was a cold late–November afternoon but somehow the world seemed to be suddenly smiling again after so many years of wearing a worried frown.

On his first visit to Washington after the election Reagan was the guest of honor at a dinner given by the Republican Senators and their wives in the Great Hall of the Library of Congress. After some informal remarks and a few Reaganesque jokes, he struck a more serious chord on a theme he and I had talked about a number of times over the years:

"We said to the American people this year, all of us, that we were going to make the government work better for the people, that we would control and limit federal spending, we'd reduce taxes, stimulate work and savings and investment, that we would relieve labor and business of burdensome and unnecessary regulations and still maintain high standards of environmental and occupational safety, that we would reduce the cost of government by eliminating billions of dollars lost to waste and fraud in the federal bureaucracy, a problem that we labeled as an unrelenting national scandal. And we pledged to restore the vitality and health of local and state governments by returning to them control over programs that would be best run at those levels of government and that we would fight to bring integrity to government. . . . I think these are very important pledges and we have to work together, all of us, to achieve them.

"But beyond those promises, I hope that we'll bear in mind that our victory in November was not a bestowal of power but a stewardship for the people. I hope we can learn to be practical but I hope we'll also never forget the ideals that brought us all here in the first place.

"Like a number of you here in this room, my first entry into national politics, Republican national politics, was in 1964 and I campaigned for a man—Barry Goldwater—who we can see now was a prophet in his own time. I hope the ideals he spoke about then, that those ideals will remain our ideals."

During this interval between the election and the inauguration of Ronald Reagan I served on the Transition Team's executive committee, which was chaired by Bill Casey and included Jim Baker, Peter Flanigan, Jack Marsh, Ed Meese, Max Rabb and William Wilson, who was the chief of Reagan's ex–officio "kitchen cabinet" and is now Ambassador to the Vatican. In addition, I was named chairman of the transition's ad hoc Committee on Federalism and the nearly three months of the transition period was one of the busiest periods of my life.

The President–elect met with our transition team in mid–January and he listened patiently to our recommendations, acting promptly on most of them, but making his own decisions on the tough appointments and issues, as he always does. The next time I saw Ronald Reagan was at his inauguration as the 40th President of the United States.

It was a bright and sunny day in Washington and the happiest I'd ever had in my long career in politics. Even my seemingly impossible logistical problem of obtaining 22 tickets for the inauguration had been solved that day. (Cabinet members were allotted six tickets each and when my wife informed me that we needed 22 to accomodate all our friends and neighbors who had come to Washington for the inaugural I almost threw up my hands in horror.) The inaugural ceremony was held, for the first time, at the West Front of the Capitol, symbolically facing westward to that section of the country which gave Ronald Reagan his start in life and beyond that to the state where he won his first political battles.

President Reagan's inaugural address summed up in less than twenty minutes the goals of his incoming administration. He made it clear that his first priority would be to control inflation, which, he said, "penalizes thrift and crushes the struggling young and fixed-income elderly alike." To accomplish this goal he reiterated his promise "to curb the size and influence of the Federal government," to reduce its spending and to "lighten our punitive tax burden."

He pledged to resume a realistic quest for lasting peace based upon sufficient military strength and promised to once again make America "the exemplar of freedom and a beacon of hope" for the whole world. "We are not, as some would have us believe, doomed to an inevitable decline," he said. Calling for an "era of national renewal," he asked all Americans "to believe in our capacity to perform great deeds, to believe that together, with God's help, we can and will resolve the problems which now confront us. And, after all," he asked, "why shouldn't we believe that? *We are Americans.*"

He closed with a quotation from the diary of a forgotten soldier killed at Chateau Thierry in World War I, Private Martin H. Treptow of Cherokee, Iowa: "America must win this war. Therefore, I will work, I will save, I will sacrifice, I will endure, I will fight cheerfully and do my utmost, as if the issue of the whole struggle depended on me alone."

It was a humble speech by a man I know to be a truly humble man. But it charted America's future course more clearly and more firmly than most of the more ambitious attempts at history-making rhetoric offered on similar occasions in this century. Moreover, between the lines one could discern in this inaugural address the primary reason why Ronald Reagan won the 1980 election, namely, that he embodies the deepest beliefs of most Americans as to what our country stands for and at the same time articulates our most fervent hopes for the future.

The day turned out to be an auspicious one for another reason. At the lunch in the Capitol after the ceremony the new President was able to announce that the 53 Americans held hostage for more than a year by the Iranians had just flown out across the border of that strife-torn country. Without participating in the negotiations, Reagan had played *the* major role in settling this crisis. The Iranians knew, and, indeed, the world knew, that Ronald Reagan would never grant them the terms his predecessor had given them to ransom our embassy people in Teheran.

With the Iranian crisis past, the way was cleared for President Reagan to concentrate on fulfilling the promises he had made to the American people to control inflation, cut taxes, reduce the size of the Federal government and strengthen our national defense.

It is not the purpose of this book to record the early history of the Reagan administration. But before he had finished his first year in office it was obvious America had finally found the President it has needed and wanted for a long, long time.

His actions in persuading the Congress, and most particularly the Democrat–controlled House of Representatives, to pass both his revolutionary budget and tax bills virtually intact was certainly one of the great political coups of the last half–century.

His firmness in dealing with the air–traffic controllers who defied the law in walking off their jobs demonstrated to the country at large what those of us who have known him for years have always recognized—that Ronald Reagan *means* what he says. That, in itself, is shaking Washington to its pragmatic roots. In a city where double–talk has been *de rigeur* for decades, Reagan's straightforward honesty has swept the capital like a welcome breath of fresh air, penetrating even to the stagnant recesses of

Foggy Bottom, the home of the Department of State. His unequivocal stand on El Salvador at the very outset of his administration
may have saved that country from falling precipitously under the
yoke of Fidel Castro and his godfathers in the Kremlin.

The big tests, of course, are yet to come. In August 1980 the
General Accounting Office, after an exhaustive study, sent a
report to the Congress verifying that "the large, sustained Soviet
program to enhance its strategic nuclear capabilities has, by many
measures, succeeded in altering the strategic nuclear balance."
The report added that "Soviet forces have significant advantages
that are not offset by United States forces." As *New York Times*
correspondent Richard Halloran noted in his story, "the report
appeared to be more pessimistic than the views expressed by many
conservatives, including members of the Reagan Administration
who deal with military issues. . . ."

There can be no doubt that rebuilding America's deterrent
force will have to be *the* priority for President Reagan if he is to
keep the peace endangered by the naive policies of his predecessors. However, the fact that Ronald Reagan recognizes this,
whereas so many who went before him did not, at least gives the
United States a chance to redress the nuclear balance which has
tipped so heavily in favor of the Soviet Union during the twenty
years we have been marking time with our strategic forces.

Tocqueville once remarked, in effect, that the genius of America was its ability to solve problems. He expressed grave doubt
that we could preserve and protect this aspect of our national
character, though I believe Toqueville would be surprised we
have hung onto it as long as we have.

What Ronald Reagan has the opportunity to give us is a new
spirit of confidence in our ability to solve our problems. This was
the spirit that made America great and, unfortunately, we came
in time to take it for granted. Thereafter, it waned, almost
imperceptibly at first, except to the relatively small band of
conservative thinkers who first detected its waning. But by 1980

our loss of confidence was apparent to the world in the erosion of our national will to deal with either internal or external problems.

Ronald Reagan was elected President at a very late hour in our history. For him to turn the foundering ship of state around before it crashes upon the rocks of history will not be an easy task, nor will it be accomplished quickly. Nonetheless, it is already, a year after his election, obvious to all that he has a firm hand on the rudder and that the good ship United States is beginning to change its course.

Whether President Reagan can swing the ship far enough around to avert the disasters which before his election seemed inevitable remains to be seen. But this much is certain. America has found a leader.

Moreover, Ronald Reagan is a leader who believes in stating plainly the direction in which he hopes to lead us. At the 1981 Conservative Political Action Conference in Washington, he set forth the nation's future course when he said:

"Those of us who call ourselves conservatives have pointed out what's wrong with government policy for more than a quarter of a century. Now we have an opportunity to make policy and to change our national direction. . . . The opportunity—yes, and the necessity—to prove that the American promise is equal to the task of redressing our grievances and equal to the challenge of inventing a great tomorrow. . . .

"This is the real task before us: to reassert our commitment as a nation to a law higher than our own, to renew our spiritual strength. Only by building a wall of such spiritual resolve can we, as a free people, hope to protect our own heritage and make it someday the birthright of all men."

Index

AFL-CIO, 24, 25, 235
Abshire, David, 59
Adams, Paul, 145
Agnew, Spiro, 110, 124, 128, 129, 149, 154
Alexander, Holmes, 46
Alexander, Lamar, 200
All the News that Fits (Dinsmore), 53n
Allcott, Gordon, 148
Allen, Richard V., 59, 61, 63, 133, 225
Allen, Robert, 46
American Broadcasting Company, 4
American Conservative Union, 69, 73, 79, 80, 124, 168, 206
American Enterprise Institute, 56, 61, 62
American Mercury, 43
American Security Council, 43, 59–60, 205
American Spectator, The, 43
Americans for Conservative Action, 58
Americans for Democratic Action, 46, 58
Anderson, John, 45, 207, 211, 212, 216, 217, 223, 231–232, 237
Anderson, Martin, 56, 63, 207, 225
Armstrong, Anne, 225, 234
Armstrong, William L., 200
Ashbrook, John, 69, 76, 79, 83, 111
Atiyeh, Victor, 201
"Austrian School," 30

Bailey, Consuela, 128–129
Baker, James, 181, 184, 211, 242
Baker, Howard, 158, 186–187, 204, 205, 207, 210, 211, 212
Baldwin, Hanson, 47
Ball, William Watts, 36
Baltimore Sun, 116
Barnes, Sullivan, 69
Barnett, Frank, 61

Barnett, Gwenn, 110
Baroody, William Sr., 21, 56
Barr, Charles, 67, 158
Barrett, Robert, 4
Barron, John, 46
Bartlett, Dewey, 83
Battin, James F., 83
Bauman, Carol, 74
Bayh, Birch, 218
Begin, Menachem, 146
Bell, Bernard Iddings, 36, 42
Bell, Jeffrey, 176
Bellmon, Henry, 83
Bentsen, Lloyd M., 161n
Bihl, Victor A., 110
Bishop, Joseph P., 156
Bisirjian, Richard, 77
Black, Charles, 207, 209, 212
Blackburn, Benjamin B., 62
Bliss, Ray, 124, 127
Boe, Nils, 110
Boyd, Forrest, 50
Bozell, F. Brent, 36, 37, 79
Bradley, Bruce, 112
Brady, James, 225
Bree, Rita, 67
Brennan, Walter, 76
Brezhnev, Leonid, 167
Brock, William, 83, 200, 222–223, 236
Broder, David, 76, 93
Brooke, Edward, 84
Brookings Institution, 59
Brown, Edmund G. (Jerry), 158, 161n
Brown, Pat, 65, 139, 158
Bruce, David, 79
Bubb, Henry, 109
Buchanan, Patrick, 47, 77
Buckley, James, 48, 144–148, 152, 155–156, 158, 159, 167, 168, 186–187
Buckley, William F. Jr., 33, 35, 36, 37, 40, 41, 42, 47, 52, 73, 79, 144, 155

Bulen, Keith, 221, 222
Bundy, McGeorge, 55–56
Burch, Dean, 14, 171, 172, 228
Burke, Arleigh, 59
Burke, Edmund, 29, 34
Burnham, James, 32, 35, 40, 79
Burt, Richard, 47
Bush, George, 1–8, 11, 12, 171, 203,
    207, 209–212, 216–219, 228
Business Round Table, 61
Butler, Caldwell, 198
Butler, J.R., 98–99, 122, 126
Buzhardt, J. Fred, 97–98, 152
Byrd, Harry F. 194, 198
Byrd, Richard E., 199
Byrd, Robert, 161n

Caddy, Douglas, 74
California, 14, 26, 28, 63, 73, 99, 106,
    115, 124, 140, 141, 149, 150, 171,
    191, 195, 219, 228, 230, 237, 239
Callaway, Howard H., 111, 124, 171,
    180–181
Campaigne, Jamieson, G. Jr., 74, 77
Campbell, James, 68
Carey, Hugh, 146
Carleson, Robert B., 140
Carmen, Gerald, 211
Carter, Anderson, 67, 156, 158, 183,
    188, 213
Carter, Hodding III, 163
Carter, Jimmy, 8, 13, 18–19, 33, 39,
    55, 142, 143, 161n, 175, 176, 184, 190,
    192–194, 196, 203–205, 220, 224,
    225–227, 231–238
Case, Clifford, 126
Casey, Robert, 148
Casey, Sophia, 209
Casey, William, 4, 48, 209, 211,
    212–214, 218, 225, 231–232,
    236, 242
Castro, Fidel, 245
Catchpole, Terry, 74
Cennarusa, Peter, 110
Center for Advanced International
    Studies, 63
Chaffee, John, 110, 194

Chamber of Commerce of the United
    States, 61
Chamberlain, John, 40, 41, 46
Chamberlin, William Henry, 40
Chambers, Whittaker, 35, 36, 40
Charleston News and Courier, 36
Cheney, Richard, 169, 184, 188, 217
Chicago, Illinois, 66, 67, 69, 105,
    150, 156, 159, 175, 227
Chicago Daily News, 46
Chicago Tribune, 17, 47, 90
China Story (Utley), 52
Chodorov, Frank, 40, 41, 42
Choice Not An Echo, A (Schlafly),
    52
Christopher, George, 65
Church, Frank, 161n, 218
Churchill, Winston, 46
Cincinnati Enquirer, 18
Citizens for Goldwater-Miller, 13, 14,
    16, 20, 24, 25, 230
Citizens for the Republic, 204
Clark, Dick, 200
Clark, George, 218
Clarke, Phillip C., 43, 50, 60
Clark, William, 121
Clements, William P. Jr., 200
Coalition for Peace through Strength,
    205
Cochran, Ted, 200
Cohn, Roy, 101
Colby, William, 171
Coleman, J.D. Stetson, 67, 198
Columbia Broadcasting System, 4, 147
Committee against Foreign Aid, 57
Committee for the Survival of a Free
    Congress, 148
Committee on the Present Danger, 61
Committee to Re-Elect the President
    (Nixon), 151–152, 153
Common Cause, 70
Communism, Communists, 23, 24, 36,
    41, 101, 133, 136, 138,
    166, 167
Connally, John, 133, 155, 158, 203,
    205, 207, 209, 210, 211, 212, 216
Conservative Book Club, 51

Conservative Caucus, 4
Conservative Digest, 43
Conservative Mind, The (Kirk), 33–34
Conservative Party (New York), 144–145, 147, 156
Conservative Political Action Committee, 48
Conservative Victory Fund, 79
Coors, Joseph, 62
Corso, Philip J., 97
Crane, Philip, 8, 58, 62, 76, 186, 205, 206, 207, 210, 211, 212, 217
Crisp, Mary, 223
Cronkite, Walter, 4
Cross, Travis, 85
Crow, Wayne, 110
Culver, John, 218
Curtis, Carl, 76, 83, 111, 148
Cushing, Ned, 67

Dailey, Peter, 221, 225, 228
Daley, Richard J., 85n
Dalton, John, 198
D'Amato, Al, 147
Damm, Helene v., 44–45
Daniel, Dan, 199
Darkness at Noon (Koestler), 35–36
Davidson, Donald, 42
Davis, Phillip, 14, 15
Davis, Dr. Loyal, 127
Day, James, M., 198
Deaver, Michael, 11, 121, 168–169, 189, 207, 209–210, 222, 225, 240
deBloom, Carl, 47
DeGaulle, Charles, 46
Democratic Party, Democrats, 8, 9, 13, 17, 18, 22, 23, 26, 27, 54, 56, 65, 69, 82, 83, 92, 96, 99, 100, 106, 107, 118, 133, 139, 140, 141, 145, 161, 166, 168, 175, 178, 184, 190, 193, 195–196, 197, 199, 200, 204, 217, 225, 226, 227, 244
Dent, Harry, 87, 97, 117–119, 121, 122, 123, 126, 184
Derwinski, Edward, 83
Des Moines Register & Tribune, 210
Detroit Free Press, 17

Dinsmore, Herman, 53n
Dirksen, Everett, 118
Dobriansky, Lev, 59
Dolan, Anthony, 48
Dole, Elizabeth, 190, 234
Dole, Robert, 189, 205, 207, 210, 211, 212, 217, 234
Doolittle, James, 14
Draft Ford Committee, 216
Dreyfus, Lee, 200
Durbrow, Elbridge, 60

Eagle Forum, 58
Eastman, Max, 40
Eberle, Bruce, 74
Edison Institute, 59
Educational Research Institute, 79
Edwards, James, 120
Edwards, Lee, 43, 74, 75
Edwards, Willard, 47, 90
Eisenhower, Dwight D., 16, 29, 88, 137, 170
Eliot, T.S., 29
Ellis, Thomas, 147, 178, 185
Equal Rights Amendment, 2, 3, 8, 58, 220, 223, 231
Evans, M. Stanton, 47, 48, 52, 74, 79, 131
Evans, Rowland, 99, 114–115
Evans, Thomas, 216, 234

Fabian Society, 33, 72
Falwell, Jerry, 3–4, 37, 51
Fat City (Lambro), 52, 77
Fay, Albert E., 68
Federal Bulldozer, The (M. Anderson), 56
Fellers, Bonner, 57
Feulner, Edwin, 62
Field, Mervin D., 114
"Firing Line" (W. Buckley), 47
Fischer, Louis, 35
Fisher, John M., 59, 60, 205
Flanigan, Peter, 86, 242
Flynn, John T., 41
Ford Foundation, 56, 57
Ford, Betty, 189, 190

Ford, Gerald, 1–5, 7, 39, 44, 59, 124, 154–155, 161, 164–173, 174–181, 182–190, 192–196, 204, 215–217, 223
Foreign Policy Research Institute, 62
Fortune, 49
Foundation for Economic Education (FEE), 30, 32, 41
Founding Father, The (Whalen), 49
Franke, David, 74
Franklin, Benjamin, 80
Freeman, The, 41
Freeman, Neil, 43
Frichette, Woody, 147
Friedman, Milton, 31, 32

Gallup, George, 174
Galvin, Suzie, 68
Gardner, James C., 115
Gardner, John, 70
Garrick, Robert, 225
Garrison, Denzil, 68
Garrity, Devin, 51
Garth, David, 146
Gavin, William J., 48–49
Georgetown University Center for Strategic and International Studies, 49, 59, 61, 62, 63
Gide, Andre, 35
Gidwitz, Gerald, 51
Gill, William J., 17, 60, 152
Gillespie, Ty, 68
Gipson, James Herrick, 51–52
Gipson, Lawrence Henry, 52
God and Man at Yale (W. Buckley), 33, 52
God that Failed, The (Koestler), 35
Godwin, Mills, 198
Goldthwaite, Alfred, 122
Goldwater, Barry, 13–19, 20–21, 25, 33, 38, 39, 51, 52, 56, 57, 66, 73, 75, 76, 82, 83, 84, 85, 87, 98, 103, 107, 111, 126, 144, 148, 156, 174, 183, 193, 205, 223–224, 226
Goodell, Charles, 144, 146
Graham, Daniel, 60
Gray, Nellie, 3

Great Depression, 70
Great Society, 22, 32, 72, 84, 95, 197
Great Society, The, (Wallas), 33
Greenspan, Allan, 4
Grenier, John, 14

Haerle, Paul, 158, 159, 172
Haig, Alexander, 59, 63, 234
Hall, Durwood, G., 83
Hall, Leonard, 85, 112, 209
Halloran, Richard, 245
Hallowell, John, 36
Hanighen, Frank, 40
Hannaford, Peter, 8, 221
Hansen, Clifford, 84
Hapsburg, Otto v., 41
Hard Core, The (White and others), 67, 68, 69, 156, 158, 169, 183, 213
Harkins, Robert, 68
Harrigan, Anthony, 36, 37, 42, 47, 61
Harriman, Averell, 204
Harrington, Ione, 67
Harris, Fred, 161n
Hart, Jeffrey, 47
Hartke, Vance, 194
Harvard University, 57
Hatch, Orrin, 194, 216
Hatfield, Mark, 84, 123, 125
Hathaway, Stanley, 207
Hawkins, Paula, 120
Hay, Samuel, 67
Hayakawa, S.I., 89, 138, 194
Hayek, Friedrich, 30, 32, 33
Hazlitt, Henry, 32, 41
Heinz, H. John III, 194
Helbert, James, 95
Helms, Jesse, 7, 8, 58, 147–148, 168, 178, 182–183, 216
Hempstone, Smith, 47
Henle, Ray, 50
Herberg, Will, 35
Heritage Foundation, 62, 171
Hickey, Edward, 135, 241
Hinkel, John V., 53n
Hinman, George, 112
Hiss, Alger, 35
Hitler, Adolf, 35, 46

Holton, Lynwood, 198
Hoober, Richard T., 110
Hoover Institution, 56, 61, 62, 63
Hope, Bob, 114
Hope, Paul, 155
Hruska, Roman, 148
Hubler, Richard G., 25n
Huie, William Bradford, 43
Human Events, 40, 168
Humphrey, Gordon J., 5, 200
Humphrey, Hubert, 116, 131–132, 193
Hurleigh, Robert, 50
Huston, Thomas, 112
Hutar, Patricia, 67

Ideas Have Consequences (Weaver), 34
Indianapolis News, 48
Institute for American Strategy, 59, 60
Institute for Foreign Policy Analysis, 62
Institute for Strategic Studies, 137
Intercollegiate Review, 42
Intercollegiate Society of Individualists, later Intercollegiate Studies Institute (ISI), 42, 196–197
It Didn't Start with Watergate (Lasky), 152n

Jackson, Donald, 26
Jackson, Henry, 161n
Janklow, William, 200
Javits, Jacob, 144, 147, 152
Jepson, Roger W., 200, 210
John Paul II, 239
Johnson, Lyndon, 15, 16, 22, 23, 32, 33, 55, 56, 60, 71, 72, 73, 78, 84, 86, 97, 99, 100, 105, 131, 132, 133, 137, 163, 175, 193, 226
Jones, David, 59, 74, 77, 112, 122, 145
Jorgensen, Earle, 236
Judd, Walter, 43, 45

KGB, The (Barron), 46
Kaye, Peter, 180
Keating, Kenneth, 144
Kemp, Jack, 8, 162, 205, 216
Kempster, Norman, 93

Kendall, Willmoore, 34, 40
Kennedy, Edward, 217, 226
Kennedy, John F., 17, 32, 55, 56, 85–86, 88, 97, 100, 132, 133, 137, 163, 193, 199
Kennedy, Joseph P., 49
Kennedy, Patricia, 101
Kennedy, Robert F., 90, 92, 99–100, 101, 104, 106, 133
Kerwitz, John, 156, 159
Kerr, Clark, 73, 89
Keynes, John Maynard, 32, 33
Kilpatrick, James Jackson, 47, 52
King, Martin Luther Jr., 105
Kings Row (movie), 25
Kingston Group, 205–206
Kintner, William, 42
Kirk, Claude, 83, 119, 126
Kirk, Russell, 30, 32, 33, 36, 37, 40, 41, 42, 52
Kirkpatrick, Jeane, 63, 232–233, 234
Kissinger, Henry A., 3, 4, 5, 59, 133, 166–167, 185–186, 204, 216, 234
Kitchel, Denison, 21
Kluckholm, Frank, 53n
Klumb, Charles, 68
Knight, John S., 17
Knowland, William, 65, 117
Koestler, Arthur, 35, 36
Krock, Arthur, 53n, 76, 138
Kuchel, Thomas, 230
Kuehnelt-Leddihn, Erik v., 40

Laird, Melvin, 158–159
Lake, James, 207, 209, 212
Lambro, Donald, 52, 77
Lane, Thomas, 58
Lasky, Victor, 152n
Latham, Robert F., 40
Lawford, Peter, 101
Laxalt, Paul, 2, 3, 6, 7, 83, 171, 177, 183, 188, 204, 206–207, 216, 221, 222, 225, 236
Leadership Foundation, 58
Le Vander, Harold, 110
Levine, Isaac Don, 41
Lewis, Drew, 179–180, 223

Lewis, Fulton Jr., 50
Liberal Party (New York), 145
Liebman, Marvin, 53, 74, 79
Lilly Foundation, 57
Lindsay, John, 107
Lindsey, Robert, 230
Lippmann, Walter, 33
List, Robert, 200
Lodge, Henry C., 85–86
Lofton, John, 43, 47
London *Times*, 118, 124
Los Angeles Times, 17
Love, John, 110, 143
Lowery, William, 76
Luce, Claire Booth, 14
Lugar, Richard G., 194
Lukens, Donald E., 77, 125
Lundigan, William, 76
Lyons, Charlton, 111

McCaffrey, Neil, 51
McCall, Thomas, 110
McCarthy, Eugene, 80, 99, 106, 175
McCarthy, Joseph, 35, 101
McClure, James, 4, 148
McCormick, L.W., 110
McDonald, John, 112
McFadden, James, 74
McFadzean, William, 67
McGee, Gale, 194
McGovern, George, 151, 152, 193, 237
McGrory, Mary, 76
McHugh, Raymond J., 47
McManus, Charles, 58
McNamara, Robert Strange, 60

MacArthur, Douglas, 55, 57
Mack, James, 68
Magruder, Jeb, 152
Mahoney, G. Daniel, 145, 156
Making of a New Majority Party, The (Rusher), 167
Making of the President—1968, The (White), 87
Manafort, Paul, 222
Marathon (Witcover), 164–165

Marcus, Kim, 44
Marsh, John O., 4, 217, 242
Martin, James, 111
Matthews, Robert, 68
Meese, Edwin III, 4, 11, 12, 63, 121, 207, 212, 221, 225, 242
"Meet the Press", 43
Memoirs of a Superfluous Man (Nock), 41
Mencken, H.L., 29, 43
Methvin, Eugene, 45–46
Metzenbaum, Howard M., 194
Meyer, Frank, 32, 35, 36, 40, 41, 52, 74, 79
Miami Herald, 125–126
Michel, Robert, 222
Middendorf, William, 67, 69
Milbank, Jeremiah Jr., 69
Milione, Victor, 42, 196
Milliken, Gerrish, 69
Milliken, Roger, 67, 69
Milliken, William, 12, 200, 219
Mises, Ludwig v., 30, 32, 33
Mitchell, John, 122, 123, 152
Modern Age, 42
Moley, Raymond, 41
Mollenhoff, Clark, 47
Molnar, Thomas, 36
Mont Pelerin Society, 31, 32
Moore, Roger Allen, 68, 127, 183, 222
Moorer, Thomas, 59
Moral Majority, 4, 37, 220–221
Morley, Felix, 40
Morrell, Benjamin, 58
Morton, Rogers C.B., 124, 170, 181, 184, 186
Motion Picture Industry Council, 229
Mowrer, Edgar Ansel, 46
Moynihan, Daniel Patrick, 133, 187
Mueller, John, 77
Mundt, Karl, 84
Murfin, William, 97, 119, 121, 122, 123, 125
Murphy, George, 26–27, 80

Nader, Ralph, 70
Nashville Banner, 47
Nathan, George Jean, 43

National Association of Manufacturers, 61
National Broadcasting Company, 147
National Draft Goldwater Committee, later National Goldwater for President Committee, 13, 14, 20, 29 43, 53, 67, 68, 69, 75, 76, 77, 80, 83, 86, 93, 98, 111, 198, 222
National Journalism Center, 48, 79
National Press Club, 64, 149
National Review, The, 29, 35, 40, 41, 66, 67, 74, 79, 168
National Strategey Information Center, 61, 62
New Deal, 32, 33, 51, 56
New Frontier, 32, 33
New Guard, 43–44, 75, 77
New Orleans Times-Picayune, 47
New York City, 16, 51, 76, 124, 147, 150, 155, 239
New York Times, 47, 49, 50, 52, 53, 76, 85n, 96, 109, 138, 215, 230, 245
Newsday, 209
Nichols, David, 68
Nixon, Richard, 26, 39, 50, 59, 65, 80, 84–87, 90, 91, 92–94, 97, 106–116, 117–129, 131–134, 148–149, 151–154, 158, 161–162, 164, 166, 172, 187, 193, 223, 237
Nock, Albert Jay, 29, 41
Nofziger, Lyn, 47, 66, 121, 207, 221, 225, 240
Novak, Robert, 99, 114–115
Nunn, Louis, 122

Oakland Tribune, 117
Oberdorfer, Don, 125, 126
Obershain, Richard D., 198, 199
O'Brien, Edward, 47
O'Doherty, Kieran, 145
O'Donnell, Peter, 75, 98
Ogilvie, Richard B., 83
Olmstead, James, 198
O'Neill, Thomas P., 102, 140
O'Sullivan, John, 62
Otepka, Otto, 101
Ottinger, Richard, 146

Paine, Thomas, 9
Pearlman, Donald, 68
Pearson, Drew, 17
Percy, Charles H., 84, 90, 158–159
Perrin, Eugene, 67
Phillips, Howard, 4, 74
Phillips, Kevin, 47
Pickett, Roscoe, 115
Pittsburgh Post-Gazette, 62–63, 96
Pittsburgh Press, 95
Plain Talk, 41
Poe, Edgar Allen, 47
Poirot, Paul L., 41
Policy Review, 62
Public Philosophy Reader, A (Bisirjian), 77

Quie, Albert H., 200, 201

Rabb, Max, 242
Randolph, Edmund, 153n
Ray, Robert D., 200, 210
Read, Leonard, 30, 41
Reader's Digest, 45–46, 77
Reagan for President Committee, 206–207, 209, 221, 225
Reagan, Nancy, 8, 9, 16, 27, 102, 114, 127, 131, 134, 150, 156, 189, 190, 191, 202, 228, 232, 236, 238
Reagan, Neil, 202
Real Reagan, The (van der Linden), 101–102
Realm Foundation, 57
Reed, Clarke, 97, 119, 121, 124, 183–184
Reed, Gordon, 88
Reed, James A., 68
Reed, Nell, 68
Reed, Thomas, 66, 68, 87, 88, 94, 100, 109, 121, 128–129, 137, 156, 216, 217
Regnery, Henry, 37, 40, 51, 52
Regnery, Alfred, 76
Rehmann, John Keith, 68
Reilly, John Francis, 101n
Republican National Committee (RNC), 14, 68, 79, 115, 189, 200, 204, 216, 222, 223
Reston, James, 96, 97

Rhodes, James A., 83, 200
Rhodes, John, 83, 126, 185
Richardson Foundation, 57
Richardson, Elliot, 170
Richardson, H.L., 190–191
Richardson, Randolph, 51
Richmond News Leader, 49
Rivers, Mendel, 60
Road to Serfdom, The (Hayek), 32
Roberts, Oral, 51
Robertson, Pat, 51
Rockefeller Foundation, 55, 57
Rockefeller, Nelson, 13, 14, 77, 82,
  84, 85, 89, 92, 96–97, 107, 110–113,
  116, 119, 121, 122, 125, 126, 144,
  145, 152, 155, 170, 174, 185
Rockefeller, Winthrop, 110
Rodino, Peter, 58
Rohrbacher, Dana, 76
Romney, George, 82, 84, 85, 89, 90, 92,
  94, 107, 112
Roosevelt, Franklin Delano, 32, 46, 51,
  61, 151 199, 200
Roosevelt, Franklin Delano Jr., 145
Roosevelt, Theodore, 132, 174
Ropke, Wilhelm, 30, 33, 40
Rosenbaum, Richard, 187
Rosensweet, Alvin, 96
Roth, William, V., 194
Rountree, Martha, 43, 50, 58, 59
Rubel, A.C., 27
Rumsfeld, Donald, 169, 170
Rusher, William A., 29, 47, 67, 69,
  74, 77, 79, 111, 121, 156, 167
Rusk, Dean, 55
Russo, Paul, 222, 229
Ryskind, Allan H., 40
Ryskind, Morrie, 46

Sacramento Union, 45
St. John, Jeffrey, 47
St. Louis Globe Democrat, 17, 47
Salinger, Pierre, 27
Salvatori, Henry, 27, 172
San Diego Union, 18
Sandman, Charles, 154
Saturday Evening Post, 85n

Scaife, Frannie, 64
Scaife, Richard Mellon, 57, 62, 63, 64
Schlafly, Fred, 52
Schlafly, Phyllis, 3, 52, 58, 59
Schlamm, Willi, 35, 40
Schlesinger, James, 170
Schmitt, Harrison, 194
Schriever, Bernard A., 60
Schuchman, Robert, 74
Schulz, Charles, 234
Schulz, William, 77
Schweiker, Richard, 179, 182, 183–184,
  186, 188
Scott, Hugh, 110
Scott, Paul, 46
Scranton, William, 13, 174
Screen Actors Guild, 24, 27, 229
Sears, John, 87, 157, 162, 164–165,
  169, 178, 179, 182, 206, 207,
  209–212, 215
Sentner, David, 47
Shafer, Raymond P., 82, 110
Shafto, Donald, 75
Shapp, Milton, 161n
Sharbutt, Del, 50
Sheen, Fulton J., 51
Shorey, Gregory, 67
Shriver, R. Sargent, 161n
Silone, Ignazio, 35
Simon, William, 207, 234
Simpson, Alan, 200
Sincerely, Ronald Reagan (von Damm),
  44–45
Sirhan Sirhan, 106
Sleeper, Raymond, 60
Smith, Dale O., 60
Smith, Howard K., 50
Smith, Loren, 222
Smith, Margaret Chase, 84
Smith, Richard, 77
Smith, Tad, 68
Snelling, Richard A., 200
Sokolsky, George, 41, 74
Soviet Union, 36, 41, 46, 60, 78–79,
  94, 97, 108, 137, 138, 166–167, 170,
  180, 192, 204, 245
Spencer, Stuart, 180, 217

Spender, Stephen, 35
Spivak, Lawrence, 43
Stalin, Josef, 35
Steen, John, 47
Stevens, Theodore, 200
Stockman, David, 232
Stone, Roger, 77
Strauss, Robert, 233–234
Street Corner Conservative, The (Gavin), 49
Streeter, James, 148
Strausz-Hupe, Robert, 42
Sundquist, Donald, 77

Taft, Robert A., 29, 194
Taft, Robert A. Jr., 194
Taft, William Howard, 132, 174
Tampa Tribune, 47
Taylor, Henry J., 46, 50
Teague, Kathleen, 79
Teague, Randal, 144
Teller, Edward, 60, 100
Thimmesch, Nick, 90
Third World Liberation Front, 138–139
Thomas, John, 68
Thomasson, Daniel, 113
Thompson, James R., 200
Thompson, Michael, 74
Thompson, Richard, 148
Thone, Charles, 67, 200
Thorin, Duane, 52
Thornburg, Richard, 200, 201, 218
Thurmond, Strom, 4, 83, 87, 97, 98, 108–109, 111, 115, 116, 119–124, 126, 128, 158, 200, 205, 216
Time magazine, 95
"Time for Choosing, A" (Reagan), 22–27
Timmons, William, 3, 6, 7, 112, 124, 128, 171, 172, 221, 222, 225, 228
To Catch a Falling Flag (Whalen), 49
Tocqueville, Alexis d., 245
Toledano, Ralph d., 35, 46
Tope, John, 67
Totten, Donald, 218
Tower, John, 4, 74, 76, 83, 98, 111, 121, 124, 200, 205, 234
Treptow, Martin H., 243

Trohan, Walter, 47
Truman, Harry, 55, 170, 199
Tunney, John V., 194
Tuttle, Holmes, 27
Tyrrell, R. Emmett Jr., 43
Tyson, Charles, 221

Udall, Morris, 45, 161n
United States Industrial Council, 61
University of California at Berkeley, 71, 73, 89, 134
University of Pennsylvania Foreign Policy Research Center, 42
Unruh, Jesse, 139
Utley, Freda, 40, 52

van der Linden, Frank, 47, 101–102
Vanocur, Sander, 88
Van Sickle, Suzie Galvin, 68
Van Sickle, Tom, 68, 77, 156, 159
Veterans of Foreign Wars, 227
Vietnam, War, 23, 55, 71, 72–73, 78, 84, 100, 105, 118, 131, 133–134, 135, 136, 137–139, 166, 227
Viguerie, Richard, 43, 53, 54, 74, 75, 206
Vinovich, Paul, 222
Vivas, Eliseo, 42
Volker Fund, 57
Volpe, John, 83, 99
Voss, Earl, 47, 52

WABC, 146–147
WRAL, 147
Walker, Charles E., 234
Walker, Robert C., 157, 159, 162, 164
Wall Street Journal, 66, 89, 90
Wallace, DeWitt, 45
Wallace, George, 98, 108, 116, 132, 161, 168
Wallas, Graham, 33
Wallop, Malcolm, 194
Walters, Barbara, 4
Walton, Frank, 171
Ward, Chester, 53
Ward, Leo R., 42
Waring, Thomas R., 36
Warner, John, 199

Washington, D.C., 14, 16, 21, 22, 25, 47, 105, 113, 152, 165, 169, 172, 196, 206, 213, 229, 239, 241, 242, 243, 244, 246
Washington Post, 49–50, 63, 232
Washington Report, 43
Washington Star, 47, 76, 155
Washington, George, 153n
Waste Land, The (Eliot), 29
Watergate, 50, 129, 150, 151–155, 158, 159, 165, 179, 189
Watson, Albert, 83
Watt, James, 63
Weaver, Richard, 33, 34, 40, 41, 42, 52
Webb, Beatrice, 33
Webb, Sidney, 33
Wedemeyer, Albert C., 60
Weinberger, Caspar, 207
Weyrich, Paul, 148
Weyl, Nathaniel, 35
Whalen, Richard J., 49
Where's the Rest of Me (Reagan), 24–25
Whetstone, Frank, 68, 156, 158, 159, 183, 188, 213, 222
White, Bunny, 201
White, Carole, 128
White, Theodore, 87
Whiteford, Charles, 116
Wick, James, 40
Wicker, Tom, 109–110

Widener, Alice, 46
Wilhelmsen, Frederick, 36, 42
Will, George F., 47
Wills, Chill, 76
Wilson, Francis, 36, 42
Wilson, William, 242
Wilson, Woodrow, 132
Winter, Thomas, 40
Wirthlin, Richard, 4, 222, 228, 236
Witcover, Jules, 164–165
World War I, 243
World War II, 30, 35, 46, 50, 57, 60, 152, 179, 229
Wright, David McCord, 42
Wright, Leonard, 197–198, 230
Wright, Richard, 35

Yale University, 34, 95
Yarborough, Ralph, 99
Yerger, Wirt, 68
Young Americans for Freedom (YAF), 43–44, 73–75, 76, 77, 78–79, 80, 111–112, 121–122, 124, 125, 144, 145, 168
Young Republican National Federation, 77, 78, 80, 112, 171
Young, Coleman, 12

Zimbalist, Efrem Jr., 76
Zumwalt, Elmo R., 194